Palgrave Studies in Literary Anthropology

Series Editors
Deborah Reed-Danahay
Department of Anthropology
The State University of New York at Buffalo
Buffalo, NY, USA

Helena Wulff
Department of Social Anthropology
Stockholm University
Stockholm, Sweden

This series explores new ethnographic objects and emerging genres of writing at the intersection of literary and anthropological studies. Books in this series are grounded in ethnographic perspectives and the broader cross-cultural lens that anthropology brings to the study of reading and writing. The series explores the ethnography of fiction, ethnographic fiction, narrative ethnography, creative nonfiction, memoir, autoethnography, and the connections between travel literature and ethnographic writing.

More information about this series at
http://www.palgrave.com/gp/series/15120

Oscar Hemer

Contaminations and Ethnographic Fictions

Southern Crossings

Oscar Hemer
School of Arts and Communication, K3
Malmö University
Malmö, Sweden

Palgrave Studies in Literary Anthropology
ISBN 978-3-030-34927-1   ISBN 978-3-030-34925-7   (eBook)
https://doi.org/10.1007/978-3-030-34925-7

Cover illustration: Ponte City, 2016: The Core (photo by the author)

This Palgrave Macmillan imprint is published by the registered company Springer Nature
Switzerland AG
The registered company address is: Gewerbestrasse 11, 6330 Cham, Switzerland

For Thomas and Beata

SERIES EDITORS' PREFACE

Palgrave Studies in Literary Anthropology publishes explorations of new ethnographic objects and emerging genres of writing at the intersection of literary and anthropological studies. Books in this series are grounded in ethnographic perspectives and the broader cross-cultural lens that anthropology brings to the study of reading and writing. By introducing work that applies an anthropological approach to literature, whether drawing on ethnography or other materials in relation to anthropological and literary theory, this series moves the conversation forward not only in literary anthropology, but also in general anthropology, literary studies, cultural studies, sociology, ethnographic writing and creative writing. The "literary turn" in anthropology and critical research on world literatures share a comparable sensibility regarding global perspectives.

Fiction and autobiography have connections to ethnography that underscore the idea of the author as ethnographer and the ethnographer as author. Literary works are frequently included in anthropological research and writing, as well as in studies that do not focus specifically on literature. Anthropologists take an interest in fiction and memoir set in their field locations, and produced by "native" writers, in order to further their insights into the cultures and contexts they research. Experimental genres in anthropology have benefitted from the style and structure of fiction and autoethnography, as well as by other expressive forms ranging from film and performance art to technology, especially the Internet and social media. There are renowned fiction writers who trained as anthropologists, but moved on to a literary career. Their anthropologically inspired work is a common sounding board in literary anthropology. In the endeavour to foster writing skills in different genres, there are now courses on ethnographic writing, anthropological writing genres, experimental writing and even creative writing taught by anthropologists. And increasingly, literary and reading communities are attracting anthropological attention, including an engagement with issues of how to reach a wider audience.

Palgrave Studies in Literary Anthropology publishes scholarship on the ethnography of fiction and other writing genres, the connections between travel literature and ethnographic writing, and Internet writing. It also publishes creative work such as ethnographic fiction, narrative ethnography, creative non-fiction, memoir and autoethnography. Books in the series include monographs and edited collections, as well as shorter works that appear as Palgrave Pivots. This series aims to reach a broad audience among scholars, students and a general readership.

Deborah Reed-Danahay and Helena Wulff
Co-Editors, Palgrave Studies in Literary Anthropology

Advisory Board
Ruth Behar, University of Michigan
Don Brenneis, University of California, Santa Cruz
Regina Bendix, University of Göttingen
Mary Gallagher, University College Dublin
Kirin Narayan, Australian National University
Nigel Rapport, University of St Andrews
Ato Quayson, University of Toronto
Julia Watson, Ohio State University

ACKNOWLEDGEMENTS

This book is the end result of a project I embarked on as a fellow at Stellenbosch Institute for Advanced Study (STIAS) in the beginning of 2015. It was formulated within the Institute's longer-term theme "Crossing Borders" and had on the outset the provisional double title "Writing Across Borders/In Praise of Impurity". I am immensely grateful to STIAS for offering me the privilege to be part of their creative environment for three full months, during which I enjoyed the inspiration from a wide range of fellow researchers who happened to share this crucial moment in recent South African history with me. Whether they like it or not, many of them appear with their forenames in the text, and I wish to especially thank Simon Bekker, Michael Blake, Denis-Constant Martin, Francis Nyamnjoh, Elmi Muller, Anne Phillips and Mats Rosengren for providing input of specific relevance for my own research. Although not a STIAS fellow at the time, but previously and later, Aryan Kaganof has also been a very important reference point and is subsequently a recurrent protagonist in my text. Susan Hayden, my former student and proof-reader, is likewise in that category of long-term relationships.

The stay at STIAS was fundamental for the realisation of this kamikaze project. But it had a prehistory and an aftermath. My first attempt at genre transgression in the borderlands of literature and anthropology, *Hillbrow Blues* (2008; 2012), was an offspring of my then ongoing artistic research project on *Fiction and Truth in Transition*, and I thank Magnus Ödmark for being so insistent on having me contribute to his literary anthology *Scenanvisningar för ett större sällskap* [Stage directions for a larger group]. The English version was also produced on commission for an anthology, to celebrate the 15th anniversary of the *Time of the Writer* Festival, in which I had participated in 2007. Time of the Writer in Durban was at the time arguably one of the most vital annual cultural events in South Africa, and being a participant with writers from all over the continent was for me personally a watershed moment; my decision to write in English, not only for academic but also literary purposes, was founded there. I salute the former Festival General Peter Rorvik for inviting me and Michael Chapman, the editor of *Africa Inside Out,* for selecting my contribution. Peter was also a partner, with Keyan Tomaselli and Ruth Teer-Tomaselli, on the *Memories of Modernity* project (2005–2007) that brought me back to South Africa for the first time, after my primordial visit as a reporter in 1991. *Memories of Modernity*'s transgressive attempt at artistic and academic collusion, including the art exhibition *Houses of Memory* which travelled from Durban to Malmö, served as a kind of dress rehearsal for my Fiction and Truth project.

Kathrine Winkelhorn, my cherished former colleague at Malmö University, had co-coordinated the Durban collaboration and was also my partner on the sequel *Mediating Modernity* project in Bangalore (2012–2013), which was to provide the material for the second "ethnographic fiction", *Bengaluru Boogie* (2015; 2017). For the Bangalore material, I am enormously indebted to our Indian co-coordinators Jyothsna Belliappa and Deepak Srinivasan, and artist Ayisha Abraham who contributed the photos that form an intrinsic part of the collaborative "transdisciplinary intervention".

Like the *Hillbrow Blues*, the Bengaluru Boogie has been published previously, in both English and Swedish. I regard them, however, as "prequels" to the *Cape Calypso*, and hence integral parts of the grander project—which I half-jokingly refer to as the World Waltz—and I thank UKZN Press and Lit Verlag for generously permitting me to include revised versions of them in this volume, as an overture to the main text.

After the three months at STIAS, which was my seventh journey to South Africa, I have obsessively returned another six times, whereof two were short stop-overs in Johannesburg on the way to Mozambique. I am especially grateful to Mariekie Burger for inviting me to give a seminar at the University of Johannesburg and Cheryl Stobie for hosting me as a visiting researcher at UKZN. In March 2018, I spent four decisive weeks in Pietermaritzburg, working on the second part of the diptych, which

I finalised in October the same year on an equally productive private "retreat" in Paris. Cheryl has been one of my most trusted readers, and her advice and encouragement have been immensely important for the conclusion of the project.

Except for the STIAS grant, the main part of this project has been carried out without any external funding, within the confines of my professorship at Malmö University and largely as self-financed research. Malmö's School of Arts and Communication (K3) has as always provided an inspiring environment, and I especially thank my colleagues on the Communication for Development M.A. programme and the fellow researchers in the *Conviviality at the Crossroads* network, which now forms part of the wider research platform *Rethinking Democracy* (REDEM). It is not a mere coincidence that *Cape Calypso* was finalised in parallel with my coordination of the Conviviality network, which is centred around another book project, in close collaboration between Malmö University and Bard College Berlin.[1] I am grateful to all the network members for valuable feedback at workshops and seminars, and especially to my Berlin colleague Kerry Bystrom, the only other researcher I know that shares my specific obsession with South Africa *and* Argentina. My heartfelt thanks also to Mary al-Sayed and Madison Allums at Palgrave Macmillan for the smooth and efficient editorial collaboration on both these book projects. Working with them has been a pleasure from the very first contact.

Many others, colleagues and friends, have in different ways influenced the trajectory—my ComDev accomplice and former Ørecomm co-director Thomas Tufte (now at Loughborough, but we are still making grand plans together); Gezi co-editor Hans-Åke Persson; Asu Aksoy in Istanbul (and Kevin wherever he may be); Johan Härnsten in Paris (and Per-Olof in Tuna)—but two "influencers" were more decisive than others for the conception of this book. Ivan Vladislavić, whom I first met in 1991, has been my principal South African reference point ever since, as interlocutor, advisor and inspiring example, as the outstanding writer he is. Incidentally, I also met Thomas Hylland Eriksen in 1991, at the Nordic Summer University's session in Hurdalsøen, Norway. In the years that followed, we were to co-coordinate a NSU "circle" on the *Globalisation of Culture*, which at the time was as controversial as it remains today.

[1]Hemer, Povrzanović Frykman & Ristilammi (2020).

The issues we discussed then, in the wake of an apparently brave new world, were very much the issues that I interrogate in this book, at an historical moment that apparently is the diametrical opposite to the optimistic 1990s (which parenthetically may have been the only moment that the South African transition could have happened).

Lastly, I bow with immense love and respect to my most merciless critic, Chinook, who has remained my life companion over almost forty years. She gave me the absolutely crucial advise for the completion of this endeavour: to be ruthless to myself.

Sandby, Sweden
September 2019

Reference

Hemer, O., M. Povrzanović Frykman, & P.-M. Ristilammi (eds.) (2020). *Conviviality at the Crossroads: The Poetics and Politics of Everyday Encounters.* Basingstoke: Palgrave Macmillan.

CONTENTS

1 Contaminations, Ethnographic Fictions and What-What   1

2 Hillbrow Blues   11

3 Bengaluru Boogie   17

4 Cape Calypso I   37

5 Cape Calypso   89

6 Cape Calypso II   107

7 Melville Medley   191

Correction to: Bengaluru Boogie   C1

References   201

Index   209

LIST OF FIGURES

Fig. 3.1   The city   18
Fig. 3.2   One way   21
Fig. 3.3   Border   26
Fig. 3.4   Basement theatre   31
Fig. 3.5   A storm   36

CHAPTER 1

Contaminations, Ethnographic Fictions and What-What

On the Convergence of Literary and Academic Writing

© The Author(s) 2020   1
O. Hemer, *Contaminations and Ethnographic Fictions*,
Palgrave Studies in Literary Anthropology,
https://doi.org/10.1007/978-3-030-34925-7_1

THE TEXTS THAT constitute this book intend to explore the possible merging of academic and literary practices. The aim is not experimentation for its own sake, but the search for a form—*forms*—that is/are congenial with the subject of interrogation: the world in transition, with South Africa as the main focal point.

What I least want is to "explain" my transgressive attempt by means of a conventional academic introduction. I regard this as a literary work as much as an academic one, and it is a golden rule that literary writers not attempt to analyse their own work, as such self-reflection runs the imminent risk of appearing as primitive or even irrelevant in comparison with the meta-level inscribed in the structure of the work itself.[1] The latter is never fully apprehended by the author (if it were, it would not be literature). Yet, my interrogation also aspires to stand the test of academic scrutiny, and for the sake of transparency, I will in the following make some preliminary reflections in order to provide a background and rationale for the *opacity*.[2]

*

The sudden outburst of xenophobic violence in South Africa in March 2015, which was even more virulent than the similar incidents in 2008, formed the backdrop of my three-month stay at STIAS, as did the parallel student revolt and symbolic battle about public memory—starting at the University of Cape Town and culminating with the removal of the Cecil Rhodes statue from its campus on 9 April. Both these seemingly disconnected events informed my emerging interrogation, which had also been motivated by the rise of right-wing populism and neo-nationalism in Europe—manifest long before the refugee migration of 2015/16—and the ticking bomb of communal violence on the Indian subcontinent, which I had touched upon in a previous study.[3]

I claimed, as a hypothesis, that the underlying structure in the regularly resurging nationalism, xenophobia and identity politics, in Europe, South Africa and, possibly, everywhere, can be framed by the discourse of *Purity/Impurity*, as outlined and analysed by British anthropologist Mary Douglas 1966. Douglas theorized purity and impurity in terms

---

[1] Söderblom 2009: 64.

[2] I use the term *opacity* in Édouard Glissant's sense, which I elaborate on in the second part of the main text.

[3] Hemer 2015, republished in this volume.

of instantiation and disruption of a shared symbolic order. Simply put, purity conceals the preservation of that order, whereas all that threatens the social equilibrium is encoded as impurity. Influential, and disputed, as Douglas has been,[4] the purity/impurity discourse arguably holds an as yet unrealised potential for both social theory and social action. By way of the cross-genre and transdisciplinary methodology—finding a form that is probing in and by itself—my aim was hence to explore the phenomenology of impurity, and specifically the notion of *creolisation, for which* South Africa (counter-intuitively) is a very apposite case.

*

The project I first formulated at STIAS can be regarded as a sequel to two preceding projects that were partly carried out in parallel. In my artistic research project *Fiction and Truth in Transition,*[5] I used South Africa and Argentina as comparative cases to explore the relationship between literary fiction and society's dramatic transformation in the two countries over the past three decades. That interrogation brought me, to my own surprise, to the crossroads of literature and anthropology (fiction and ethnography), where this project starts.

After completing the artistic research project, which I defended as a dissertation in Social Anthropology,[6] I returned to fiction and wrote the concluding novel in a trilogy that I had begun working on in the late 1990s.[7] These two major long-term projects (academic and literary) definitely informed each other, and in retrospect I can clearly see how they were really two complementary forms of interrogating some common themes. Complementary, yet distinctly different. And, contrary to my preconception, the difference seemed to be emphasised rather than blurred as I moved between them—from the academic straitjacket to the freedom of fiction. Even though I had retained the perspective of the literary writer, and incorporated elements of essay, reportage and memoir, there was a limit as to how far I could challenge the format of the dissertation.

---

[4]When the *Times Literary Supplement* in 1995 listed the "hundred books which have most influenced Western public discourse since the Second World War", *Purity and Danger* was on the list, alongside the more expected works of Orwell, Sartre, Wittgenstein and others.

[5]Hemer 2012.

[6]Hemer 2011.

[7]Hemer 2014.

(For me, the principal challenge was to write an academic dissertation, not another novel.) And it was indeed a great relief to return to writing fiction. The title of the concluding part of the Argentina trilogy, *Misiones*, had been in the back of my mind ever since I wrote the second part, and I would certainly have written it some five years earlier if the dissertation had not come in-between. But then, it would as certainly have become a quite different novel. On the one hand, the systematic research into the ethnographic and historical material that I was beginning to explore in the second novel (*Santiago*) provided my writing with a more solid ground. On the other, and more importantly, the subsequent greater confidence in my own authority enhanced my ability and motivation to *invent* more freely. For example, Misiones is a province in North-Eastern Argentina with a fairly large and largely unknown community of Swedish immigrants, who arrived in the late nineteenth and early twentieth century. I had been there twice, very briefly, and I was all the time planning to go back and do some proper ethnographic research for my novel. But that journey was always postponed and in the end I decided to write the novel anyway, almost completely based on imagination and hardly making use of any of the "real" history, let alone current ethnographic empirics. Hence, in the end, the *literariness* of my literary approach was actually accentuated.

So, what about *transgression*? To what extent do the academic and literary practices actually converge? Is it even desirable *that* they fuse into new genres? It would appear that the somewhat discouraging answer is "No". Moreover it may be, as Norwegian writer and anthropologist Thomas Hylland Eriksen suggested already in the early '90s, that literature and anthropology are relevant to each other only as long and in-so-far as they remain aware of their fundamental difference.[8] And given the current fictionalisation of journalism and politics, with proliferation of "fake news" and *fact resistance*, it may no longer even be a discouraging conclusion. But the question of convergence has continued to intrigue me. This project is my second take on it, my implementation in practice, if you like. I have pursued it, well knowing that it may be a dead-end street.

[8] Eriksen 1994: 192. On my direct question, in a panel on "Writing Across Borders" at EASA in Tallinn, 2014, he admitted to having nuanced, if not abandoned, his rather categorical standpoint, which primarily had been motivated by his concern that aspiring anthropologists would too willingly adopt literary ambitions and inadvertently confirm the mocking epithet as "failed novelists" (ibid.: 194).

*

"In Praise of Contamination" is an intermediate headline in one of the chapters of Ghanaian American philosopher Kwame Anthony Appiah's *Cosmopolitanism: Ethics in a World of Strangers.*[9] By evoking Roman (Carthagian) playwright Terence (Publius Terentius Afer), whose mode of combining tragedy and comedy was known as *contamination*, Appiah outlines a literary tradition that goes back at least two thousand years and he suggests Salman Rushdie to be its most articulate contemporary proponent. In fact, he says little more about this supposed tradition. The only writers he mentions are Terence and Rushdie. I see it more as a tentative idea, in a category similar to Argentinean writer Juan José Saer's definition of fiction as "speculative anthropology",[10] and I am happy to take on the challenge of outlining and exploring this tradition—but possibly in another direction than Appiah intended.

There are of course innumerable examples in the two millennia between Terence and Rushdie. One key work would be Montesquieu's *Lettres persanes* (1721), a satirical novel that tells the experience of two Persian noblemen's journey from Isfahan to Paris. US American anthropologist James Clifford, one of the editors of the ground-breaking anthology *Writing Culture* (1986), defines ethnography as *hybrid textual activity*, traversing genres and disciplines, and traces its origin to the Greek historian Herodotus on the one hand, and "Montesquieu's Persian travellers" on the other.[11] Jorge Luis Borges' elusive *ficciones*, sometimes described as "fictional essays", would be another outstanding feature in this marginal canon (marginal in the sense that it thrives where the literary imagination is the most creative, at the limits of its extension). Borges famously coined the idea that an author creates his/her own predecessors, but I don't think he would have minded that we invented this tradition for him. After Rushdie's *The Satanic Verses* (1988), contaminations have arguably proliferated even more. Chris Kraus' infamous novel *I Love Dick* (1997) is but one example, which I find particularly interesting, of what literary critic Joan Hawkins in the

---

[9] Appiah 2006: 111–113.
[10] Saer 1997.
[11] Clifford 1986: 2–3.

afterword labels *theoretical fictions*.[12] And, in fact, I would not regard Salman Rushdie as the principal contemporary proponent of *contamination* in my understanding—as a cross- or trans-genre between literary and discursive writing. My first candidate would be J. M. Coetzee, for whom the relation between the two writing practices has always been a crucial concern, and whose recent work, from 1999 and onwards, combines and even fuses the two formerly separate yet communicating practices, in more and less innovative ways. Coetzee made a short sojourn at STIAS during the time I was there. Our stays overlapped less than a week, but it so happened that we attended each other's seminars.

A possible contender, if he were still alive, would be Édouard Glissant, whose fusion of poetry and philosophy, *Poétique de la Relation* (1990) is the key reference for *Cape Calypso*, alongside *Purity and Danger*. Glissant was the mentor for the three Caribbean writer colleagues Jean Bernabé, Patrick Chamoiseau and Raphael Confiant, who in 1989 proclaimed what became known as "The Creole Manifesto". *Éloge de la creolité* [*In Praise of Creoleness*] is a key text in the creolisation debate that preceded and informed the discussion on "globalisation", which *nota bene* did not emerge among economists or political scientists, but in cultural studies.[13] Incidentally, the Creole manifesto was parallel in time with *The Satanic Verses* and ayatollah Khomeini's subsequent fatwa against Rushdie, and although there are no explicit cross-references, Rushdie's essays (1992) reflect on many of the crucial concerns of the creolisation debate.

I probably wouldn't have thought of bringing Glissant and Coetzee together under other circumstances, but they do somehow meet in *Cape Calypso*, and their imaginary (mute) conversation is in my view perhaps the most surprising possible achievement.

*

[12] Hawkins in Kraus 2016 [1997]: 247. Kraus herself called an early manifestation of her genre-bending "Lonely Girl Phenomenology" (ibid.).

[13] The coining of the term "globalisation" is commonly attributed to US American cultural sociologist Roland Robertson, who defined it (1992) as "the compression of the world and the intensification of the consciousness of the world as a whole".

Although my dissertation abided to the academic rules, the Fiction and Truth project also had "literary" offspring. *Hillbrow Blues* was conceived while I was working on the South African part of the comparative study, more specifically on a chapter about "writing the city" (Johannesburg). It was a way of approaching the same material from a slightly different angle. The difference is the component that would be defined as fictional; the stream of consciousness, the subjective distortion of reality, and most importantly, the simple distancing device of the third person, which I added in the English version. Yet it remains ethnographic in the sense that it is conveying the experience of a *real* place. It's a condensation of many journeys, and with two registers in time, a now and a past, a before and an after; in this case, before and after the transition to democracy.

The sequel *Bengaluru Boogie* is similarly based on two temporal registers, a before and an after; the emerging IT metropolis of the first years of the new Millennium and the combusting mega city ten years later.[14] The breakneck feature of that text is the protagonist's change of gender. The "he" now becomes a "ze",[15] creating a compositional challenge, and by all means a disturbing difficulty, which adds new meaning to the term *third person*.

The *Cape Calypso* diptych takes the protagonist's transformation even further and definitely blurs, if not erases, the border between fiction and auto-ethnography. Here, the supposedly congenial form is elaborated as two distinct yet correspondent texts that run in parallel; one is a fictionalised report from "the Institute", in the present tense of March and April 2015; the opposite text is in the first part a close reading of *Purity and Danger*, and in the second a similar reading of *Poetics of Relation*.

---

[14] In fact, there are three time layers, as the "after" is viewed from the perspective of two different journeys, both in 2013, one of which is written in the future tense.

[15] This improvised turn was partly inspired by the recent introduction in Swedish of the neutral gender term "hen" (as between the masculine "han" and the feminine "hon"), which at the time had no officially recognised correspondent in English. In the original English version, I used the not quite adequate "s/he". When reading it a few years later, Cheryl Stobie suggested that I replace "s/he" with "ze", and also made me aware that this is a contested term with a number of contenders. Moreover, the common convention has lately become to use the—in my view extremely awkward—pronouns they/them/theirs for trans or non-gendered persons. My insistence on the invented ze/hir pronouns may not be a deliberate political statement, but I simply prefer them and have grown accustomed to using them.

The first part (*Impurity and Danger/Sounding Stellenbosch*) was largely finalised in 2015, during and shortly after my stay at STIAS, and I presented it in draft versions at the IAMCR conference in Montreal in July and at a workshop at Bard College Berlin in November the same year. The second part (*In Praise of Relation/Waiting for Señor C.*) is written at three years' distance from the frame story, in 2018 (in Pietermaritzburg and Paris). The two parts are (dis)connected by the *Interlude* (*Allesverloren*) which essentially was conceived after my revisit to the Cape in 2016. That year's journey is also the timeframe of the concluding *Melville Medley*, which although written after the diptych should be read as another interlude rather than as an epilogue, referring back to the Hillbrow Blues and thus closing the incomplete circle.

Both as a theoretical concept and as cultural practice, *creolisation* is in the common debate primarily associated with the Caribbean and, to a lesser extent, with Latin America (the *New* World); not with Europe, or Asia, and certainly not with South Africa, which in the second half of the twentieth century was the epitome of its negation: *apartheid*. But, as already hinted, South Africa provides a very apt case for cross-exploration, not only because its apartheid policy (1948–94) was one of the foremost large-scale applications of a politics of purity,[16] but also because that same policy of separation, which goes longer back than Afrikaner nationalism, was a reaction to and suppression of one of the world's epicentres of creolisation. Like the Caribbean, the Western Cape has literally been a cultural crossroads for centuries and is today in fact the region with the highest genetic variation in the world.[17]

The long-term relationship is a prerequisite for the multi-layered diachronic and synchronic perspective of whatever I choose to call this cross-genre (contamination, ethnographic fiction or what-what) with its elaboration of a tense that could be described as a future past.[18] I would not claim any "regional expertise" on South Africa (the very notion of regional studies is profoundly colonial), but I have a thicker experience

---

[16]The elective affinity between purity discourses and black-and-white worldviews (Duschinsky 2013: 72).

[17]Elmi Muller, STIAS seminar, March 2015.

[18]I owe that term to Juan José Saer, who skilfully uses the tense of the future past in his novels, for example *Glosa* (1986), translated to English as *The Sixty-Five Years of Washington* (2010).

with its complexity than I have with most other parts of the globe (the only contenders outside Scandinavia would be Spain and Argentina). And I have a historical perspective on the South African transition and post-transition that many—in fact, most—South Africans do not have. Twenty-seven years is more than a quarter of a century, and although the legacy of apartheid is still very tangible, and will remain so for decades to come, the South Africa that I first knew in 1991 is just as distant in time and mind as the German Democratic Republic. But enough with preludes now. Let the contamination begin!

REFERENCES

Appiah, K. A. (2006). *Cosmopolitanism: Ethics in a World of Strangers*. New York and London: W. W. Norton.

Clifford, J. (1986). "Introduction: Partial Truths", in Clifford, J. & G. E. Marcus (eds.). *Writing Culture: The Poetics and Politics of Ethnography*. Berkeley: University of California Press.

Douglas, M. (1966). *Purity and Danger: An Analysis of Concepts of Pollution and Taboo*. London: Routledge & Kegan Paul.

Duschinsky, R. (2013). "The Politics of Purity: When, Actually, Is Dirt Out of Place?" *Thesis Eleven* 119 (1): 63–77.

Eriksen, T. H. (1994). "The Author as Anthropologist: Some West Indian Lessons About the Relevance of Fiction for Anthropology", in Archetti, E. P. (ed.). *Exploring the Written: Anthropology and the Multiplicity of Writing*. Oslo: Scandinavian University Press (Universitetsforlaget).

Glissant, É. (1997 [1990]). *Poetics of Relation*. Transl. by B. Wing. Ann Arbor: University of Michigan Press [*Poétique de la Relation. Poétique III*. Paris: Gallimard].

Hemer, O. (2011). *Writing Transition: Fiction and Truth in South Africa and Argentina*. Diss. Oslo: University of Oslo.

Hemer, O. (2012). *Fiction and Truth in Transition: Writing the Present Past in South Africa and Argentina*. Berlin: Lit Verlag.

Hemer, O. (2014). *Argentinatrilogin* (e-book). Stockholm: Vulkan.

Hemer, O. (2015). "Bengaluru Boogie: Outlines for an Ethnographic Fiction", in Hansen, A. H., Hemer, O. & T. Tufte (eds.). *Memory on Trial: Media, Citizenship and Social Justice*. Berlin: Lit Verlag.

Kraus, C. (2016 [1997]). *I Love Dick*. London: Serpent's Tail.

Robertson, R. (1992). *Globalization: Social Theory and Global Culture*. London: Sage.

Rushdie, S. (1992). *Imaginary Homelands: Essays and Criticism 1981–1991*. London: Granta in association with Penguin.

Saer, J. J. (1997). *El concepto de ficción*. Buenos Aires: Seix Barral.

Söderblom, S. (2009). "Anteckningar om senfärdigheten – om ansatser till konstnärlig forskning inom det litterära området", in Lind, T. (ed.). *Konst och forskningspolitik: konstnärlig forskning inför framtiden*. Stockholm: Vetenskapsrådet.

Hillbrow Blues

(2007)

IT GOES FAST. Pretoria Street is shorter than ze remembered; ze's looking for the hotel on the right side whose name ze has repressed, no, simply forgotten, but ze doesn't see any signs at all, nor any traces of bookshops, cafés or lunch restaurants. Lots of people in the street, mostly young men, no suits or ties, a few older women, no commerce, shutters closed, the entire Carlton Hotel shut down like a ghost tower, the garage doors locked with chains, but no roadblocks or burning oil drums... *The Nigerians and the Zimbabweans have ruined the place,* says the taxi driver with a matter-of-fact distaste that reminds hir of hir first taxi ride in Joburg fifteen years ago, that time with a white driver venting his contempt over the black hordes that had invaded the formerly secluded city. Ze stayed in the hotel whose name ze doesn't remember, with a view to the street, noisy, without air conditioning, cockroaches in the bathroom but otherwise neat and tidy. Apartheid was already history, like Communism in Eastern Europe, TV showed Hill Street Blues dubbed to Sesotho (*ze believes*), interspersed with commercials for Ohlsson's lager, the beer for the New South Africa in the making. Double-deckers ran like shuttles along Hillbrow's busy artery, studded with shops, cinemas, bars and restaurants where you could have breakfast at any time of the day; a block or two further down were open-24-hours cafés and bookshops, some of them amalgamated into book cafés. At Café Zurich, ze had met Ivan Vladislavić, then in his early thirties, editor at the semi-clandestine Ravan Press and the author of a well-received collection of short stories. Ze retained the memory of Ivan's smile, leaning on the red PVC-coated sofa in the spacious venue. Café Zurich was to merge with nearby Café de Paris into the imaginary Café Europa, the centre around which Hillbrow's and South Africa's transition evolves in the eyes and mind of retired proof-reader Aubrey Tearle, the main protagonist of *The Restless Supermarket* (2001), a regular at the café and, in his own words, an incorrigible European, although he has never set foot outside South Africa. Tearle finds himself utterly disturbed by the rapidly declining standards of the emerging new order whose semiotics he is unwilling or unable to understand. In all his rigid conservatism and unreflecting racism, he evokes sympathy as he helplessly witnesses the crumbling of the world, as he has known it. Café Europa is eventually trashed, just like its real-life models. On his last visit, Tearle literally wades through the debris of paper cups, toilet paper, bottles, crunched cheese snacks and scattered newspapers *with their pages curling from the wooden spines, like moths that had flown too close to the chandeliers.* But there is a certain ambiguity in the loathing; he is in the company of a young coloured woman who takes him out in the streets, out into the luring, frightening, violent, beautiful banality of Hillbrow.

Phaswane Mpe's *Welcome to Our Hillbrow*, published almost simultaneously with Vladislavić's novel, is set in the period immediately after, when the formerly orderly district, mostly inhabited by Eastern European émigrés, has already transmuted into the diverse, disorderly transit station for today's new immigration from the rest of Africa. Mpe's novel tells a dark and melodramatic story of a young man who arrives as a stranger to a Hillbrow reigned by violence, aids and xenophobia, where elemental humanity and civility have constantly to be negotiated. To be welcomed to Mpe's Hillbrow is to be embraced by vulnerability, compassion's and hospitality's weakened immune defence against the real politics of hatred and prejudice that the taxi driver so confidently conveys. But now the car is already out of the turmoil of Pretoria Street, tension is starting to wane as they turn towards Observatory. There, towering over the border to Berea, is Ponte City, once South Africa's and the entire continent's grandest residential building, a self-sufficient city within a city, fifty-four storeys upon seven levels of parking; now a ghost tower, the Carlton's twin, abandoned but not empty, taken over by the detested *makwerekwere*. A *drug den*, snorts the driver, and the mere sight of the rows of black windows is sufficient to assure anyone that it is a place you would not want to live or even visit, ze wonders how it is possible at all to inhabit the top floors, without an elevator—although one of the elevators is rumoured to function occasionally, hir associations run to the hidden shantytown of Buenos Aires, *Ciudad Oculta*, where squatters occupied the skeleton of an uncompleted twelve-storey construction, an authentic ruin from the recent Argentinean melt-down; but this is different, this is unfathomable, as if Malmö's Turning Torso within a few years were to be seized by asylum seekers pouring in from the Eurasian mainland, while the former tenants sought refuge behind triple security systems in the garden suburbs nearby… Is that a proof of prosperity, to simply abandon your tallest buildings and move onward when the imminent arrival of the barbarians is announced? Of a certain mentality, at least, to accept that existence is purely provisional and that the moment will inevitably come, sooner rather than later, when it is time for the tribe to move on… Hence, Ponte City turns into an ambiguous symbol of the transformation that has indisputably taken place since ze was here the first time; yes, exactly, *taken place*, because it is a transformation inscribed in the physical and imaginary shape of the city, as in the contemporary literature, which to a large extent is *writing the city*; mapping the territory, crossing the still visible demarcation lines, connecting and inhabiting the nightmarish no-go-zones and in-between-places.

Ze meets Ivan Vladislavić again at De Boekehuis in Melville, a smaller and more exclusive book café in a much more suburban setting, far from Hillbrow, but perhaps the closest current correspondent to what Hillbrow was at the time as well; the entertainment district of the intellectual middle-class. Ivan has recently published *Portrait with Keys: Joburg & What-What*, a mixture of journal, reportage, memoir, prose poem and collage on life in present-day Johannesburg, with all its absurdities and ambiguities. He looks astonishingly the same as fifteen years ago; it is almost as if they picked up an interrupted conversation, although none of them remembers what they were actually talking about. Now they talk about the mythical aura that has come to surround the Hillbrow of the late '80s, not unlike the one framing the Sophiatown of the '50s, the Southern off-shoot of the Harlem Renaissance that was levelled to the ground to give room for white trash Triomf, the literal emblem of apartheid's pyrrhic victory over urban modernity. If it were not for *Drum*'s defiant predecessors of new journalism, even the name Sophiatown might have vanished. Now the myth lives as strongly as ever, also in its inversion as *Triomf*, for which Marlene van Niekerk has secured a haven in the new national imaginary. But the myth of Hillbrow is another one; it is not the myth of a quashed modernity-to-be, the cradle of a contra-factual non-apartheid South Africa. Hillbrow is the metaphor for the *real* transformation, for the emerging *Afropolis* ... The first night in the home of hir hostess, Nomsa from Harare, ze was to hir surprise offered *dagga* after dinner. It happens very seldom, ze can't even recall the previous time, but in the sharpened perception and illusory clarity of inebriation, standing on the terrace, overlooking the veritable urban jungle below, when Nomsa's husband David told hir about the series of burglaries that had stripped them of all valuables, the last time at gun-point and in the conviction that the last thing the burglars would take before leaving would be their lives, ze could almost physically sense the fear, the quiet menace from the glimmering slums, little more than a stone's throw away ... The novel of the new metropolis is soberly prosaic. Affirmative, at most, but without lyrical overtones. Yet writing the city is re-inhabiting it, crossing the barriers, connecting the forbidden zones; reclaiming the effectively shattered public space.

Alone, ze is a sorry victim. But in Nomsa's company, ze returns to Hillbrow, contained by her calm; walking down Pretoria Street, attentive, perceptive, possessed with a peculiar resigned assurance.

References

Mpe, P. (2001). *Welcome to Our Hillbrow.* Scottsville: University of KwaZulu-Natal Press.

van Niekerk, M. (1999 [1994]). *Triomf.* Transl. by Leon de Kock. London: Little, Brown.

Vladislavić, I. (2002). *The Restless Supermarket.* Claremont: David Philip.

CHAPTER 3

Bengaluru Boogie

with Photos by Ayisha Abraham

(2013)

The original version of this chapter was revised: Figure text citations have been removed. The correction to this chapter is available at
https://doi.org/10.1007/978-3-030-34925-7_8

Fig. 3.1   The city

TEN YEARS EARLIER ze, that is *he*, was another person. The altered perspective does not entirely have to do with the change of gender, but the manifestation could not have been timelier, with the daily new gruesome disclosures of "the Delhi case". The gang rape of the twenty-three-year-old physiotherapist student and the demonstrations of protest all across the subcontinent have been breaking news ever since hir arrival two weeks ago. As a woman (hermaphrodite), ze is being seen with other eyes, but ze is also seeing other things than last time, because ze is looking for other things. Jyothsna talks about the metropolis of the drowsy millennium as the "pre-broken Bangalore". Then ze, that is he, was only here for three or four days, at the end of a twelve-day condensed grand tour Bombay-Ahmedabad-Varanasi-Delhi-Bangalore-Delhi, whereof all-in-all at least two full days were spent at Delhi airport, which the coldest winter in forty years had wrapped in coal smog and fog. Ze hardly remembered anything about Bangalore, except the nice weather. *The air-conditioned city*, an as worn-out cliché as *India's Silicon Valley*—and not even the weather is persistent.

Ten years ago, he was in the company of Madan, a cheery IT researcher who had invited him to stay in the living-room of his two-room apartment in some lush suburban neighbourhood (*ze has no recollection of the direction, but ze remembers that the view from the balcony over green as yet un-drained swamps evoked a long-lost memory of hir childhood's Almhög; the view from their balcony over farmlands about to be expropriated for the expanding Malmö*). He had met Madan the week before at a disastrous ICT and Development conference in Varanasi, where they had both felt out-of-place; an instant friendship of the kind he used to make on his travels, mutually beneficial, as it were to turn out. Madan had recently published his *Asia Pacific Internet Handbook*, the first comprehensive overview of the digital revolution in South and East Asia, including Australia, with the subtitle "Episode IV: Emerging Powerhouses". The Star Wars allusion indicated that he saved the pre-history for later, moving straight into the second round of the global Internet race, the one that had just started, about the mobile and the wireless; a round in which Asia had already taken the lead. The hardware producers Japan and South Korea were in the forefront, but the emerging powerhouses were of course China and India with their giant markets; they were the ones to generate the coming veritable explosion (the third, take-off stage of the digital revolution) … The first night in Bangalore, Madan had taken him to an outdoor concert with the violinist virtuosi Lakshminarayana Subramaniam and Jean-Luc Ponty and afterwards they went to a party at the house of Rajesh Reddy, the executive director of July Systems, who had just got back from San Francisco, his other home, to which he commuted once a month. A mix of old and new pop music streamed from the digital jukebox on the S-shaped bar, where bourbon and Drambuie were blended on the rocks in heavy glasses, the soft conversation moved from complaints over the increasingly hostile climate in the USA to jokes about America's lagging behind in the digital race, "they have only recently discovered SMS" (*giggle*). Ze could recall the scene because he had described it in his last reportage; that is, ze did not remember, but that was the way he had reconstructed it, with exactly those significant details, the clichés of the IT metropolis, juxtaposed to the pilgrim town by the Ganges, whose murdering cold by contrast still evoked chills of discomfort. *Death in Varanasi* … People froze to death by the hundreds, while the pilgrims continued performing their morning rituals in the cold and highly polluted water and the gold-diggers poked for tooth fillings and nose jewellery in the ashes of the funeral piles. He laid awake a whole night in a shivering fit at the pension whose name ze does not remember (*why didn't he ever memorise hotel names?*) thinking about Death in Varanasi.

He wrote his last reportage on commission, and received a decent honorarium, but it was never published. He waited for the next issue of the journal, then the next and the next again, until it was too late to offer it to someone else. It was not his best reportage, but it still nags hir that it never went to print. Ten years later, ze is also reading what he wrote with other eyes; that which had been in the forefront, the very point about *India's Catch 22*, that the competitive advantages over other developing economies would cease the moment it started to move up the global IT chain, *blah blah*, now appeared to be trivial, or even irrelevant, whereas the second register of the reportage, which was then in the background, points towards that which now preoccupies hir: the latent holocaust, group psychosis, the outbursts of unfathomable bestiality. Ten years ago, the pogroms of Gujarat were fresh in the minds of victims and perpetrators. He had been shown the cleansed residential areas in Ahmedabad, but without paying much attention to what he saw, without trying to induce the evil *genius loci*. There were no traces, no bloodstains, no stink of stale clotted horror (as the one that would nauseate him many years later in Rwanda, where the mouldering clothes of the murdered had been put in neat bundles in the pews), but it still astounded hir that he had not been more profoundly stricken by the moment. Obtunded, or simply absent-minded? On the verge of the second Iraqi war, anti-Islamic rhetoric permeated the public debate, security controls were as rigorous as in the USA (*or Israel, where he had never been*), and although he may have intuitively grasped that in India the exception had been the rule ever since the disastrous partition in 1947, the mother of all pogroms, it was only many years later that he would realise the full extent of the hecatomb. No, it was still unfathomable, just like the gruesome popular festival in Rwanda, or the extermination of Europe's Jews and Gypsies … Unfathomable, but not unintelligible; Arjun Appadurai dissects the logic of genocide with chilling exactitude in *Fear of Small Numbers*; the majority's fear of the minority that stands in the way of the completion of wholeness, and which must be destroyed because if proportions were inverted the then majority would do exactly the same. India has no memorials over the butchered; nobody wants to be reminded because everyone is incriminated, more or less; even the untouchable.

Mass Violence is not only the consequence of antagonistic identities, the violence in itself is one of the means by which the illusion of fixed and loaded identities is shaped and maintained … The minority is the symptom, but the underlying problem is difference. Therefore, the purpose is the elimination of difference; that is the hallmark of large-scale predatory narcissism. Remember Philip Gourevitch's statement about Rwanda: Genocide, after all, is an exercise in community-building.[1]

---

[1] Appadurai 2006; Gourevitch 1998: 95.

Fig. 3.2 One way

INDIA OVERWHELMS hir. "An assault on all the senses", as V. S. Naipaul so accurately has put it, ze does not know where but has it from a reliable source. Ten years ago, *he* had experienced the ambivalence, too, but now it is physical, a dyspnoea, a threatening nervous breakdown. The crowds, the sweat, the odours from exhaust pipes and sewers, the hands that furtively stroke hir body, the exposure in the auto-rickshaws that fearlessly crisscross in the constant rush-hour traffic, a wonder that it is at all possible to travel unhurt, just a few dents and scratches in the paint, like caresses, a word that connotes carcass … *car-casses, car-kisses* … Every transport a strenuous enterprise, Nandi Durga Road, where the pension is, an almost insurmountable barrier; once back at Droog House, ze is so exhausted that ze stays in hir room the rest of the day. In the reportage he had likened Bangalore to *a botanical garden traversed by motorways* and regardless of whether it was an accurate metaphor or just another cliché, it is completely out of place now, ten years later, when the number of inhabitants, the human mass, has grown from sixty to a hundred *lakhs*, and the cars, motorbikes and auto-rickshaws must have tripled or quadrupled; the few sorry trees left along the extinguished pavements look like the burnt tree trunks that miraculously survived a forest fire. Out of place, yet predictable. Banal (*like the contrast to Varanasi*); The Botanical Garden, Lal Bagh, is Bangalore's only attraction, according to *The Lonely*

Planet (*but he never visited it then*); an extensive oasis, in the centre of which Gondwana raises its bald pate of gneiss, three, maybe four billion years old. Immemorial, without memory.

Now ze is in Bangalore to participate in a conference, *Mediating Modernity in the 21st Century*, for which ze hirself is one of the organisers. The city changed name in 2006, but ze never heard anyone pronounce the revived Bengaluru. It is not laden with ideology like Bombay—Mumbai, where M still might signal Hindu nationalism, whereas B (as in Bom Bahia) connoted cosmopolitanism rather than colonialism, although Bengaluru does signal *Kannada* nationalism, while Bangalore remains inseparably associated with the British Empire, the garden city of its retired servants. In fact, although ze does not realise that yet, it is two cities that have lived side by side and only merged during the second part of the twentieth century, the City and *the Cantonment*, which turned its back on the City² ... Cantonment, *containment*, the English enclave imported their house serv-ants from Madras, not Mysore ... The origin of coordinates is somewhere in Cubbon Park, but the borderline between the twin cities is nowadays an invisible seam, like the difference between Tamil and Kannada for the inex-pert; the subcontinent's forty languages and almost as many scripts is yet another warp in the composite fabric. Hardly any traces remain of the old Bengaluru, before the English conquest; a fragment of Tipu Sultan's fort, embedded by the bus station and the market (*the rickshaw driver had never heard of it*); an air of the eternal market's extravagance, the cones of spices in the warm register of the rainbow, the sea of guillotined flowers, but the light of their petals does not banish the stink of putrid oil; the basic colour is russet to black.

Let it wither! says Vasanthi, who is coordinating a Swedish-Indian collaboration project on Cultural Heritage. A metropolis that did not forget would soon be buried in its own memorials. But Bengaluru's amnesia is exceptional! It is not denial, or suppression, but blindness, self-delusion, *simulacrum*. The symbol is Singapore. Hir only image of Singapore is the one that William Gibson engraved in a reportage in *Wired* in the mid '90s: *Disneyland with the Death Penalty*.³

² Nair 2005; Pani, Radhakrishna & Bhat 2010.

³ Gibson 1993.

Ze witnesses the demonstrations against the sexual violence on TV, not in the streets of Bangalore, the cries for capital punishment for the arrested perpetrators, the youngest in particular, the one who has committed the ghastliest violation, an iron rod in the vagina. The editor's column in *The Times of India*, which is hung in a bag on the door handle to his room every morning, makes a comparison of the last month's two globally mediated tragedies: the gang rape in Delhi and the school massacre in Connecticut; Obama's decisive and upright behaviour versus the gawky Manmohan Singh, but also the lack of protests against the weapon industry and easy access to firearms versus the wrath and indignation of the Indian middle class. But those who protest in the streets, says writer and activist Harsh Mander, are indifferent to the street children who get raped every night. Mander gives an open lecture on *Unequal India* in the location that a few days later will be the venue of the *Mediating Modernity* conference. He defies his middle-class audience by comparing today's India with the US American South in the 1960s. The elite schools' reluctance to accept quota-based admission of Dalit students is like the resistance against the Civil Rights movement and the desegregation of the schools in the South. The same confusion of privilege and merit; the horror of putting your children in the same school as the children of the servants, to find out that the gardener's or the housemaid's kid is smarter than your own. The listeners unashamedly confirm his observations by their comments and questions. (*No anxiety of showing your colours here, as opposed to South Africa. At a dinner in the home of one of the design teachers at Srishti, where all housework is carried out by servants, the hostess smiles and remarks that "this is the privilege of living in India".*) But the challenging question is left hanging in the air, ze is not sure what hir own answer would be: Are you prepared to understand—and forgive—the juvenile rapist in Delhi?

The next evening, William Dalrymple gives a lecture at the National Gallery of Modern Art about the last Mughals; one and a half century, from 1707 to 1857, which the History books describe as a period of decay, that is, times characterised by miscegenation and cultural mélange. *The White Mughals* are predominantly Scots, transferred from the Empire's Western outpost in North America, who fall in love with India to the extent that they take Indian wives and convert to Islam. As radical as ever Sir Richard Burton, and in any case the negation of hir preconceptions about Brits in India. That is, hir conception of British colonialism is marked by the experience of Durban, and of Kenya. Now, all of a sudden, the concept *Anglo-Indian*, a term that encompasses all children of Indian mother and European father, attains a different meaning. Even the offspring of Frenchmen, Dutchmen and Germans are Anglo-Indians, just as all immigrants to Argentina travelling with Ottoman passports became *turcos*. When ze asks how many they are, nobody seems to know the answer, not even an estimate. It is almost like asking for the number of Brahmins.

IN SIX MONTHS ze will sit at hir late found favourite place, Indian Coffee House *on Church Street, pale blue walls, wooden tables, laminate-clad wooden benches, waiters in white, classical Mysore garment* (ze believes), *heavy belts and ornamented headgear, like loosely tied turbans; the cashier in round steel-rimmed glasses looks like a teacher, or intellectual. At the table in front of him, by the opening to the kitchen, a barefoot man puts his signature on the bills before the waiters take them to the cashier. The guests are all old or middle-aged men, alone or in company, immersed in soft conversation or reading the paper, one is playing with his mobile. The posters on the walls could have been the retro props of a hipster bar, but these have most certainly hanged there since before Independence: a proud bearded man and a plate with roasted coffee beans, a fine type, a* fine coffee, both are Indian. *The coffee is exquisite, and so is the* dhosa, *hir simple lunch.*

The third journey settles over the second, nuancing the picture ... it will wonder hir that ze gets so little out of the on-going sojourn, in spite of its three week duration, ze will explain it partly with the isolation at Droog House (next time ze is staying at Elanza Hotel on Richmond Road and the city is accessible in a completely different manner), *partly with hir insufficient preparations, ze is not well-enough-read ... As a reporter he could be unprepared and still find his way, by intuition and improvisation, but now there is no compelling force, unlike ten years ago ze is not doing any interviews, none of that dialectic generated by the hyper-active reporter mode, a state of mind that requires solitude, he would never have been able to work in pairs, not even with a photographer, because every social concession would disturb his concentration ... Now it is something else that ze is after, uncertain what exactly, perhaps impossible or not even desirable, it remains obscure six months ahead,*

when ze recapitulates this already distant now. Then, as now, ze worries
about the insensibility, no doubt a form of blunting, or habitual blind-
ness and numbness, as devious as alcoholism; blasé is the wrong word,
because ze is still curious, radical also in a conventional political sense
(more radical now than ten years ago) ... *Even though ze sets hir mind*
on absorbing, registering, remembering all the significant details, it is as
if the impressions pass hir perception without a trace, the travels of recent
years merge in hir memory, muddle, fade. Is there simply a limit as to how
much you are able to remember? He used to assure himself that everything
was there, somewhere, subliminally, below the surface, in the darkroom
of consciousness, like undeveloped film ... *But keen eyes and ears were*
never his distinctive characteristics, his foremost asset as a reporter was
the reflection, the surprise association, the ability to think in new direc-
tions, new even to himself ... *Boldness requires a certain innocence, an*
undaunted ignorance, too much preparation prevents audacity ... *The*
revisit six months from now will strengthen hir conviction that ze is on
to something important, both in terms of the form, the ethnographic fiction, *and the subject, the phantom of partition and the silence about the*
unhealed wound. But hinting is not enough, ze has to go to the marrow ...
At the table next to hir, two Muslim men are sitting forehead to forehead
in their white skullcaps, beside them, with his back to hir, a man in jeans
and a t-shirt that says Shakespeare and Company Network of Writers,
maybe a Westerner or Anglo-Indian ... *That would be another alterna-*
tive, an ethnographic study of the Anglo-Indian minority, a compara-
tive study of marginalized hybrid communities in racially and culturally
segregated societies; Anglo-Indians, South Africa's "coloureds", the creo-
lised Swedes of Misiones ... *Then three young women sit down at the table*
to his left, and behind them a man reading a Kannada newspaper (ze
assumes); *it can just as well be Tamil, but not Hindu, because ze rec-*
ognises the South Indian characters, rounded in order not to destroy the
fibres of the palm leaf). It is a fine point from which to observe and reflect,
nobody pays hir any attention.

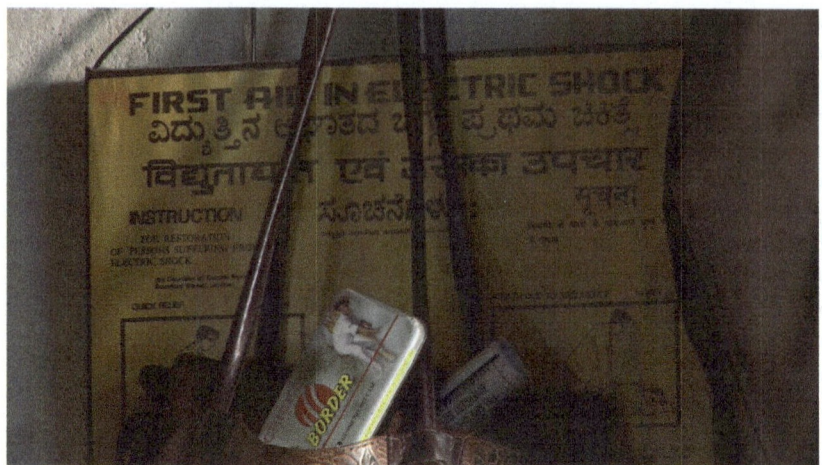

Fig. 3.3 Border

WHY ARE THE middle classes so angry? Arjun Appadurai, escorted by his stunning Slovenian wife, is shorter and darker than ze had imagined him. He is the keynote and draw of the *Mediating Modernity* conference, but that is not the reason for his visit to Bangalore, the modest conference has on the contrary been timed according to his schedule; he is invited by the Tata group's National Institute of Advanced Studies, and on his main performance he speaks to a full auditorium at the Institute on the subject *Corruption as Participation in Neo-Liberal India.* Appadurai distinguishes the traditional vertical corruption, the one that consists of gifts and tips, from the modern, global one, which is horizontal and fraternal. India is a cash economy. Credit cards are scarce, half the population is unbanked (*a peculiar word, ze loses hirself for a moment in search of a Swedish translation*) ... The motif for economic liberalisation in the '90s was more transparency, but the result turned out to be the opposite. Today half the economy is informal. There is of course a correlation here. The cash economy is, according to Appadurai, a more important explanation to contemporary India's peculiarity than all the cultural factors put together. But, why this sudden fury? There are two things that make the upwards-striving middle classes take to the streets to demonstrate: sexual violence and corruption. It is partly an anger turned inwards, frustration over dependency, over being so intrinsically involved in the corrupt transactions, horizontal and vertical. India is a beast that has wakened and started to move—not the wise elephant that venture capitalist Gurcharan Das envisioned ten years ago, in contrast to the East Asian tigers; the elephant who moves forward steadily and surely, pausing occasionally to reflect on its past and enjoy the journey[4]—but a brute whose face the world has barely begun to divine.

The middle classes strive for the obscene opulence of the richest ten percent, while at the same time trampling on the likewise upwards-struggling Dalits. The caste hierarchy is multiplex and unfathomable (incomprehensible to an outsider), with new alliances that allow a certain social mobility; corruption is the sphere of convergence ... *a charismatic interruption in the bureaucratic routine* (did he really say that?) ... Corruption as opposed to communalism? The violence against the Dalits, the casteless, is perpetrated by those second lowest on the ladder, the low-castes who are not favoured by *reservation*. Inciting communal violence is an efficient way of diverting the frustration of the poor and preventing the low-castes from rising against the high-castes. Muslims, the majority among minorities, Pakistan's alleged fifth column, is the national scapegoat, but in Bangalore the eruptions of communal violence have also occurred along linguistic lines, Kannada against Tamil and Urdu.

In the hotel room ze zaps between the TV channels, all *Fox News* lookalikes. The Delhi case has had to stand aside for the breaking news about a killed frontier guard in Kashmir; beheaded, as far as ze can decipher from the agitated commentators who stir up the hatred and demand retaliation. In one of the channels, the foreign minister tries hard to fend off the fiery interviewer's accusations of indulgence towards the archenemy. It has not occurred to hir until that moment that the resentment rests so immediately underneath the surface, ze can sense the latent holocaust; the reversible pogroms that are only waiting for the signal to be unleashed; if ze were to imagine the possibility of a nuclear war, it would be here. *People are as easy to set fire to as matches.* Ze remembers those exact words from his reportage from Istanbul in 1998, during the Öcalan crisis, when people burned spaghetti in the streets prior to Galatasaray's draw with Juventus in the Champion's League.[5] One of his Kurdish informants used the phrase to evoke the riots in Smyrna/Izmir, the population swap between Greece and Turkey, a

---

[4] Das 2002.
[5] See Hemer & Persson 2017: 4–6.

minor scale parallel to India's partition when twelve million people were replaced across the new border and one million murdered. Is it possible to imagine anything worse than the ethnic (or religious) narcissism, the excuse and prerequisite for genocide? A deceptive simplification, perhaps, fundamentalism vs. cosmopolitanism—maybe *cosmopolitanism from below* is just illusory wishful thinking, like Anarchism's faith in human altruism, the fundament of libertarian socialism … But what else could one rely on? The terror balance of self-interest.

TEN YEARS earlier he had travelled in a flying saucer. Electronic City, the largest in the corridor of IT parks, *IIIT-B*, India's cutting-edge academy for IT engineers, an already faded hyper-modernity rising over the stalls and cartridges of the rudimentary subsistence economy, but on the interior a space station, manned by the rebels against the Empire. Open source against Microsoft's monopoly (long before Facebook and Google). *The Linux Spirit*, like the electronic frontier of the early '90s, The California ideology, but with a social conscience.

It was easy to imagine how old Everett Rogers on his tour around India's tech parks had been taken in by these young enthusiastic engineers and entrepreneurs. India's road to the future seemed as obvious as appropriate: *the informatisation strategy*.[6] The last five years had implied a greater change than fifty years of independence, was the mantra that could be taken for an incantation. But "informatisation" never became an accepted sequel to industrialisation. And what happened to the expected exponential growth of Internet teashops, community centres and local radio stations, that would spread the blessings of the IT metropolis to the villages and light up the compact rural darkness? He did not see anything of village India then, and ze hardly does now either, but ze cannot avoid the slums, just a few blocks from Nandi Durga Road. *In Bangalore even the poor make an impression of prosperity*, was one of the statements in his reportage. That sentence is the only one ze shamefully regrets.

[6] Singhal & Rogers 2001.

The transformation is simple. A long purple *kurta* over white cotton trousers, white cloth shoes, a shawl over head and shoulders, a little eye-shadow, and eyeliner under the eyes. But when ze finally gets half a day on hir own, ze puts away the shawl and the make-up, to stroll in the district Shivajinagar, ten minutes rickshaw ride from the hotel. Filled with the notion of vernacular cosmopolitanism, ze feels part of the millennial urbanity, an unusual but not unfamiliar element in the multitude. Here ze wanders undisturbed, but there is nowhere to go; the mosques are forbidden, as are the Hindu temples with their towers of smurf-like multi-coloured idols, and ze would not step into the dark of any of the few bars even if someone invited hir. There is a smell of oil, of dismantled engines and gearboxes, the canal is a dry ditch, clogged with garbage, refuse (*what's the difference?*), sewage, the sweet human smell, ze comes to think of a book title, *Den deodoriserade skunken* [The Deodorised Skunk], an insignificant work from the late 1960s, a completely misplaced association, baroque, a defence against the galvanised reality around hir, like the lens of the mobile: he used to be a good photographer, or could have become, with his restored Leica M2 from 1962 which he bought in Stockholm in 1976 at the prize of 1200 kronor, which at the time corresponded to 250 US Dollars and today would be the equivalent of 2500 or more. He used to slosh about in the dark room at the School of Journalism, 25 ASA on Portriga Rapid, melancholy pictures from his monk-like existence in a summer house eighty kilometres north of Stockholm; later it would be slides from his travelling in Africa and Latin America. The camera ceased to function in 1992 in Tanzania; he had shot a whole film on villages on the shore of Lake Tanganyika that had been taken over by baboons, and on chimpanzees in Jane Goodall's reserve, where one of the males had made a charge at his Italian travel companion, but nothing had been exposed on the non-unrolled film, and afterwards—now—it is as if that journey never took place, or was a dream. After the Leica he had a cheap Nikon that caught everybody's attention every time the shutter opened and closed, then a couple of digital cameras that all broke down after less than a year, and ever since he made do with the mobile, but never got the feeling back for photography. The overflow of instant images has blunted the gaze, or the will, ze has never even held a video camera in hir hand, a limitation, no doubt, like the aversion against social media, ze really *hates* Facebook, intensely and irrationally, an eccentric whim, maybe preposterous, but not a matter of snobbery; no nostalgic lamentation over

Fig. 3.4 Basement theatre

worldly shallowness or disenchantment, only light-hearted sadness at mediocrity ... Ze has no pretentions to be more than an observer, a tourist, although that word is so circumscribed by contempt, both for vulgar charter tourism and as a metaphor for the new mobile elite, as opposed to those who are displaced by force, or who can't move, tourists and vagabonds (*or which was Bauman's dichotomy?*).[7] The people ze meets in the alleys of Shivajinagar, who hardly notice hir, or at least don't turn their heads, are they even vagabonds, or for ever banished to this periphery? Swarming, stinking Shivajinagar, an Anti-Singapore in the heart of the IT metropolis, the remains of the vast semi-slum that the English called Blackpally, of which the most muddled parts were levelled to the ground after the plague to give space for Fraser Town. On the other side of the railway lies Cooke Town, where both Jyothsna and Ayisha live.

THE GLOBALISATION of Indifference. The new Pope, Francis, is to be credited for that expression, but it could just as well have been Harsh Mander's; the very visible limit for the empathy of the middle class, in India as in Argentina and in the entire brave new world ... Cubbon Park has been fenced in, to shut the masses out; in the middle-class

---

[7] Bauman 1998.

metropolis, plebeian democracy is a private nuisance. But no matter how one entrenches oneself behind fences and walls, it still permeates with its noise and its smells—like an *entropy of diversity*—if only as scenes outside the toned car windows on the way to the office or the private school.

Hir own indifference is challenged daily, but not until ze returns in six months will anyone reach behind hir shield. A beggar girl follows hir high pace a couple of blocks, ze does not routinely whisk her away as ze uses to do, sometimes without even noticing, but ze does not have any change, only five-hundred rupee bills; the girl senses hir indecision, as if she sees through hir dissemblance, and to escape the humiliation ze stops at the first street shop they pass to buy eight different ayurvedic soaps. When ze gets the change back, he gives the girl thirty rupees—sixty cents!—and regrets it the moment she disappointedly slouches away. Why didn't ze give her fifty, or a hundred, or five hundred? Ze can't scatter money about, that would serve no purpose, but why couldn't ze surprise the girl—and hirself? That elusive meeting with a snotty-nosed girl, twelve, thirteen, fourteen years old, perhaps a cunning scrounger, will be hir only close encounter with anyone other than the deliberate colleagues at Srishti— with the exception of rickshaw drivers, but then the relation is strictly regulated by the situation, a non-relation, a transaction, eventually even without negotiation, according to the meter, but the girl whose hopes ze raises to immediately dash shall grieve hir the rest of the third journey.

Six months from now the rapists are convicted, the rebellious spirit has vanished and the media are already saturated with the upcoming election campaign, Hindu fundamentalist and opposition leader Modi's measures and statements being the serial story. Ze shall seriously doubt hir own usually reliable judgement when one of the colleagues at Srishti, whom ze had instantly found very likable, comes out as a devoted Modi supporter. "If India as a whole were to be governed like Gujarat, it would be a completely different country". She sounds like an echo of her husband, who at dinner the night before had explained China's advantage over India by its racial homogeneity and strong central power. Hir suggestion that caste might have something to do with it had been whisked away with a sigh resembling a snort. In the original Hinduism, caste was like a guild, something you acquired, not something you inher-ited. The distortion was due to the Muslim invasion. In the beginning of time, there were no minorities. Everybody was a Hindu. As a mat-ter of fact, he had declared, India was more divided now than before Independence, because of the *Reservation* policy. "For how long are we as Brahmins going to pay for our forefathers alleged wrong-doings?" "Instead of lifting the Dalits to a higher level, the standard is lowered for everyone." … The usual arguments about flattening and vulgarisation, the propertied classes' defence of their hereditary privileges … [propertied *is a strange word, as if they were burdened, weighed down, owned by their property … And why does it provoke hir so? Where does the sudden sensation of* class hatred *come from* (if that is the proper word)? *Ze, who grew up in one of Malmö's dismal inner suburbs, but always felt out of place, superior to the working-class neighbours* (that was from hir mother, not hir father). *The first time hir brother could vote, in the local elections 1966, he voted for a liberal-conservative coalition that challenged the ruling social democrats; one year later all the siblings were communists … A string of memories inadvertently pop up from that year of grace of pre-puberty, when ze fully lived up to hir parents' expectations* (mother's minion; father's favourite was hir eldest sister); *ze accompanied them on a public debate at the Amiralen dance hall between a rising Olof Palme and his ten years' younger liberal adversary Per Ahlmark* (although ze was supposed to support Ahlmark, ze secretly considered Palme to be the winner; Palme, the newly appointed Minister of Communications, who shortly afterwards—or was it before?—was welcomed with rotten tomatoes in Malmö, after closing the pirate radio station Radio Syd); *they took him to R-rated movies, Alain Resnais' La guerre est finie, endlessly slow but with nude scenes* (Ingrid Thulin with Yves Montand, hir mother's idol) *that made hir blush with innocuous indulgence, just like Ulla Sjöblom in Jan Troell's* Här har du ditt liv, *the strongest darkroom experience of all from this year of behaved and precocious contentment, before the complete and irreversible fall*] … Ze does not want to write the colleague's name, in case she is going to read it, although she would immediately recognise herself anyway and although she is not at all ashamed of her opinion—on the contrary! But maybe ze wants to retain hir first impression, which ze always used to trust. She had been silent during dinner, while the husband swaggered, ze had not for a moment identified her with his unvarnished fascism, but then the day after, in the car to Srishti, she is not only an echo of her spouse, but even worse. The sweet little mouth, which ze had associated with a little girl, becomes the jaws of a trooper. Modi, the butcher from Gujarat, prime-minister-to-be in the world's largest democracy … If that happens, Jyothsna says she is going to emigrate. Maybe regardless of the outcome of the elections. She can't stand being a woman in India, every time she goes abroad she

can feel her entire body language change, relaxing and becoming herself
... Ze understands what she means, although ze can only imagine what
it would be like to live here; ze is white, twenty years older, and not a
woman, too big, too manly, a butch or a tranny ... everywhere else in
the world ze would be more vulnerable as a third gender, but not here,
where the hermaphrodite is less offensive than the young woman who
does not prove her subjugation by avoiding the men's glances or stepping aside when they meet. The glances ze receives may be defamatory,
but not threatening, and most often simply indifferent; ze is neither nor,
invisible, harmless, neutral, like the untouchables who undisturbed plun-
dered both Muslim and Hindu homes during the mutual massacres of
the Partition; whereas the women, the vessels of religious chastity, were
not to be soiled. They were forced to commit suicide, or executed by
their husbands and fathers, in order not to end in the arms of the enemy.
The concept of honour killing attained henceforward a very concrete
meaning. Wells filled with dead women, the last ones to jump in survived
if there was not water enough to drown them all.

ZE FINDS HIR Ze way to Ayisha in Cooke Town with certain difficulty. The rickshaw driver calls for instructions several times from hir Swedish mobile, the journey ends up being more expensive than a taxi ride, but taxi drivers are even worse at finding their way, Bengaluru is a labyrinth where all districts have the same street names—first, second main street, second, third cross street—but at last ze arrives and is welcomed in the stairwell by two waist-high dogs that would have scared hir stiff if ze had met them in the street, and after that, in the evening sun on the balcony, to hir complete surprise, Asu, Kevin's wife, whom ze hasn't met in many years. Ze knew that she was coming to Bangalore, to participate in the same conference, but ze had no idea that Asu and Ayisha were old friends; Ayisha had lived in Turkey for a year in the mid '90s. They tell hir a fantastic story; when Ayisha and Asu's younger sister were hitch-hiking in northern Anatolia, they were picked up by a man who took them to a deserted place up in the mountains. He could have been a rapist, a psychopath, a murderer, but all he wanted was to show them the view over the Black Sea. When they return to the valley below, an earthquake has ploughed through the landscape and buried the village where they had spent the night. The man who saved them is now Asu's brother-in-law, although her sister divorced him a long time ago. They have a grown-up son in Istanbul.

Ayisha's short films tell stories of people who live in the interstices, Anglo-Indian neighbours, the Nepalese garage guard, the Indian-Burmese dancer Ram Gopal; she calls them *quasi-documentaries*, but they are considered too arty for documentary film festivals. The raw material are restored 8 mm films, vanished colours, a very special nostalgic nimbus, her parents' first journey abroad from the newly independent India gives a flashback to the family film screenings of hir own childhood, the purring projector, the moment of awe, a very efficient way of tying the family together, the envied community, the sibling solidarity whose glossed over conflicts ze was luckily unaware of … The interstices, the passages, fragments of stories, abstract, tangible; it strikes hir that these observations in the margin are the ones that narrate the history of Bangalore, a permanence in the transformation, as the comfort ze feels in front of Ayisha's computer, watching hir films, one after the other, like an endless loop which ze wishes will never stop, while Ayisha and Asu are talking in low voices and moving around the room, as if ze weren't there.

Fig. 3.5 A storm

References

Appadurai, A. (2006). *Fear of Small Numbers: An Essay on the Geography of Anger.* Durham: Duke University Press.

Bauman, Zygmunt (1998). *Globalization: The Human Consequences.* London: Polity.

Das, G. (2002). *The Elephant Paradigm: India Wrestles with Change.* New Delhi: Penguin.

Gibson, W. (1993). "Disneyland with the Death Penalty". *Wired* 1 (4): 51–55.

Gourevitch, P. (1998). *We Wish to Inform You That Tomorrow We Will be Killed With Our Families: Stories from Rwanda.* New York: Farrar, Straus and Giroux.

Hemer, O. & H.-Å. Persson (2017). *In the Aftermath of Gezi: From Social Movement to Social Change?* Basingstoke: Palgrave Macmillan.

Nair, J. (2005). *The Promise of the Metropolis: Bangalore's Twentieth Century.* New Delhi: Oxford University Press.

Pani, N., S. Radhakrishna, & K. G. Bhat (eds.). (2010). *Bengaluru, Bangalore, Bengaluru: Imaginations and Their Times.* New Delhi: Sage.

Singhal, A. & E. M. Rogers. (2001). *India's Communication Revolution: From Bullock Carts to Cybermarts.* New Delhi: Sage.

CHAPTER 4

Cape Calypso I

Impurity and Danger
(Sounding Stellenbosch)

(2015)

© The Author(s) 2020
O. Hemer, *Contaminations and Ethnographic Fictions*,
Palgrave Studies in Literary Anthropology,
https://doi.org/10.1007/978-3-030-34925-7_4

THE CRADLE

YOU CAN GET LOST IN STELLENBOSCH. The first day at the Institute, ze walks out in the wrong direction, following Marais street instead of van Riebeck, and when ze realises the mistake and tries to correct it, without either a map or the direction of hir residence, ze soon gets disoriented in the lofty labyrinth of shaded pave walks and white rectangular buildings, departments, dormitories, all belonging to the University; like a city plan by Le Corbusier, sanitary, modern, conspicuously white, buzzing with students who have just returned from the summer break, Afrikaans-speaking, conspicuously white with scattered exceptions in pairs or small groups, their faces shades of brown, not black, *bruin-mense*, as they were benevolently branded by their white superiors. Ze is going to walk these streets every day in the coming months, but this first impression of disorientation will persist in a latent feeling of estrangement. Where is ze? It could be a campus town anywhere in the affluent West, California, Australia, a subtropical Holland—*Hottentot Holland*—a garden city with vineyards climbing the backdrop of the majestic mountains. This is the cradle of apartheid. It's hard to believe, unless you think of it as benevolent evil. D. F. Malan, the first prime minister of the apartheid state was chancellor of Stellenbosch University when his National Party ascended to power in 1948. His hat and pipe, a rock-hanger and a few bookshelves are left as curious props in a corner of the University museum, between the ethnographic display of tribal cultures and the dull mimicry of modern art. Dr. Hendrik Verwoerd, the engineer rather than the architect, the brutal implementer of the master plan, had been Professor of Sociology at this same university in the formative 1930s, but his imprint is somehow retouched from the records (*Where did all his busts go? All of them could hardly end up in Orania, the Afrikaner reserve in the semi-desert Karoo*). His as staunch successor, B. J. (John) Vorster, was a former Law student at Stellenbosch, and Verwoerd's closest collaborator in the Ministry for Native Affairs, Werner Eiselen, had held the chair as Professor in *Volkekunde*, the science of physical and cultural anthropology that formed the academic basis for the ideology of apartness and separate development. Eiselen, the benevolent racist; loyal bureaucrat and perverse visionary, proposing total separation as the only way in which African cultures could be protected from the pernicious effects of urbanisation.[1] Ze looks

[1] Kross 2002: 60.

for vestiges of oppression, of surveillance, the fencing off of the barbarians at the gate, but dividing lines are invisible or internalised, not blurred; the campus security policing the streets is so discrete that one could take them for road workers in their orange vests. While xenophobia rampages the country, Stellenbosch remains a bubble; even when load shedding blacks out the streets, the whites confidently torch their way back to their moderately armoured residencies.

A DISCRETELY GREY hard-cover copy of the third impression (from 1970) is delivered with the eminent library service that brings whatever ze orders from the anonymous librarian all the way to hir desk within a day or two. The yellowed pages are full of pencil underlining and notes, and ze finds these reader's comments, made during the dark times, as intriguing as the text itself; the first library stamp is from 1975, the book has been frequently borrowed in the late '70s and early '80s, but only sporadically thereafter. How was it read, ze wonders, during the State of Emergency; as subversive critique or as ideological support of the politics of purity outlined and implemented by Afrikaner academics, all affiliated with Stellenbosch University. This was arguably the ideological cradle of apartheid (*although two of the Afrikaner fellows protest vehemently against hir allegation, made in passing over lunch, and stress that the racial segregation was long established as an integral part of the British colonial indirect rule; group area laws were implemented already in 1913, after the formation of the union, long before the Nationalist Party's takeover in '48*).

Ze imagines the author of these notes as one and the same Afrikaner student, who has struggled with the English, dictionary in hand, and had to look up and translate "consecrated" (*heilige*) and "profane" (*goddelose/heidense*). Written in 1966, in High Modernity, in the heyday of Western rationality and Technology-Optimism (*in the vacuum after the continental genocide yet to be named the Holocaust*), *Purity and Danger* is a radical cultural self-examination—...*[W]e shall not expect to understand other people's ideas of contagion, sacred or secular, until we have confronted our own*[2]— which portents the civilization critique and the postmodern breakup of the '70s and '80s. High Modernity coincides with High Apartheid; a yearly growth rate of six to seven per cent, dislocations, evictions, expulsions, obscene exploitation; the negation of modernity, reversing the influx from country to city, returning unwanted labour units to the miserable reservoirs called homelands (later *Bantustans*), while the white citizens prosper in unprecedented wealth.[3]

[2] Douglas 1966: 28.
[3] Dubow 2014: 99–101.

Dirt is essentially disorder. Separating, purifying, demarcating and punishing transgressions have as their main function to impose system on an inherently untidy experience. Only by exaggerating differences (within-without, male-female, black-white) is a semblance of order created.[4]

A semblance of difference? False diversity—as the apartheid regime's encouraging of the Coon festivals in the Cape[5], letting the coloured show their colours; even the queers come out of the closets to parade at the white masters' back. The queer coloured, that is, subject to the indifferent white gaze in the non-existent public sphere, the non-public non-space of absent contagion.

[4]Douglas 1966: 4.

[5]The New Year *Coon*—or *Klopse*—*Carnival* has, since it started in the 1920s, been a locus for the symbolic confrontation of opposed conceptions of "coloured" identities. For a thorough study of the Carnival's impact on Capetonian and South African culture, see Martin 1999.

WHY?

SIMON, one of hir fellows at the Institute, gave hir the book with this intriguing title, by the late sociologist Charles Tilly.[6] Written under the verdict of a terminal cancer, which most certainly added a special clarity to the thought, it is, as the subtitle reads, about "what happens when people give reasons … and why". Ze starts reading it in parallel with many other readings and will finish it (four weeks later), not for the obligation of returning it with a comment, but because ze is enthralled to know why Simon gave it to hir in the first place. They had only just met over lunch. After that first conversation, the same afternoon, ze comes across Simon's name as a reference in one of the books ze is reading for hir project on *Purity and Contamination*. Simon was one of the first to analyse the outbursts of deadly violence against "foreigners and strangers" in May and June 2008, a carnage reminiscent of and as abhorrent as the "black-on-black" butchery of the interregnum years. As ze is reading, new vile xenophobic attacks are being carried out, in Soweto and other black holes of the persisting apartheid cityscape, targeting Somali vendors, often in the presence of the police, who in some instances even participate in the looting. A month later Durban will explode in murderous rage, instigated by the Zulu king in leopard-skin garment, spreading inwards from the dreary townships to the city centre. Yesterday's breaking news of the bullying and harassment of black secondary school children by their white peers and self-appointed superiors will be forgotten. The concerned expert panels assembled on prime time in all the news channels to discuss why race is re-emerging as top obsession of the South African mind twenty years after the demise of apartheid, will reconvene to explain the xenophobic logic of inclusion and exclusion.

Why? is indeed the most pertinent question. Ze is back in South Africa for the seventh time. Three months as a fellow at the Institute, one of the privileged to have been invited to this creative space for the mind, as the slogan reads. Ze has not been anywhere abroad for so long, not since Ethiopia in the late 1980s. And for three months, ze will hardly set foot outside Stellenbosch, except for weekend excursions down the coast, and a five-day trip with J. to Namaqualand and Namibia (and a second trip to Namibia, to renew the residence permit). Ze is playing

[6]Tilly 2006.

with the thought of being in exile, imagining hir new career in a new country … (*Why is that preposterous? If ze were to emigrate, ze would possibly choose between Argentina and South Africa.*)

Why do victims become perpetrators? Have the former guest workers in their own country—potential criminals by definition, guilty until proven innocent—simply internalised the *Bantustan* mentality?[7] It may be more accurate to talk about *afrophobia*, the self-hate of blacks, a psychological disease of the mind that has killed more black people in the last five hundred years than any epidemic or plague.[8]

Ze sees Heribert Adam and Kogila Moodley for a coffee at the Institute, after just having finished reading *Imagined Liberation*, their comparative study on "xenophobia, citizenship and identity in South Africa, Canada and Germany". It's their second meeting; last year at about the same time, a few weeks after the book launch, just before their return to Vancouver, they had received hir in their Cape Town summer home. The chillingly premonitory analysis could not have been timelier. Why? Apartheid is only part of the answer, and Neo-liberalism but another partial reason. Xenophobic attitudes are equally strong among elites, black as white, and increasing in all groups, with Indians being slightly more tolerant than others. On the other hand, ecumenical tolerance still prevails; neither Islamism nor Islamophobia are as yet featuring in the public debate. The South African divided society has long learned to co-exist with diversity. That, says Heribert, is the main hope to overcome xenophobia. And yet now, in contrast to 2008, ANC leaders are coming out with coded xenophobic statements, Zuma's own son even breaking the code, in allegiance with the Leopard-skin pillbox king.

AT THE DAWN OF **Anthropology, Edward Burnett Tylor tried hard to prove that civilisation was the result of gradual progress from an original state similar to that of contemporary savagery. His understanding of cultures had obvious semblance with Darwin's handling**

---

[7]D. Everatt in special issue of the journal *Politikon*, 2011, in Adam & Moodley 2013: 37.

[8]Hassim, Kupe & Worby 2008, in Adam & Moodley 2013: 39–40.

of organic species, although Tylor was not so much interested in the survival of the fittest as in the lingering survival of the unfit. William Robertson Smith, inheriting the idea of evolution, was not interested in dead survivals, but in what modern and primitive experience had in common. Tylor founded folklore; Robertson Smith founded social anthropology.[9]

Robertson Smith inspired Emile Durkheim to develop "the germinal idea that primitive gods are part and parcel of the community, their form expressing accurately the details of its structure, their powers punishing and rewarding on its behalf".[10] Durkheim quarrelled with the English political philosophers, particularly Herbert Spencer, refusing to subscribe to utilitarian psychologism. He claimed the need for "a common commitment to a common set of values, a collective conscience" in order to correctly understand the nature of society. Magic, to Durkheim as to Robertson Smith, was an evolutionary residual, yet a form of *primitive hygiene*.[11]

Louis Moulinier, a French classicist, made a study of purity and impurity in Greek thought—"excellently empirical by current anthropological standards but free of anthropological bias"—and finds Greek thought to have been relatively void of ritual pollution in the time described by Homer, while later littered with clusters of pollution concepts, as expressed in the classical dramas. [littered *is not Douglas' word, but* clusters *has that derogatory tinge; litter as opposed to dirt*]. The study is condemned in the *Journal of Hellenic Studies* by an English reviewer for wanting in 19th century anthropology.[12]

[9] Ibid.: 14.
[10] Ibid.: 19.
[11] Ibid.: 20.
[12] Moulinier 1952, in ibid.: 26.

THE RACIST WITHIN

THE MOST CAPTIVATING part of Heribert and Kogila's book is the couple's concluding autobiographies; she, an Indian from Durban, granddaughter of indentured labourers, he a German war child, a catholic conservative turned radical rebel of the Frankfurt Institute for Social Research, their fates unite in Durban during high apartheid, transgressors of the Immorality Act, forced in exile for loving across the race barrier; now Canadians, world citizens, intercontinental commuters …

Hir own biography has none of the cosmopolitan ingredients. Ze was privileged middle-class, though growing up in one of Malmö's "Million programme" inner suburbs, and naturally assumed an attitude of superiority and alienation. Only after moving to Stockholm, to become a journalist, did ze start to identify with Malmö, and precisely for the "cosmopolitanism" ze had hardly experienced hirself. The Yugoslav immigrants, ze remembers, were commonly patronised (*Bosko, hir class-mate in high school, was popular among the girls, and his gallantry, physical fitness and dancing skills only added to the condescending contempt*). Southern Europeans in general, including Italians and Spaniards (*if there had been any*), were looked down upon. In retrospect, it is hard to understand where this inherent prejudice came from. Hir family was liberal, open-minded. Culturally homogeneous Sweden of the 1960s was programmatically modern and affirmatively anti-racist (*avant la lettre*), with its prominent jazz scene (Alice Babs and Duke Ellington) and mixed marriages (Gösta and Fatima Ekman, Svenne and Lotta Hedlund). The Swedish Sin was transgressive, the most defiant degree of Immorality. Ze received Stokely Carmichael's *Black Power* as a guerdon in 7th grade, while never even reflecting on hir own assumed sense of privilege and superiority. Ze recalls with shame the bullying of the few Jews, not for being Jews, but because they were strange, nonconformant, yet trying hard to appease, bearing the humiliation with resignation, and how ze never interfered in their defence but rather added to the insults. As late as in the mid-'70s, one of hir peers in the School of Journalism was generally disliked for his arrogance and the jokes and slander behind his back always hinted at his Jewishness: *Omskuret är bäst.*[13] This is as unfathomable to hir now as ever the celebration of the Aramburazo to Beatriz Sarlo,[14] and definitely just as shameful. As are hir blatantly racist declarations after the first rough encounters with the US reality on hir great tour of the Americas. In the course of the journey's first three days, ze was robbed twice, at the YMCA in New York and the Greyhound Bus station in San Francisco, and then next to raped by a Vietnam veteran who helped hir report the second robbery and offered hir his place to stay, only to demand that ze gives him a handjob, and barely letting hir get away with that (*c'mon suck it for a while, it won't hurt you*). Ze escaped and barricaded hirself at the nearby Elk Hotel (*for once ze actually recalls a hotel name*), where ze had to pay a week's rent in advance for a filthy room with red plastic covered chairs and a sullen broadloom, percolated with smoke and sweat, and ze hardly dared to walk out through the front door in the morning, expecting that hir sobered and regretful tormentor would be waiting to pick hir up (promising to make up for everything).

At lunch the next day, Ulrike from Austria, who was surprised that Swedes would go to Turkey—and even Iran!—for transplantations, and who, when confronted, admitted her prejudice, says that the interesting thing about studying apartheid at its roots is that it forces you to confront the racist in yourself.

SIN IS FUNDAMENTALLY conceived as a material impurity. Blood, a holy substance endowed with miraculous power, is expected to remove the stain of sin.[15] But since the common verb for making atonement can be translated as both "wipe away" and "cover", the

---

[13] The English translation of the Swedish expression *Osvuret är bäst* would be that it is best not to be too confident or to promise too much. By substituting *Osvuret* for *Omskuret*, the sense is radically transformed while the expression sounds alike: *Circumcised is the best*, the meaning of which becomes mockingly ironic.

[14] The abduction and execution of the former Argentinean president, general Aramburu, by the guerrilla organisation Montoneros in 1970, was at the time celebrated by the supporters of Juan Perón, whom Aramburu had toppled in a military coup in 1955. In Sarlo 2003, literary critic Beartriz Sarlo analyses her own reactions to the event in retrospect.

[15] Eichrodt 1933, in ibid.

meaning may just as well be interpreted as "covering up one's guilt from the eyes of the offended party by means of reparation".[16]
  Covering up one's complicity... *Responsibility-in-complicity.* Ze orders Mark Sanders' analysis of the intellectual and apartheid [*connect vessels that have not consciously communicated, that is part of hir responsibility as researcher-writer; perhaps the most important part; it would be preposterous to assume any kind of (intellectual) originality, other than as bricoleur, facilitator of flows between vessels, miscegenator of ideas, prolific and promiscuous*]; ze was aware of its existence, but never read it before; although ze did read Sanders' later book on the TRC.[17] Now *Complicities* appears as one of the really important analyses of the complexities at the core of the South African transition (*a good verdict for a book, to mature with age*).

> When opposition takes the form of a demarcation from something, it cannot, it follows, be untouched by that to which it opposes itself. *Opposition takes its first steps from a footing of complicity.*[18]

Therefore, the negotiation of complicity should be an essential moment in intellectual responsibility.
  A year later, on hir return to the Western Cape, ze will disclose another correspondence; Jacob Dlamini's Askari, *the beautifully disturbing "story of collaboration and betrayal in the anti-apartheid struggle". How different would the history of apartheid sound, asks Dlamini rhetorically, if told not as the story of racial war but of what we might call* a fatal intimacy between black and white South Africans?[19] *It is an intriguing assumption, given that the subject of the interrogation is Glory Sedibe, the defector, traitor, sell-out, turn-coat, collaborator,* Comrade September *turned apartheid agent* Mr X1, *abhorred by both his former fellow freedom fighters in the ANC and his later white trash superiors at Vlakplaas. Complicity is mutual, collaboration always marked by ambiguity ... The ruthless Askari, perpetrator and* victim, *fell outside the frame of the TRC. Nobody wants to acknowledge that in the apartheid dusk most cats were grey.*

---

[16] Ibid.
[17] Sanders 2007.
[18] Sanders 2002: 9.
[19] Dlamini 2014: 2. The notion of "fatal intimacy" is borrowed from Njabulo Ndebele.

STELLENBOSCH STOMP

FOR SOME REASON, ze is obsessively associating Stellenbosch with The Snobs. The godforsaken English pop group, performing in Regency costumes and wigs, whose one hit, *Buckle Shoe Stomp*, never made the charts in Britain but became a big success in Scandinavia (*big in Japan!*). Recorded live, as ze now learns, at Medmenham Abbey, where, two centuries earlier, prostitutes dressed as nuns had been provided to the prominent guests of the legendary Hell Fire Club. 1964. The year Barry Goldwater ran for president in the USA (and Nelson Mandela was sentenced to life-time imprisonment, barely escaping the gallows). Ze is scarcely old enough to remember the silly song and the silly group, but why does that stupid memory pop up in the face of the pious white-washed Dutch mansions of this neat University dorp? The porticoes look like elegant veils, like the Droste Cocoa lady, *was she a nun?*, no, that association is too far-fetched; ze had no idea of the peculiarities of the Hell Fire Club before ze googled it (*nowadays all this crap information that ze used to take pride in storing is ubiquitous, only a mouse click away*). It must be the stomp, the alliteration with Stellie, the somehow blasphemous, ridicule (dråplig *is the Swedish word, literally meaning murderous*) coupling of high-brow conservative Stellenbosch with vulgar Dixieland jazz or, better, Bavarian or Balkan *oompa-oompa* … What does the *Stellenbosch Stomp* sound like?

WHEN ZE COMES upon the central passage on *Dirt as matter out of place*, ze finds to hir surprise that there are neither notes nor underlining in four pages. Has the reader jumped them, or skimmed them so extensively that the reading literally has left no marks? Ze thinks of the scribbled notes as reflections of the words' imprint on the reader's mind; reading as a physical, bodily, sensual practice, the tangible text tattooed over yellowish pages of living skin.

Where there is dirt there is system. Dirt is the by-product of a systematic ordering and classification of matter, in so far as ordering involves *rejecting inappropriate elements*. Hence, our pollution behaviour is the reaction which condemns any object or idea likely to confuse or contradict cherished classifications.[20]

[*What comes first? What are the cherished classifications? Con-fusion, con-tradiction, contra-tradition, contra-order, dissolution, declassification* ...]
Since place in the hierarchy of purity is biologically transmitted, sexual behaviour is paramount for preserving the purity of the caste. Therefore, in the higher castes, boundary pollution focuses particularly on sexuality. Caste membership of an individual is determined by the mother (like Jewish matrilineality); even if she marries into a higher caste, the children take their caste from her. Women are the gates of entry to the caste. Female purity is carefully guarded and a woman who is known to have had sexual intercourse with a man of lower caste is brutally punished.[21]

The Other Side of Silence... Remember Urvashi Butalia's account of the horrendous brutality of the Indian partition; wives and daughters being killed by their husbands and fathers and brothers, women voluntarily killing themselves to defend the chastity of the community ... the communal carnage targeting the women in particular.[22]

In South Africa, by contrast to India, it's not the clash between dogmatic conflicting identities, but the very opposite: insecure, fragile identities searching to assert themselves, develop self-esteem, escape humiliation and reverse denigration.[23] Hence, it's rather a lack of identity that instigates murder. Xenophobic violence as identity assertion—Adam and Moodley borrow the example from writer Jonny Steinberg: the unemployed South African on welfare bullying the Somali shop owner; both hold each other in utter contempt, but the powerless customer empowers himself (*asserts his identity*) by ordering the *kwerekwere* around, and he in turn has to react with superior discipline not to provoke potentially lethal fury.[24]

[20] Ibid.: 35.
[21] Ibid.: 125.
[22] Butalia 2000.
[23] Adam & Moodley 2013: 193.
[24] Steinberg, in Adam & Moodley 2013: 194.

Xenophobic violence reverses daily humiliation. Reverses and relieves. Perpetration is apparently joyful, as noted by Simon (*funny that ze comes across his quote just after eating lunch with him*); the emotional dimension of xenophobia symbolically frees the perpetrators from the real deprivation.[25]

The re-appearance of *necklacing*, the powerless community assuming power by deciding over life and death in a gruesome ritual. *Punishment by burning tyre.* The stabbing of Emmanuel Sithole in Alexandra in front of the camera captures the moment of murderous impulse, whereas the necklacing of Angolan shebeen owner Joseph Hipandulwa in Khayelitsha is unbearable to even imagine.[26] Like the beheading by knife of IS prisoners. Is the gruesomeness the perversion of this humiliation in reverse? Cleansing by fire, by fear, by fury—targeting the vulnerable, powerless *makwerekwere*, while the real culprits for the misery of the murderers are immune from their rage, since they have the power to retaliate. Julius Malema's young supporters put tire necklaces on statues commemorating World War I … (*Hans-Dieter, the new German fellow, warns that the removal of Cecil Rhodes from the UCT campus will be the beginning of a Culture War:* Soon they'll start burning books that remind of colonial times).

---

[25] Bekker 2010: 137, in ibid.
[26] Adam & Moodley 2013: 195.

LEIWATER

ZE'S BEEN GIVEN an apartment in a rental house for undergraduate students, almost like a dorm, Leiwater on Rattray straat, ten minutes' walk from the Institute, five minutes from the dorp centre. The location is perfect, but the end of January, when ze arrived, is when students come back from the summer holidays, and they party days and nights on end before submitting to the chores of the new semester. Ze's literally surrounded by them; walls and floor vibrating with an incessant dull hit parade (*bland* is a word that comes to hir mind), cars roaring on the parking in front, hysterical laughter, especially two high-pitch voices in chorus, an octave above the others; they virtually drive hir to the brink of grabbing the kitchen knife and stepping into the backyard terrace screaming BLOODY BOER BRATS... (*Ze did in the end walk out and ask the young hostess on top to, PLEASE, lower the volume; she silently abided, turning it down two or three steps to a still loud but bearable level, until someone a few minutes later turned it up to normal again.*) Ze tries hard but ze can't help becoming the grumpy old neighbour, nagging the girl next door for letting her visiting sister use *hir* parking lot, although ze doesn't have a car to park there, as yet. (*She looked at hir in awe and apologized a hundred times and ze was struck with sudden sympathy for the spoiled and curled and inoffensive girl who could have been hir niece, knowing that she would turn to her sister and burst out in laughter as soon as she had shut the door.*)

ZE DWELLS WITH DEPRAVED DELIGHT in the chapter on Leviticus. The irrationality of the abominations. The rational assumption, that what was forbidden to the Israelites was prohibited solely to protect them from foreign influence, is not a comprehensive argument, since some heathen practices were accepted. Sacrifice, for example, which is moreover given an absolutely central place in the religion. Maimonides explains the acceptance of sacrifice as

> a transitional stage, regrettably heathen, but necessarily allowed because it would be impractical to wean the Israelites abruptly from their heathen past.[27]

[27] Maimonides 1881, in Douglas 1966: 48.

The word *transitional* stands out in the context as premature, a premonition; only decades later will it attain a central standing, and yet retain its ambiguity. Transition, as opposed to evolution, or development, is the in-between, a neither-nor, the very process of change, instability, metamorphosis; not development as unfolding, realization, but disruption, revolution. If development is clean, orderly, pure, transition is dirty, messy, contamination...

> Van Gennep likens society to a house with rooms and corridors in which passage from one to another is dangerous. Danger lies in transitional states, simply because transition is neither one state nor the next, it is indefinable.[28]

Any cosmological enquiry, says Douglas, should start by seeking the principles of power and danger. In the Old Testament we find the blessing as the source of all good things, and the withdrawal of blessing as the source of all dangers. Holiness—in its root *set-apart*—becomes equated with wholeness and completeness, which is extended to species and categories.[29]

> And you shall not lie with any beast and defile yourself with it, neither shall any woman give herself to a beast to lie with it: it is perversion.[30]

The rare Hebrew word *tebhel* is significantly mistranslated as perversion, whereas the actual meaning is mixing or confusion. Hybrids and other confusions are abominated:

> You shall keep my statutes. You shall not let your cattle breed with a different kind; you shall not sow your fields with two kinds of seed; nor shall there come upon you a garment of cloth made of two kinds of stuff.[31]
>
> You Bastard! You Pervert! That which is abominated shall not be eaten. (*He who does not dance, neither shall he eat.*)

---

[28] van Gennep 1909, in Douglas 1966: 96.
[29] Douglas 1966: 53.
[30] Leviticus: xviii, 23.
[31] Leviticus: xix, 19.

The fear of blood mixing haunts not only the Boer, but all white settlers; no, the English are not *haunted*, they would rarely imagine the temptation of miscegenation (*as Israeli soldiers are allegedly not raping Palestinian women*), whereas the Afrikaners know that they are bastards on the outset, sons and daughters of one *hottentot* ancestor (not necessarily female)[32];

> in an abyssal historical irony, given the origins of the tongue in which Afrikaner nationalists ground their identity, it shuns hybridity and measures purity.[33]

Not only the hybrid is abominated, but everything that breaks the classifications, stated by the merciless God. An English-speaking black is the most frightening abomination. Even the opponents of apartheid (*avant la lettre*) opt for racist solutions. Olive Schreiner, writer and feminist pioneer, and explicit opponent to Cecil Rhodes' colonial savagery, talks of South Africa as "a mixture of races", but only in a social sense, since she, like everyone else, opposes miscegenation; her vision of a federation of South African states, as opposed to the Union of 1910, is a vision of a racially separated society that clearly resembles the radical apartheid visions of ethnic nations in separate development.[34] (Anne McClintock, one of the foremost contemporary Schreiner scholars, would maybe protest vehemently against that allegation, but then, even McClintock, in her otherwise exemplary analysis of "race, gender and sexuality in the colonial contest",[35] is curiously insensitive to the notion of creolisation.)

The crux is of course simply that the whites are a minority, and in a state where all citizens were given equal opportunities, they would (*in their capacity as whites*) be a powerless minority. In a state of unchecked miscegenation, they would be "ploughed under" by the black masses, tarnished, vanished ... *tainted by the tar brush.*

---

[32] Rabie 1964, in Sanders 2002: 146. Denis-Constant Martin comments that even if the Afrikaners may *know* about it, very few will acknowledge their Khoisan ancestry.

[33] Sanders 2002: 82.

[34] Ibid.

[35] McClintock 1995.

God's stepchildren (1924) by Sarah Gertrude Millin. Shame lies in the sexual unions that give rise to racial mixing, spreading the "degenerate seed" that is inherited from one generation to the next and always threatens to erupt, *thereby retrospectively revealing all the past white generations of its carriers as frauds, false whites.*[36] Coetzee points to the direct parallel to the Christian ideas of "falling from grace" and "original sin".[37]

Shame is not strong enough to denote the original mixing of fluids because black blood is a form of defilement; a formless horror evading description—much like the HIV virus, which can be kept at bay, at best, but never cured. The only way the polluted community can cleanse itself is by expelling the polluter. And the only way that the responsible polluter can put an end to the suffering is by sexual abstinence, thereby killing the taint (virus) and extinguishing the bloodline that carries it—the ever-damned tradition of hybrid impurity.[38]

Yet, the fear of miscegenation is not solely an obsession among whites. Sol Plaatje's novel *Mhudi* from 1930, one of the fundamental works of black South African literature, fervently warns against the Bechuanas' alliance with the Boers, as the Boers will "take Bechuana women to wife and, with them, breed a race of half man, half goblin".[39]

[36] Millin's influential discourse, as interpreted by Coetzee 1988 (italics added).
[37] Coetzee 1988: 141.
[38] Hemer 2012: 135–136.
[39] Citation from *Mhudi* in Wicomb 1998: 100; 2018: 54.

"Boarding school"

THE INSTITUTE is a refuge. After three weeks, ze had still not taken in the privilege of having 24/7 access to a spacious air-conditioned office with a view to the rolling foliage of a lush botanical garden; a creative space for the mind, precisely, not the "soul", although the scaled Nordic architecture and interior design also may evoke the idea of a spiritual retreat. Nobody disturbs hir; the only requirement is to be there, in situ, to participate in the lavish lunches, Monday to Friday, and the afternoon seminar every week, when the researchers present their findings to each other. After seminars there is always wine and snacks, generous yet moderate; what remains in the bottles is left to self-service when tables are cleaned, but nobody would dream of overdoing the welcome, let alone go somewhere else to continue the party. Some even go back to their offices after the seminars. Michael, the composer, artist in residence since more than half a year, virtually lives in his room on the ground floor, with an electric piano and a mattress, on which he naps after lunch, and the note blades of his work in progress papering the walls. But he is receding to Cape Town over the weekends, where his wife is soon going to meet up from their second home in London. Marlene, an archaeologist from Johannesburg, is always in place when ze arrives in the morning; she sits with her back to the open door staring at the computer screen, even on a Sunday morning when ze discovers that ze has forgotten the key to hir office and has to go back to Leiwater, only to discover that ze hadn't forgotten the key, only put it in the outer pocket of hir shorts, but it doesn't matter, because it's less than ten minutes' walk, and ze needs some exercise anyway. Being so close to the workplace is a luxury ze hasn't enjoyed for decades, if ever, commuter as ze has been all hir professional life, spending two-three hours a day in the limbo of transit, a bubble in the time-space-continuum to which ze has become so accustomed that ze takes it for granted, a fact of life; ze even enjoys the morning limbo, as a reserved moment of focused reading, but dreads the late afternoon return, when ze's too tired to read anything other than the sports section of the major tabloid.

Lunch is the meeting point where the fellows gather between 12.30 and 12.40, not too early, not first in line, and absolutely not too late, when the others are already having the dessert. One of the fellows that arrived after hir, Eddie, from Johannesburg, a hardened sociologist in his seventies, complains jokingly that it is like a boarding school. Eddie is the former tutor of Jonny Steinberg (proudly announcing Steinberg's recent decision to return to South Africa from his exile in England), refreshingly void of the bitterness that English-speaking white liberals almost unanimously developed from the mid-'90s onwards; he is rather like a British labour intellectual, naturally loyal to the New South Africa, if not necessarily to the current government, his white skin so tanned by the African sun that it may appear as if he's got psoriasis.

One of the unwritten rules is to circulate, not sitting down with the same people at the same table every day; but, of course, some are socialising more than others, dominating both seminar discussions and lunch conversations, and of course ze feels more connected to some than to others. Hir first acquaintance is Simon, some five years hir senior, professor emeritus in sociology at Stellenbosch, who can count to ten in unbroken Swedish with rasping r:s (he had a Swedish girlfriend in his youth). Simon, who lent hir the Tilly book, introduced hir to Michael, the composer, who in his turn happens to be a friend of Aryan, one of hir reference points ever since they first met in Malmö, in 2008, when ze was working on the South African material for hir dissertation and Aryan was a visiting professor at hir department (*the incredulous official at the Visa section of the Swedish embassy in Pretoria had asked him: "Are you a visiting professor? Or are you visiting a professor?"*).

Ze relates less actively to the many Swedes; Lars, an archaeologist from Lund, "the Stone Age man", reminding hir of hir elder brother; Peter, the cognition philosopher, also from Lund, whom ze is slightly acquainted with from decades back, just as ze distantly knows his wife, Susanne, although ze didn't know that they were a couple; Susanne is working on a project on the global organ trade and transplantation industry, with Elmi, a surgeon from Cape Town. Elmi commutes from home and is sometimes late or not appearing at all, because she has been summoned to her clinic. "I had to do a kidney", she excuses herself with a smile and looks as if she had just come from an invigorating session of Pilates at the nearby gym.

The interdisciplinary mix appeals to hir generalist curiosity; the archaeological richness of Southern Africa and the speculation on how *homo* became *docens*, or the difficulties in matching organ donors and recipients when the genetic variation is as vast as it is in South Africa (*ze pricked up hir ears: did ze get that right? Is genetic variation a euphemism for racial differences? Does mixing augment or diminish the genetic*

variation? Are there strictly medical arguments to support creolisation and contamination?) Ze knocked on Elmi's door for an answer, but she couldn't give hir a straight one. In the long run, yes, but in a short perspective there is vulnerability.
In the long run, we are all coloured. But in the short run we are all dead. *Vanitas vanitatum omnia vanitas.*

For the architects of apartheid, apart-ness means the self-determination of every nation, and the principle that no nation be dominant over another. Those who take this notion seriously propose *Total Separation.* Werner Eiselen, the founder of *Volkekunde* never described African cultures as explicitly inferior to "white" culture, but regarded them as being in a state of decline, due to the corrupting contact with "white" society. Subsequently, they ought to be protected from foreign (white, modern) influence and given the chance to develop in line with their own particular cultural imperatives.[40] The favoured metaphor to illustrate that each culture contained its own dynamic for development was Hans Christian Andersen's fairy tale about the ugly duckling that is able to flourish only when it finds itself among its own kind.[41]

Malinowski, at the time seen as a progressive thinker who opposed racist assumptions, envisioned a future "common society", with a "new type of culture, related both to Europe and Africa, yet not a mere copy of either".[42] This idea of a potential "hybrid culture" inspired Z. K. Matthews, future executive member of the ANC, but never took root in the organisation. (*Why is this idea always dismissed at an embryonic stage? Why this obsession with blood purity, also among black intellectuals?*)

Eiselen conjures the image of Bantu barbarians at the gate, ironically alluding to the white paranoia provoked by "black-peril"

[40] Kross 2002: 53–73.
[41] Eiselen 1948, in Kross 2002: 65.
[42] Malinowski 1938, in Kross 2002: 60.

propaganda.[43] But, instead of enhancing the advancement of black intellectuals, his conclusion is that they should be saved from the inevitable disappointment of realising that, however hard they tried, they would never be accepted members of the white society, due to racial prejudice. The mission-educated blacks (*the abominable English-speaking blacks, mimicking English gentlemen*) were doomed to be an "intellectual proletariat".[44] (*Eiselen, a German, and Verwoerd, a Dutchman, overcompensate their foreignness by becoming more Afrikaner than the caricature* Voortrekker.)

The only proponent of mixing is Breyten Breytenbach, who launches the idea of *Zuid-Afrikanerdom* as opposed to the nationalist purism of Afrikanerdom, and defines it as a culture of hybridity (*basterskap*).

> We are a bastard people with a bastard language. Our nature is one of bastardy. It is good and beautiful thus. We should be compost, decomposing to be able to combine again in other forms. Only, we have walked into the trap of the bastard who has acquired power. In that part of our blood which comes from Europe was the curse of superiority. We wanted to justify our power. And to do that we had to consolidate our supposed tribal identity. We had to fence off, defend, offend. We had to entrench our otherness while retaining at the same time what we had won. We made our otherness the norm, the standard— and the ideal. And because our otherness is maintained at the expense of our fellow South Africans—and our South Africanhood—we felt threatened. We built walls. Not cities, but city walls. And like all bastards—uncertain of their identity—we began to adhere to the concept of purity. That is apartheid. Apartheid is the law of the bastard.[45]

Note the ambiguous value in the word bastard... *Bastervolk, bastertaal, basterskap* are positive notions, on which a new inclusive identity can be built—but the baster is a *bastard* in the conventional sense that the word has attained. And when Breytenbach returns to Paradise a decade later, at the beginning of the transition, it's only the latter meaning that remains:

[43] Eiselen 1920, in Kross 2002: 61.

[44] Ibid. The term "intellectual proletariat" was borrowed from historian Arnold Toynbee.

[45] Breytenbach 1982, in Sanders 2002: 144.

The Afrikaners aren't such reprehensible bastards after all. If you leave them to their own devices, they don't really bother other people. The problem is that their minds were warped by European exclusivism. At least they have a modicum of respect for nature and for animals.[46]

[*Is there self-irony at play here? Maybe inadvertently. Afrikaners, like Swedes, have difficulties detecting irony. Marlene, the archaeologist, was shocked by hir use of the words* hotnot *and* kaffir.]

---

[46] Breytenbach 1993: 80.

Load Shedding

Dining at De Wijnhuis in darkness. No chips served, but meat, presumably grilled over open fire; a meagre portion with one piece of beetroot and one of squash, and a tomato salad on the side. Maybe to compensate, the waiter pours the glass full with Fairview Caldera, an excellent wine in the non-exclusive range. The candlelit restaurants are oases in a pitch-black desert. The atmosphere warm, almost intimate. Afrikaans all around hir, a more inclusive language than English... *why does ze think that?* ... Ze watches the people strolling by on the pavement: young Afrikaners in knee-long shorts, flabby, often of dark complexion, and it suddenly becomes so evident that it is just because the border is diffuse that the bordering has been so important. For some reason that somehow contradicts hir reflection, ze finds it relieving that in the Cape, Afrikaans is the first language among both blacks and whites. Then the power comes back, to the applause of all guests.

Magic, according to James George Frazer, author of *The Golden Bough*, interpreted by the scornful Douglas:

as if primitive tribes were populations of Ali Babas and Aladdins, uttering their magic words and rubbing their magic lamps.[47]

Malinowski uncritically developed this idea of a rite based on the magician's physical enactment and deluded wish-fulfilment,

a kind of poor man's whisky, used for gaining conviviality and courage against daunting odds.[48]

Miracle, on the other hand, is independent of rite; a gift, a grace, which could be expected to erupt anywhere, at any time, in response to virtuous need—or the demands of justice [*The Saving Grace*].

[47] Douglas 1966: 58.

[48] Ibid.: 59. Only at the second revision of this text, three years later, do I notice the word "conviviality" here. Going back to Douglas, I find that it is not a word with any added meaning attached to it, as in the later interpretations of Ivan Illich (1973) and Paul Gilroy (2004). For a discussion of conviviality in relation to cosmopolitanism and creolisation, see Hemer, Povrzanović Frykman & Ristilammi 2020.

Any religion must swing between the poles of interior will and exterior enactment... The rage of the Old Testament prophets was continually renewed against the parading of empty external rites instead of humble and contrite hearts. But the Messiah of the New Testament relegates Mosaic Law as "the old dispensation". After the Sermon of the Mount, any person, man or woman, leprous, bleeding or crippled, is welcome to approach the altar. Sin (impurity) is turned into a matter of the will and not of external circumstance.

Yet, the ideas of pollution persist; the Penetential of Archbishop Theodore of Canterbury enjoins penance of three weeks' fast on any woman, lay or religious, who enters a church or communicates during menstruation.[49]

Is Purity of the Heart the most treacherous? Interior will implies pious communalism, parish, Gemeinschaft, whereas exterior enactment connotes pragmatism, commerce, trading of tricks, Gesellschaft... The Barefoot Boer in the City of Gold.

As a social anima, man is a ritual animal ... [I]t is very possible to know something and then find words for it. But it is impossible to have social relations without symbolic acts.[50] Basic, banal things, like the days of the week, cannot be experienced without ritual. [W]e cannot experience Tuesday if for some reason we have not formally noticed that we have been through Monday.[51]

Ritual changes perception because it changes the selective principles. It can permit knowledge of what would otherwise not be known at all. It does not merely externalise experience, bringing it out into the light of day, but it modifies experience in so expressing it. Thoughts that have never been put into words are after framing changed and limited by the very words selected.[52]

This is a beautiful passage, opening an abyss of awe. Is Art the attempt at challenging, circumventing or at least illuminating the limitations of language? And is Literature that illumination in the words themselves, transformed, dissolved, like letters in the *Book of Sand*?

---

[49] McNeill & Gamer 1938, in ibid.: 61.
[50] Douglas 1966: 62.
[51] Ibid.: 64.
[52] Ibid.: 66.

Imaginary Exile

A CAT AMONGST ERMINES. Ze can't free hirself from that feeling, a sensation ze actually experiences in literary circles as much as in academic ones; but maybe that is simply a constitutive human complex which some are better at masking than others. In the eyes of the other fellows, ze probably makes an impression of self-confidence, and moreover seniority, which is something ze still hasn't really apprehended. In the academy ze remains, in hir own eyes, an outsider, although hir position in the university hierarchy is nowadays solidly established, as opposed to that in the wrecked cultural public sphere, where ze is practically forgotten.

Three weeks is normally an ocean of time, or rather an interregnum which ze has learnt to seize with utmost efficiency. Hir last novel was in substance written during two weeks in Athens, in October 2011, when ze worked in such a manic fervour to the very last minute that ze did not even allow hirself the intended, long-awaited excursion to Hydra, and during a prolonged week (ten days) in Visby on Gotland, exactly one year later, when ze was so totally immersed that ze finalised the project with the exact margin of the extra three days. Now ze has three months, an unfathomable amount of mind space, but ze is also in another mode, another calendar (chronology), which more resembles the stumbling first year of the *Fiction and Truth* project. Back in the garden of forking paths; the traces of hir coming endeavour barely discernible. Three months are more than sufficient for a well-defined writing task, but barely enough to even get started with a major research project. Ze is not obliged to produce anything, but ze knows that the conditions are as good as can be, that the days are numbered (*vanitas vanitas*) and time is now. Ze started writing after a week, well aware that writing itself is hir main method, not only the subject of methodological reflection. Ze writes in English, and just as last time it is not a matter of course. Then the choice had been more natural, despite of hir little experience, because the format was a dissertation, albeit with elements of reportage and memoir. At the time, ze would not even have considered writing fiction in another language than Swedish. Now, when the ambition is to write across borders, to let genres and practices contaminate one another, ze decides to hold on to English and, once made, ze feels impudently assured about hir choice.

Ze has no nostalgic or other attachment to the Swedish language, other than the confidence in mastering it quite well. There is one Swedish writer that ze holds in highest esteem—Lars Norén—but there is no Swedish literary tradition that ze would adhere to (in fact, ze takes pride in being mistakenly listed in the Immigrant Institute's register of immigrant writers in Sweden; that curious discovery sparked the idea of imagining a personal history in Argentina). So, ze is fine with English, but a broken English, or rather English with an accent, although ze would not know how to define that twang. Scandinavian, perhaps, but then, no, that would not be its significant characteristic. *Cosmopolitan*, in the sense of being a second (or third) language; the global lingua franca of non-native English speakers, like hirself. Migrated—*deterritorialized*—English. Moreover, ze has no Swedish publisher, and ze is determined to never again humiliate hirself by trying to persuade one. Writing in Swedish would be like writing a diary, for oneself. Whereas in English, ze can address a presumptive South African public.

On the spur of the moment, ze also decides to aim at a form that is neither academic nor literary (in alignment with the apartheid classification of the "coloured" as neither black nor white). A claim to be both literary and academic would not only be immensely pretentious, but somehow banal, aiming at all and nothing, and it would miss the point that ze believes ze is trying to make. Neither-nor, by contrast, challenges the very border, *limes*, as an uninhabited (*but possibly booby trapped*) no man's land. Not one text, no monograph, but several, parallel and traversal, in different tenses and registers. *Transdisciplinary interventions*, as ze so fancifully coined it for the Bangalore project. The "ethnographic fictions" would be one layer, a diary in Swedish another, perhaps. A pamphlet for a politics of contamination, radical in the fundamental meaning of the word, written from an imaginary exile, as if ze had actually left Sweden behind. Which would hir imaginary new homeland be? Hardly Argentina, after all; contrary to the counter-factual fantasy of hir last novel, Argentina apparently remains stuck in its evil circle; Cristina Kirschner, on official visit to China, is a laughing-stock in the *Late Nite News* (along with Mugabe and the bully of bullies, Jacob Zuma). Australia? Canada? Well, why not South Africa? For sure a "violent democracy", in Eddie's words, like Mexico or Colombia, but also an immensely vital culture, capable of ironic introspection. *Ze muses at the weekly satire of the* Late Nite News:

> *When the ANC was fighting for power, it was clearly not electric power…*
>
> *Zuma made a call to the voters to ask them what they wanted him to address in his speech to the nation. He got two replies: 1. Legalise marijuana! 2. Resign!*

DOUGLAS DEFENDS the dichotomy Primitive–Modern, insisting on the unity and variety of human experience. Progress means differentiation; thus primitive means undifferentiated and modern means differentiated.[53] The primitive culture must be taken to be unaware of itself, unconscious of its own conditions.[54]

To what extent is the modern culture (world) aware of itself and conscious of its own conditions? Certainly, only to a limited extent in 1966, pre post-modernity's coming to awareness of its own historicity.

> The European history of ecclesiastical withdrawal from secular politics and from secular intellectual problems to specialised religious spheres is the history of this whole movement from primitive to modern.[55]

Again: Douglas writes in Modernity's zenith, when the return of Religion to the political and intellectual arena seemed as unlikely as a regression to pre-industrial feudalism. Yet, she does not dismiss the primitive. Among "continental" scholars, she says, *le primitif* enjoys honour.

> The only conclusion that I can draw is that they are not secretly convinced of superiority, and are intensely appreciative of forms of culture other than their own.[56]

---

[53] Ibid.: 77.
[54] Ibid.: 91.
[55] Ibid.: 92.
[56] Ibid.: 93.

The War Diary

HIR SISTER AND brother-in-law are transcribing hir father's diaries. It is a mammoth project that has gnawed the conscience of the children ever since his death in 1998. The sixteen diary volumes and the close to a hundred 8 mm films have been in hir youngest sister's possession, and she has done some occasional transcribing of selected parts. Now the approaching 100th birthday seems to have prompted her to resume the effort in a systematic manner. Ze feels that ze ought to help, that this is a task for hir, rather than hir brother-in-law; ze has had the intention for so many years to make it hir "next project", but something has always come in-between. Now ze is both physically and mentally entirely somewhere else, but that is perhaps the prerequisite for breaking the resistance to try to get under the skin of hir father, whose physical traits are appearing with ridiculous resemblance in hir own reflection. Ze recalls how ze mercilessly cleaned out his workroom, until only one box remained; a whole work life reduced to some folders, compendiums, and a collection of stamps and first-day covers. The box is stowed-away in hir attic ever since. Ze has never opened it. But ze has read the diaries, in parts. After completion, they were put in the living-room bookshelf, for anyone to read. On birthdays and other special occasions, hir father used to read out loud; it was a family ritual, like the regular screening of the 8 mm films, an initiation rite for all presumptive boyfriends and girlfriends of the five siblings. Ze never had any difficulty deciphering the minuscule handwriting (*whereas ze is increasingly unable to interpret hir own notes from yesteryear or sometimes even yesterday*). But the two three last diaries became gradually unintelligible, like the ever more fractured films. They never contained any secrets, only notes about occurrences in the family and the world. An occasional glimpse of something untold, a hint, between the lines, but mostly measured, dry recollections and reflections. Ze is not sure whether ze really wants to dig deeper. Ze doesn't expect to find anything new below the surface. Date and class restrain his accurate account. A distanced observer, sharp and sensitive, but neither bold nor radical; a social liberal who always voted *Folkpartiet*. Anyway, ze reveres him, only too well acquainted with his lethargy, and now also reconciled with his contentment. At the 60th and 70th birthdays (and 65th, too?), ze had repeatedly urged him to write something other than the diary, to sum up and synthesise his immense experience and knowledge. Although well intentioned, it was a note of deception, and ze wonders how he took those remarks from the prodigal son. He was content. Yet, there was something encapsulated, an absolute vulnerability. The hermit crab. Obsessively social; emotionally dependent. Ze can see why hir brother-in-law identifies with him, and maybe that is the explanation of hir own estrangement ... After all, ze ought perhaps to write hir journal in Swedish. A diary. But how sincere could ze be? A diary in third person, perhaps. The future past tense. The pluperfect future ... In a fictional diary, ze could disclose anything (*even the truth*). Yes, the Swedish retains a function even though ze impudently dismisses it in hir public writing. As already stated, no monograph but a plurality of layered texts. A screwed-up diary may be one of them.

A year later, interrogating the parts of hir father's "war diary" that have not as yet been transcribed (or deliberately left out?), *ze will make the unsettling discovery that he, in the spring of 1939, as a student in Uppsala, attended the infamous meeting at* Bollhuset, *where the admission of ten to twelve Jewish intellectual refugees from Nazi Germany was discussed. Not only did hir father attend; he voted with the majority, fore the protest against "refugee import". This revelation will come as a complete shock and overshadow the centenary, which passes without celebrations, almost unnoticed ... Then, reading the above ze will realise that a note or comment* en passant *is not satisfactory. Nor is an easy dismissal.* (How would ze have voted?) *Ze is intent on eventually pursuing this path, juxtaposing hir own diary from the correspondent time in hir own life (the late '70s in Stockholm). But not now. Not here. In another interrogation. In Swedish.*

IN VAN GENNEP'S HOUSE of rooms and corridors in which passage from one to another is dangerous, the person who must pass from one room to another is himself in danger and emanates danger to others.[57] Initiation rites are supposed to be dangerous, possibly lethal, but are in fact often perfectly safe; the dangers being trumped up to warn us from going out of the formal structure, into the margins.

---

[57] Van Gennep 1909, in ibid.: 96.

Transition in ritual is the process of death and rebirth, during which the initiate is an outcast, without place in society—allowed and even enjoined to transgress law and act as a criminal; to rape, steal, waylay [*and even kill?*] To be in contact with danger is to be in contact with power [*Endangerment, empowerment, putting one's self at risk*].

> *Contrast between form and surrounding non-form accounts for the distribution of symbolic and psychic powers: external symbolism upholds the explicit social structure and internal, unformed psychic powers threaten it from non-structure.*[58]

Now it's hir own underscoring. Ze reads the sentence again and again. What about the "aesthetic pleasure" which "arises from the perceiving of inarticulate forms"? Non-articulate, non-form, non-structure, non-power ... [*perceiving as opposed to perception? The present experience vs. the remembered past? Explicating instead of embalming ...*]

> Ritual pollution arises from the interplay of form and surrounding formlessness. Pollution dangers strike when form has been attacked. Authority is a very vulnerable power, easily reduced to nothing.[59]

Power vanishes without resistance. Who said that? Baudrillard? He, who later also claimed that the Gulf War had never happened. What if the 1980s had never happened? In retrospect the happy nihilism of postmodernity seems even more repulsive than the Marxist-Leninist puritanism that preceded and provoked it.

Transitional is ambiguous, neither-nor and both-and, in-between loyalties and double loyalties, those outside the structure are dangerous and vulnerable to (protective) violence from those belonging fully in the structure. *Witches* are "the social equivalents of beetles and spiders who live in the cracks of the walls". They attract fear and dislike; the power attributed to them symbolises their ambiguous, *inarticulate* status.[60]

---

[58] Douglas 1966: 99.
[59] Ibid.: 104.
[60] Ibid.: 102.

Baraka is witchcraft in reverse It floats between the segments of the formal political structures. Like witchcraft or sorcery, it is detected and proved post hoc. If witchcraft is institutionalised jealousy, Baraka is institutionalised admiration. "People in fact become possessors of baraka by being treated as possessors of it".[61] [*Being possessed = being polluted? Baraka Obama.*]

> Pollution (only) occurs where the lines of structure, cosmic or social, are clearly defined. A polluting person is always in the wrong (having crossed some line which should not have been crossed) and this displacement unleashes danger for someone. Pollution can be committed intentionally, but intention is irrelevant to its effect—it is more likely to happen inadvertently.[62]

What is the difference between pollution and contamination? Is contamination always intentional? And mutual—an act of consent ... consensual ... crosspollination, the blurring of boundaries, the mixing of fluids, insemination, *consemination* ...

Dlamini refers to Douglas when calling collaborators "polluting people – dirt", but that is a misreading (on his or my behalf), connoting her guilt-by-association to ANC leader Chris Hani's defence of necklacing as "a weapon devised by the oppressed themselves to remove this cancer from our society; the cancer of collaboration of the puppets".[63]

---

[61] Gellner 1962, in ibid.: 111.

[62] Douglas 1966: 113.

[63] Dlamini 2014: 13.

Marikana

ELMI'S HUSBAND, STEPHANUS, is a musicologist, and also a friend of Michael and Aryan. Ze joins the three of them for the screening of Aryan's latest film, *Threnody for the Victims of Marikana*,[64] at the University of the Western Cape in Bellville. Stephanus is introducing it and moderating the discussion afterwards, and he starts his presentation by evoking Stellenbosch, "where the only thing that is not white is, perhaps, the conscience". The threnody for the striking mineworkers of Marikana in the Gauteng, who were massacred by the police on 16 August 2012, is a shortened version of the film *Night is Coming*, Aryan's contribution, as one of three invited artists, to an academic collaboration between the universities of Stellenbosch, Oxford and Harvard on "Music and Landscape". The film was supposed to be screened at Harvard, at the third seminar/workshop, but wasn't, because it was thought to have misrepresented what happened in Stellenbosch. (*Not what the prominent participants had expected, after flying in, having a good time at the restaurants and wineries and club floors, and flying back to the USK with the contention that the New South Africa has come a long way*, as Aryan put it, or as ze reads his scorn.) The threnody leaves nobody unmoved. What does it mean to look at the footage of the massacre through the eyes of the killers? Not the bragging perpetrators, as in Joshua Oppenheim's *The Act of Killing*, but yet the ones who pull the trigger, the police, the state of decision, life or death, the police state; we are looking over the shoulder of the executioners of a ritual murder, in a state of police, we are witnessing and partaking, complicit in the decomposition, seeing through listening, hearing through watching, the percussive reality of South Africa. Marikana is disturbingly absent in the public memory, a void in the story of the post-apartheid, post-transition nation in the making, the dissonance of an unimaginable Sharpeville in democracy, a Soweto uprising, a state of emergency, a red alert, again, rewinded memories erased; the violent democracy, the virulent police state. And the presence of this absence, the melancholy of the threnody ... Aryan, urged to comment, sits down among the audience and lets the images speak, that's how he works as an artist, the provocateur, *l'enfant terrible*, but never as an empty gesture, always with a purpose, a bit like Jean Rouch and Edgar

---

[64] Kaganof 2014.

Morin in *Chronique d'un été*, turning the tables, calling the viewer.[65] The productivity of inadequacy (*ze can't quite remember the meaning of that note; oh yes, it had to do with Harvard's refusal to screen Aryan's film, with the consequence that it travelled far beyond usual academic circles*). His inadequate report of an academic encounter, a conference proceeding contaminated with the brutal footage of the police state. Yes, a perfect example of contamination in the sense that ze is striving at in hir yet to outline project.

How can we live with the presence of the absence? What do we do with the knowledge? "Who is the main actor?" asks one in the audience, a student in his late twenties, scared, as he puts it, by the suggested continuity from the apartheid state. "Who is the responsible?" "You are", says Aryan. "What are you going to do now?"

The TRC, and the innumerable truth commissions before and after, have accustomed us to the dichotomy perpetrator-victim. But what about the bystanders? The silent majority, standing by, consenting or not, the amorphous system of oppression, murder; the standers-by, dreading to be defined by their omission, what they don't do. (*And who is ze to judge?*) The troubling thing about Marikana is that it doesn't go away.[66] It is not an event with a beginning and an end, it is still there, in its present absence or absent presence. We are watching it as it unfolds over the shoulder of the police, complicit in the act, in our own inaction, unable to think rationally, adequately.

Somebody asks what Musicology and Stellenbosch are getting out of it, and Stephanus rightly comments that Aryan would not have been able to do the film about Marikana without them. He needs that kind of structure. Aryan does not object. It's a brilliant example of miscegenation of art and academia, an exemplary illustration of what art and academia can accomplish—in disjuncture. Like Bill Kentridge's power point performance in the City Hall of Cape Town a few days later.[67]

Composers steal all the time, says Michael. Because they love music. Béla Bartok—was it, or Stravinsky?—said that it is just a matter of concealing it the best. Why are writers so afraid of being epigones?

---

[65] *Cronique d'un été* [Chronicle of a Summer], Paris, 1960, directed by anthropologist and film-maker Jean Rouch, in collaboration with sociologist Edgar Morin.

[66] For a thorough recollection—"the definitive account"—of the Marikana events, see Marinovich 2016.

[67] Kentridge 2015.

Inspiration doesn't come from nowhere or from within; it comes mediated through others, only slightly distorted. The voice of the old man, the witty funny lucky bastard, no not even a bastard, a silver-hair whitey, with his three muses, the giant yellow soprano, the bobbed blue megaphone—and the wondrous bald ballerina following him around like his shadow, like a monkey, tearing the books, mocking him ... What a beautiful impossible couple. Father and daughter, master and pupil, master mistress masturbating his bald ego ... The words of the old man, the admirable fool, echoing in hir mind all the way back to Stellie in the pink van, driven by a shemale in pink T-shirt, and coming back in the early morning, after having been temporarily drowned by the barren dialogue of *Pat Garrett and Billy the Kid* on the TV, semiporn-saturated Wild West clichés, Garrett in the bathtub with five señoritas and a young Kris Kristofferson shot in the bed ... In the early morning, it is the old man's witty words and sentences forwards and backwards that drags hir out of bed. *Undo unsay unsave unhappen unremember ... Unforget* is hir own unsettling contribution. *Unthink unlive.* Life is to him a fiction unlived. *Unclean unpurify unimmaculate uncleanse unclassify unbarrass unfuck.*

NAUGHTY, NO, *WICKED* **is a better word, void of erotic connotations; Douglas lustfully smashes Frazer's Golden Bough to splinters, and she gives a subtler but nonetheless sinister bashing to Norman O. Brown [** *which ze finds particularly intriguing, since Brown is a recurrent covert reference in hir* **Argentina trilogy** *that none of the few reviewers noticed***]. The wry wit comes through in sentences like this one:**

> If anal eroticism is expressed at the cultural level we are not entitled to expect a population of anal erotics. We must look around for whatever it is that has made appropriate any cultural analogy with anal eroticism.[68]
>
> [*Ze puts it down in hir notebook; a sentence to be used in a dinner conversation in a novel, if ze ever writes another one.*]

---

[68] Douglas 1966: 122.

Pollution is like an inverted form of humour (apropos Freud's analysis of jokes), it does not amuse, but the structure of its symbolism uses comparison and double meaning like the structure of a joke.[69] The symbolism of the body's boundaries is used in this kind of unfunny wit to express danger to community boundaries. The Coorgs in Karnathaka were so obsessed by fear of dangerous impurities entering their system that they treated the body as if it were a beleaguered town, every ingress and exit guarded for spies and traitors. Anything issuing from the body is never to be re-admitted, but strictly avoided.[70] (*The association inevitably goes to Jyothsna in Bangalore; thinking of her as Coorg immediately transforms the image, as if that clarified everything; what if ze were reduced to a Swede... Would that explain anything?*)

> *The sociological counterpart of this anxiety is a care to protect the political and cultural unity of a minority group.*[71]

[Again, it's hir own underlining—or, rather, hir exact transcription, supplemented with "Appadurai" and an expression mark. Ze doesn't have Appadurai at hand, but ze makes the note to check whether A. refers to D. He must! As an anthropologist he must have been fed from Douglas' breast ... But you can never be sure. The forking paths often run in parallel, without crossing. In their analysis of xenophobia, Adam and Moodely referred to Freud's narcissism of small differences,[72] but not to *Fear of Small Numbers*,[73] let alone *Purity and Danger*, which latter they of course most probably were aware of, as cultivated intellectuals, but not regarded as a relevant reference. Discipline borders are just as carefully policed as genre borders; no, not even necessarily policed, there is simply no cross-going traffic.]

Envy and narcissism. Envy turned on outsiders. The former victims turned perpetrators single out target groups for their apparently superior abilities. Violence becomes a desperate but decisive

---

[69] Ibid.
[70] Ibid.: 123.
[71] Ibid.: 124 (italics added).
[72] Freud 1961, in Adam & Moodley 2013: 191.
[73] Appadurai 2006.

method of last resort with which perpetrators compensate for their own shortcomings.[74] (The real culprits—the indigenous elite in cahoots with the old ruling-class—cannot be targeted, since they still wallow in the glory of liberation and effectively silence dissent. The government's lip-service condemnation of xenophobia conceals the fact "that ours is a neo-apartheid state managed by yesterday's anti-apartheid revolutionaries".[75])

The threat of the "nearly-we" who imperil our self-concept. "The ugliest manifestations of racism are reserved for immigrants who look, act and talk like us. The more they try to emulate and imitate us, the harder they attempt to belong, the more ferocious our rejection of them."[76] Germany's extermination of the Jews is the historical proof of this logic (and a forceful argument against assimilation, as proposed by anti-migrant nationalists). But why does minimal difference trigger hostility? Adam and Moodley quote Indian psychoanalyst Sudhir Kakar:

> The community in which we are socialised is part of our personal identity. And the clash between internalisation of social rules, i.e. *culture*, and a person's natural drives is solved through the projection of "bad" representations onto others; first inanimate objects and animals and later people and other groups.[77]

The disavowed bad representations need such "reservoirs"—Muslims for Hindus, Arabs for Jews and vice versa—which also serve as convenient repositories for rages for which no clear-cut addressee is available.[78]

Is it really reversible? Some groups are obviously more prone to become reservoirs of bad representations; currently Muslims and Gypsies, previously Jews, Kaffirs, Coolies, Boers... Aryans vs. Jews is not reversible, nor US Americans vs. Mexicans. Not even Hindus vs. Muslims, even if that would be closest to an equal and reversible demonisation. (There is an interesting passage in David Malouf's

---

[74] Du Toit & Kotze 2011: 162, in Adam & Moodley: 190.

[75] Mngxitama 2009, in Adam & Moodley: 39.

[76] Vaknin 2011, in Adam & Moodley: 191.

[77] Kakar 1996: 189, in Adam & Moodley: 193.

[78] Volkan 2006, in Adam & Moodley: 192.

novel *The Great World*, centred on the Australian World War II experience, when the Australian POWs realise that they, in the eyes of the Japanese, are no better than coolies; that the Japanese in fact wish to turn them into coolies—a fate that they, in their self-assured confidence of white superiority, regard as the horror of horrors.[79])

The psychoanalytic interpretation explains the predominance of promiscuity, drunkenness and excessive forbidden behaviour in descriptions of the enemy. The animality of the other.

Israelites were always a hard-pressed minority, and in their beliefs all bodily issues are polluting. The Hindu caste system, while embracing all minorities, embraces them each as a distinctive cultural sub-unit. The Indian case is to Douglas the principal proof that a sociological approach is more convincing than a psychoanalytical one.[80] To touch excrement is to be defiled, and the latrine cleaner stands in the lowest grade of the caste hierarchy. Yet, Hindus are not at all controlled and secretive about the act of defecation. On the contrary, "pavements, verandas, public spaces are littered with faeces until the sweeper comes along".[81]

> Ze transcribes the quote from V. S. Naipaul's *An Area of Darkness*, one of his early works with ethnographic aspirations:
> Indians defecate everywhere [...] These squatting figures—to the visitor, after a time, as eternal and emblematic as Rodin's Thinker—are never spoken of; they are never written about [...] this might be regarded as part of a permissible prettifying intention. But the truth is that Indians do not see these squatters and might even, with complete sincerity, deny that they exist.[82]

Rather than oral or anal eroticism it is more convincing to argue that caste pollution represents only what it claims to be. It is a symbolic system, based on the image of the body, whose primary concern is the ordering of a social hierarchy.[83]

---

[79] Malouf 1990.
[80] Douglas 1966: 124.
[81] Ibid.
[82] Naipaul 1964, in ibid.
[83] Douglas 1966: 125.

BUBBLES

AFTER SIX WEEKS, hir senses have been numbed, the beautiful mountains with their vineyard *kloofs* have become the quotidian setting, the running freshwater in the ditches (*that you don't want to drive into*), which ze associated with Ollantaytambo, a deeply intrenched memory from hir Grand Tour through the Americas, are as normal as the left-hand traffic, which ze never had problems with, because it's just the reverse, a parallel world in the mirror … Fellows are leaving and new fellows take their places, ze's socialising as usual but in a more reserved manner, the privilege has become routine, ze is halfway through hir sentence and worrying slightly about not using the time in the most optimal way … optimal, a strange word, how can time be used *op-timally?* Halfway and starting the descent, ze noted the angst of the long-term fellows who were doing their last week, realising that this is a moment that will never come back (although most fellows, if they behave, are actually invited a second or even third time). Everybody seems to feel this slight frustration, although nobody would speak openly about it … Unless you come here to finish a book project, as Jörg (*about the Dutch-Roman law*), with his blond German housewife taking care of their three blond daughters, you are inevitably affected by the violent vibe, even in the Stellenbosch bubble (*which, as all bubbles, one day will have to burst*).

It is already beginning to burst. Jillian, author of a remarkably open-hearted aid worker memoir,[84] whom ze met last year and whom ze invites as hir first lunch guest (fellows are encouraged to invite visitors), compares today's booming IT and tourism town to the Stellenbosch she knew in the early '90s, all white, all male, all Afrikaans-speaking (*ze comes to think of Antjie Krog's* boervrouwe, *with their "impressive cleavages"*[85]). …. For hir, the immediate comparison is Lund, where ze lived for more than ten years, to which ze has come to feel such strong and irrational resentment, Lund as opposed to Malmö, where ze grew up (and which ze hated then); ze knows exactly what it is about Lund that ze hates, the narrow-minded academic conservatism that believes itself to be open and cosmopolitan but in reality is as provincial and parochial as any of the inland villages on Österlen, where ze is now residing [*an extreme exaggeration, no doubt, to be put on the same account as hir eccentric refusal to use*

---

[84] Reilly 2012.
[85] Krog 1999.

any form of social media]. Ze can easily imagine Stephanus' struggle at the Music department, the repressive tolerance of his wild ideas about artistic research, about Ph.D. dissertation in Music not being a performance/work and a comment, but an integrated composition/reflection.

POLLUTION RULES, in contrast to moral rules, are unequivocal. They do not depend on intention or a nice balancing of rights and duties. The only material question is whether a forbidden act has taken place or not.[86] Physical crossing of the social barrier is treated as a dangerous pollution. The polluter becomes a doubly wicked object of reprobation, first because he crossed the line and second because he endangered others.[87]

When attacked from the outside, solidarity within is fostered. When attacked from within by wanton individuals, these can be punished, and the structure publicly reaffirmed. But the structure can also be self-defeating. *Perhaps all social systems are built on contradiction, in some sense at war with themselves.*[88]

Again, a lucid, revolutionary thought, against the grain of her time, defying both socialist and liberal utopianism; not the end of history, nor the realisation of classless communism, but the perpetual paradox of dual impossibilities: neither growth nor degrowth, neither black nor white.

If the social structure were weakly organised, men and women might follow their own fancies in choosing and discarding sexual partners. If the primitive social structure is strictly articulated, by contrast, it is bound to impinge heavily on the relation between men and women. The pollution ideas bind the sexes to their allotted roles.[89] However, when the principle of male dominance is accepted as a central principle of social organisation and applied without inhibition,

---

[86] Ibid.: 130.
[87] Ibid.: 139.
[88] Ibid.: 140 (italics added).
[89] Ibid.: 141.

beliefs in sex pollution are not likely to develop, Whereas, when the principle of male dominance is contradicted by other principles, such as female independence or the women's right to protection from the violence of men, then sex pollution is likely to flourish.[90]

Men's anxiety's about women's behaviour is in most cases justified, since the situation of male/female relations is so biased that women are cast as betrayers from the start.[91] But men are not always afraid of sex pollution. Among the Bemba of Zambia, the women are matrons in a matrilineal society, yet depending on their husbands' willingness to stay with them ... *Delilah on the one hand, and Samson on the other, who, if humiliated, can bring the pillars of society tumbling down.*

Why do all pollution fears cluster round contradictions that involve sex? No other social pressures are potentially so explosive. (*And how could it be different? Remember Bertrand Russell's definition of an intellectual as someone who thinks about* something other than sex *more than half an hour a day.*)

Most likely he (possibly even she) also thinks more about sex the rest of the day than the non-intellectual (whoever that is). Sexuality and creativity are so intrinsically intertwined that even noting it tends to be banal. *At night ze becomes a Man with a myriad mistresses, and unlike the muses they drain hir resources, like heroine, or some other drug that sips into hir mind and subtly alters hir personality ...* ze shudders and abruptly cuts off the stream of thoughts and memories ...

Note St. Paul's extraordinary demand that in the new Christian society there should be neither male nor female [*neither Jew, nor Greek, nor bond nor free*].[92]

The effort to create a new society which would be free, unbounded and without coercion or contradiction, required a new set of positive values. Virginity as a special positive value fell on good soil in a small, persecuted minority group [*c.f the idea of the body as an imperfect container which will be perfect only if it can be impermeable*].

---

[90] Ibid.: 143.

[91] Ibid.: 154.

[92] Galatians, 3: 24, in ibid.: 158.

Virginity *as a revolutionary concept: The idea of woman as the Old Eve, connoting fears of sex pollution, belongs with a certain specific type of social organisation. If this order has to be changed, the Second Eve, a vir*gin source of redemption crushing evil underfoot, *is a powerful new symbol.*[93]

[93] Douglas 1966: 158.

Mandela Rey

NELSON MANDELA RYLAAN—some innovative and witty Afrikaner graffitist had transformed the road mark of Nelson Mandela Driveway to DELA REYLAAN. (Koos De La Rey, one of the Boer generals of the Anglo-Boer War—politically correctly renamed the South African War—is the hero of a popular anthem for young Afrikaners, chanted at pubs, rugby games and public rallies.[94] On one of hir previous journeys to South Africa, ze visited a beach resort south of Durban where the predominantly white lower middle-class audience again and again requested that the Afrikaner entertainer sing *De La Rey*, but he as sternly declined with the argument that the song was politically incorrect[95]...)

Dutch was the official language until after the war, when the creole "kitchen Dutch", Afrikaans, was adopted as official language, besides the colonial English. *Would De La Rey have made a worse match than De Klerk?*

Eye to Eye

WHEN ZE MEETS ANTJIE KROG again, after seven years, at the University of the Western Cape, she does not recognise hir. It's a strange situation, where ze starts doubting whether the woman who just entered the meeting, ten minutes late, is in fact the famous Afrikaner writer. She is, and she does recall their meeting at *Waltic* in Stockholm in 2008,[96] but not the animated interview in Cape Town the year before, when "every question ze asked was about something she had dealt with the past week".[97]

Anne Phillips, with whom ze invites Antjie Krog for lunch at the Institute, says she admires hir courage to write about South Africa. She has herself decided not to, after realising the complexities. Antjie also

[94] Contrary to the now established legend, De la Rey was largely forgotten, even by Afrikaners, before Bok van Blerk made him famous through his song (Martin 2015).

[95] Hemer 2012: 250.

[96] WALTIC (Writers' and Literary Translators' International Congress), 29 June–2 July 2008, was initiated by Swedish writer Henning Mankell and gathered 600 participants from 90 countries. A second congress was held in Istanbul 2–5 September 2010.

[97] Hemer 2012: 251.

questions hir project in an indirect way. Writing across borders, she says, presupposes that you are confident within your borders, inferring that the vast majority of South Africans aren't; all those who are not writing in English for a white audience (and a white publisher). Ze objects and argues against the seemingly essentialist position; the same that ze criticised in hir reading of *Begging to Be Black*,[98] the somehow discouraging conclusion of the Transition trilogy, that it is impossible to imagine the other as yourself. For a moment, the lunch talk is turning uncomfortable and ze wonders why ze envisioned collaborating with her in hir research proposal. But then afterwards, in hir office, Antjie gives some valuable suggestions, as if their collaboration was already a fact, and the farewell is on a friendly collegial note.

The day after ze receives a mail from her, saying: i think why we do not see eye to eye is because both of us are trying to address the intolerance we see in our respective societies, but your intolerance is a first world one and mine a third world one and behove different strategies.

DIRT IS (ONLY) DANGEROUS *as long as some identity clings to it.* When identity is lost (pulverized, rotted, dissolved) it enters the mass of common rubbish. *It is unpleasant to poke about in the refuse to try to recover anything, for this revives identity.*[99] So long as identity is absent, rubbish is harmless and does not even create ambiguous perceptions. *Even the bones of buried kings rouse little awe and the thought that the air is full of the dust of corpses of bygone races has no power to move. Where there is no differentiation there is no defilement.*[100]

Everything said to explain the revivifying role of water also applies to dirt. Dirt is a by-product of the creation of order, starting from a state of non-differentiation, threatening the distinctions made, finally returning to its (true) indiscriminable character[101] [*Ashes to ashes, dirt to dirt*].

---

[98] Krog 2009.
[99] Ibid.: 160.
[100] Ibid.
[101] Ibid.: 161.

The quest for purity is pursued by rejection. It follows that when purity is not a symbol but something lived, it must be poor and barren. It is part of our condition that the purity for which we strive and sacrifice so much turns out to be hard and dead as a stone when we get it. [*"Purity" and "rejection" are here not only underlined but encircled by the anonymous Afrikaner student, as is the following entire sentence:*]

Purity is the enemy of change, of ambiguity and compromise.[102]

What is, then, the attraction of the barren, of that which is hard and dead as stone? Sartre portrays the anti-semite as someone who wants to adopt a mode of life in which reasoning and the quest for truth plays only a subordinate part, in which nothing is sought except what has already been found, in which one never becomes anything but what one already was.[103]

But is it a choice to reason falsely? Is it not rather an assumption that one possesses the truth? Purity cannot be consciously conceived as untrue. Yet anything that questions the assumed truthfulness and threatens the order will be condemned as pollution. Douglas, more radical in thought than Sartre, critiques the implicit division between "our thinking" and the rigid black and white reasoning of the anti-Semite. Because [*and this is doubly underlined and encircled*] the yearning for rigidity is in us all.[104]

The little perpetrator. Sanders expounds on a self-critical remark in the *TRC report*, on its failure to focus sufficiently on the dimension of "moral responsibility", stating that the attention on *the deeds of the exceptional perpetrator* led to *fail[ure] to recognise the "little perpetrator" in each of us*[105]; whereas Breytenbach adds the insight that, as an intellectual, it is not enough to resist the system in its overt manifestations, but *it is necessary to find the roots of the conversion of "foldedness with the other" into forms of complicity in its denial.*[106] This is what makes apartheid exemplary for the intellectual as a figure of responsibility-in-complicity. It is necessary to have not only

---

[102] Ibid.
[103] Sartre 1948, in ibid.: 162.
[104] Douglas 1966: 162.
[105] *TRC Report, I*, in Sanders 2002: 3.
[106] Sanders 2002: 157.

an ideal of freedom or autonomy but an account of sufficient power to capture how that ideal is, at a fundamental level, susceptible to perversion as something like apartheid.[107]

N. P. Van Wyk Louw, the poet "whom we all revere",[108] the "critic from within", who in the end becomes apartheid's ambassador, because he chooses allegiance to the *volk* before allegiance to humanity—although he tries, in vain, to incorporate the coloureds (*de bruin-mense*) into the conception of "us" *(ons mense)*. As ambassador in Holland, he attempts to universalise apartheid and make it an issue for Europe as well as South Africa (thereby rightfully making Europe complicit). He proposes "multinationalism" as the solution to the problem of racial domination, in South Africa and in Europe; separation (apart-ness) being the "ethically just" response.[109]

The lasting insight of Black Consciousness was that apartheid was not, in any essential sense, an achievement of separateness at all, but it was a system of enforced separation that, paradoxically, generated an unwanted intimacy with an oppressive other [*unwanted, or ambiguously desired?*]. In a narrow sense, it decreed apartness; in a general sense, it disavowed relation (foldedness in human-being with the other).[110]

If such a disavowal of relation is what tends toward support for apartheid, it is an acknowledgement of this complicity and its disavowal at the heart of apartheid that is the essential starting point of any opposition to apartheid.[111]

---

[107] Ibid.: 190.

[108] Breytenbach 1993: 59.

[109] Sanders 2002: 65, 90.

[110] Ibid.: 189–190. Again, only afterwards do I notice this covert reference to Édouard Glissant's concept of Relation. Sanders largely leans on Jacques Derrida, but "foldedness in human-being with the other" is a notion that I am sure would appeal to both Glissant and Zimitri Erasmus, as elaborated in the second part of the diptych (*In Praise of Relation*). Glissant *is* among Sanders' references, but only as a secondary source. He notes that Breytenbach recently has invoked *Poetics of Relation* in the name of language-based minority rights (ibid.: 146).

[111] Ibid.: 190.

RUSHDIE'S BITCH

AT THE TIME OF THE WRITER festival in eThekwini (Durban), in which ze participated eight years ago, debutant writer Zainub Dala is assaulted in the street for stating that Salman Rushdie is one of her favourite writers. The assailants call her *Rushdie's Bitch*. Dala, due to launch her novel *What about Meera*, the tale of a 22-year-old woman who escapes her arranged marriage in Durban to spiral out of control in Dublin, cancelled her performance after the assault.

THE FINAL PARADOX of the search for purity is that it is an attempt to force experience into logical categories of non-contradiction. But experience is not amenable and those who make the attempt find themselves led into contradiction. Sexual purity which implies no contact between the sexes must be literally barren.[112]

Breytenbach, on his return to Paradise, reads a wall-truth in Cape Town: "WE HAVE MOVED FROM THE INTERREGNUM TO THE INTRARECTUM". Somebody had scribbled underneath: "VICTORY HAS AIDS".[113]

After finishing reading ze still has problems to grapple the ambiguity. Dame Douglas to-be outlines a possible dichotomy between dirt-affirming and dirt-rejecting philosophies. Whereas the latter are typically incomplete but optimistic, the former tend to be more complete (complex) and also pessimistic. Yet, although fascinated by transgressions, she remains herself essentially a conservative friend of order.

[112] Douglas 1966: 162.
[113] Breytenbach 1993: 132.

THE SPRINGBOK PUB

ZE TRIES TO IMAGINE the mental regimentation and self-deception of an entire community, the complacency of complicity, maybe as banal as the evil of indifference. Or ignorance. The benevolent police state. The very building for the Arts and Social Sciences, where Volkekunde was taught until 2002, disturbs the harmonious picture with its blatant brutality. The concrete colossus, previously named after Verwoerd's successor, B. J. Vorster, was constructed on the rubble of the evicted "coloured area", Die Vlake, overlooking the new white neighbourhood on the other side of Merriman Avenue, anonymous one-storey buildings, chain-houses, villas, a huge gas station, parking lots; no traces, not even a plaque of remembrance of this Stellenbosch's own District Six. The former Lückhoff Skool, which was also given or traded to the expanding university, is now a centre for community interaction, dutifully telling its story in non-committal half-truths, like the grand display of the university's history, decade by decade, in the University Museum. It would take hir many weeks to find out, but that was where ze ended up in hir first disorientation, a lively square in what had once been Die Vlake, now, again, a fringe area, where the white city ends, a Somali coffee shop and a coloured hairdresser, where ze drops in for a haircut and asks for the direction to Dorp Straat, the only street name ze recalls; two months later ze will accidentally rediscover the hairdresser, who will smilingly recall hir and repeat the haircut, and suddenly the pieces of the inner and outer map fall together, and the contours of this other parallel city appear in a flash of illumination, like the stroboscopic lights of the Springbok Pub, less than a stone throw away in the corner of Andringa and Merriman. It all makes sense.

Already on hir first Saturday night in Stellenbosch, Aryan suggested that ze go "try hir moves" at the Springbok Pub. Ze was tired and hesitant; if it weren't for the expectation to see Aryan there, ze would not have gone, thinking that it would be a posh or hip show-off venue for the beautiful people (*why did ze expect that?*). It was the opposite. Ze had a couple of Black Label (*Black Labour, White Guilt*) in the sports bar, to dare approach the dance floor in the other room, irresistibly drawn by the drums and base and the videos projected on the wall, assuming to be viewed as a sexagenarian voyeur, a freak, the only white among coloureds, certainly the oldest on the floor. But the atmosphere is one of familiarity, the women middle-aged, in their thirties or forties, with their friends or their husbands, curiously observing hir and inviting hir to dance with them, embedding hir in unpretentious hospitality, and ze is overwhelmed by their welcoming warmth. The sound of the Cape, the progenies of this crossroads, the breed of three hundred years of intimacy, wanted or unwanted, defying the boundaries of slave and master, white and black; the *bruin-mense* as the Afrikaners called them, in affection and contempt, neither black nor white, less than white but better than black, privileged among the unprivileged, yet despised for being half-caste, for being neither-nor, without tribe, without culture, without home—the leftovers of humankind, as Madame De Klerk so lovingly called them. Bastards, like the Afrikaners, but of a darker shade; the fine divisive line could cut a family in two, siblings ending on each side of the insurmountable border.[114] Humble bastards, inconsolably compromised by their not-quite-whiteness. On hir second visit to the Springbok Pub, ze arrives at the end of a birthday party; now ze's recognised, prompted to eat and drink, and one of the pitiful husbands teaches hir to dance properly ... Syncopating hir sense of the Stellenbosch stomp, surprisingly, to—ze searches in vain for the proper metaphor—Saturday night insouciance.

References

Adam, H. & K. Moodley (2013). *Imagined Liberation: Xenophobia, Citizenship and Identity in South Africa, Germany and Canada.* Stellenbosch: SUN Press.
Appadurai, A. (2006). *Fear of Small Numbers: An Essay on the Geography of Anger.* Durham: Duke University Press.
Bekker, S. (2010). "Explaining Violence Against Foreigners and Strangers in Urban South Africa: Outbursts During May and June 2008". *The African Yearbook of International Law* 16: 125–149.
Breytenbach, B. (1982). *A Season in Paradise.* New York: Persea Books.
Breytenbach, B. (1993). *Return to Paradise.* London: Faber and Faber.
Butalia, U. (2000). *The Other Side of Silence: Voices from the Partition of India.* London: C. Hurst.
Coetzee, J. M. (1988). *White Writing: On the Culture of Letters in South Africa.* New Haven and London: Yale University Press.

[114]The racial division line was not *absolutely* insurmountable. A small number of people were "reclassified" each year. Zoë Wicomb's novel *Playing in The Light* (2006) makes a thorough investigation of the "play-white" phenomenon. See also Watson 1970.

Dlamini, J. (2014). *Askari: A Story of Collaboration and Betrayal in the Anti-Apartheid Struggle*. Johannesburg: Jacana.

Douglas, M. (1966). *Purity and Danger: An Analysis of Concepts of Pollution and Taboo*. London: Routledge & Kegan Paul.

Dubow, S. (2014). *Apartheid 1948–1994*. Oxford: Oxford University Press.

Du Toit, P. & H. Kotze (2011). *Liberal Democracy and Peace in South Africa*. Johannesburg: Palgrave Macmillan.

Eichrodt, W. (1933). *Theologie des Alten Testaments*. Leipzig: Hinrich.

Eiselen, W. W. M. (1920). "Die Naturellevraagstuk: 'n Lesing gchou op 7 Mei 1920 voor die Filosofiese Vereniging van die Universiteit van Stellenbosch".

Eiselen, W. W. M. (1948). "Die Bevolkingsvraagstuk van Suid-Afrika, Sosiologies Beskou met Besondere Aandag aan die Arbeidsgemeenskap van Blankes en Naturelle en die Implikasies van Apartheid," 'n referaat gelewer op die Simposium van i Julie, 1948, van die Jaarvergadering van die Akademie vir Wetenskap en Kuns te Orange Free State.

Freud, S. (1961). *Civilization and Its Discontents*. 1st American ed. New York: W. W. Norton.

Gellner, E. (1962). "Concepts and Society", in International Sociological Association. *Transactions of the Fifth World Congress of Sociology*, vol. 1. Washington, DC.

Gilroy, P. (2004). *After Empire: Melancholia or Convivial Culture?* London: Routledge.

van Gennep, A. (1909). *Les rites de passage: étude systématique des rites*. Paris.

Hassim, S., T. Kupe, & E. Worby (eds.) (2008). *South Africa: Go Home or Die Here: Xenophobia and the Reinvention of Difference in South Africa*. Johannesburg: Wits University Press.

Hemer, O. (2012). *Fiction and Truth in Transition: Writing the Present Past in South Africa and Argentina*. Berlin: Lit Verlag.

Hemer, O., M. Povrzanović Frykman, & P.-M. Ristilammi (eds.) (2020). *Conviviality at the Crossroads: The Poetics and Politics of Everyday Encounters*. Basingstoke: Palgrave Macmillan.

Illich, I. (1973). *Tools for Conviviality*. New York: Perennial Library.

Kaganof, A. (2014). *Night is Coming: Threnody for the Victims of Marikana* (Digital Video). Cape Town: African Noise Foundation.

Kakar, S. (1996). *The Colors of Violence*. Chicago: The University of Chicago Press.

Kentridge, W. (2015). *Refuse the Hour*. A collaboration with Philip Miller, Dada Masilo, Catherine Meyburgh, Peter Galison. Cape Town. 26 and 27 February 2015.

Krog, A. (1999). *Country of My Skull*. London: Vintage.

Krog, A. (2009). *Begging to Be Black*. Cape Town: Random House Struik.

Kross, C. (2002). "W.W.M. Eiselen: Architect of Apartheid Education", in Kallaway, P. (ed.). *The History of Education Under Apartheid, 1948–1994: The Doors of Learning and Culture Shall Be Opened.* New York: P. Lang.

Maimonides, M. (1956 [1881]). *The Guide for the Perplexed.* 2nd ed. New York: Dover Publications.

Malinowski, B. (ed.) (1938). *International Institute of African Languages and Cultures. Memorandum XV, Methods of Study of Culture Contact in Africa.*

Malouf, D. (1990). *The Great World.* London: Chatto & Windus.

Marinovich, G. (2016). *Murder at Small Koppie: The Real Story of the Marikana Massacre.* Cape Town: Penguin.

Martin, D.-C. (1999). *Coon Carnival: New Year in Cape Town, Past and Present.* Cape Town: David Philip.

Martin, D.-C. (2015). "Le general ne répond pas... Chanson, clip et incertitudes: les jeunes Afrikaners dans la "nouvelle" Afrique du Sud". *L'Homme: Revue Française d'Anthropologie* 215/216: 197–231.

McClintock, A. (1995). *Imperial Leather: Race, Gender and Sexuality in the Colonial Contest.* New York and London: Routledge.

McNeill, J. T. & H. M. Gamer (eds.) (1938). *Medieval Handbooks of Penance.* New York: Columbia University Press.

Millin, S. G. (1924). *God's Stepchildren.* London: Constable.

Mngxitama, A. (2009). "We Are Not All Like That: Race, Class and Nation After Apartheid", in Hassim, S., Kupe, T. & E. Worby (eds.). *Go Home or Die Here: Xenophobia and the Reinvention of Difference in South Africa,* 189–208. Johannesburg: Wits University Press.

Moulinier, L. (1952). *Le Pur et l'impure dans la Pensée des Grecs, d'Homére à Aristote.* Paris.

Naipaul, V. S. (1964). *An Area of Darkness.* London: Deutsch.

Rabie, Jan (1964). *Die Groot Anders-Maak.* Cape Town: Human & Roseau.

Reilly, Jan (2012). *Shame: Confessions of an Aid Worker in Africa.* Cape Town: Jillian Reilly (e-book: lulu.com).

Sanders, M. (2002). *Complicities: The Intellectual and Apartheid.* Durham, NC: Duke University Press.

Sanders, M. (2007). *Ambiguities of Witnessing: Law and Literature in the Time of a Truth Commission.* Stanford: Stanford University Press.

Sarlo, B. (2003). *La pasión y la excepción: Eva, Borges y el asesinato de Aramburu.* Buenos Aires: Siglo Veintiuno Editores.

Sartre, J.-P. (1948). *Anti-Semite and Jew* [*Réflexions sur la question juive*]. New York: Schocken Books.

Tilly, C. (2006). *Why?: [What Happens When People Give Reasons... and Why].* Princeton, NJ: Princeton University Press.

Vaknin, S. (2011). *Malignant Self-Love: Narcissism Revisited.* Prague: Narcissism Publishers.

Volkan, V. (2006). *Killing in the Name of Identity*. New York: Ingram.

Watson, G. (1970). *Passing for White: A Study of Racial Assimilation in a South African School*. London: Tavistock Publications.

Wicomb, Z. (1998). "Shame and Identity: The Case of the Coloured in South Africa", in Attridge, D. & R. Jolly (eds.). *Writing South Africa: Literature, Apartheid and Democracy 1948–1995*. Cambridge: Cambridge University Press.

Wicomb, Z. (2006). *Playing in the Light*. New York and London: The New Press.

Wicomb, Z. (2018). *Race, Nation, Translation: South African Essays, 1990–2013*. Johannesburg: Wits University Press.

Cape Calypso

Interlude
(Allesverloren)
(2016)

O. Hemer, *Contaminations and Ethnographic Fictions*,
Palgrave Studies in Literary Anthropology,
https://doi.org/10.1007/978-3-030-34925-7_5

J.

ZE'S A LONER, has always been, will always be. It is as if ze's back to normal, after all these years of partnership, so precious to hir and yet something ze might leave behind, as everything else … It's a horrible thought, so horrible that ze whisks it away, but it stays nonetheless (like an evil omen). When J. comes to visit, ze has an inexplicable pain in the jaws, like toothache but not located to a particular tooth; it's like a paralysis, as ze imagines the effects of a stroke or a brain tumour (*the dark thoughts rise easily from hir inner void*) … Ze wants so much to please him, to make him feel comfortable, to have him enjoy hir solitary company, the twosomeness, without family or friends, their being lonely together; he's a loner, too, and that's why ze loves him, the reason why they put up with each other … But he takes hir down, unintentionally, with his obsessive remarks on hir tics, on hir obvious restlessness. He suggests that ze start with the anti-depressive medication again, the pills ze proudly ceased to take from one day to another, as ze regularly used to stop smoking, just for the sake of being able to do it—especially if ze had just bought a carton (or *ten*, as ze did in Buenos Aires once, without realising that ze would have to declare it on arrival to the EU, between flights in Frankfurt, and pay a hundred Euros in tax for something ze didn't even want). Now ze had almost literally a suitcase with drugs that ze wouldn't use. He takes hir down, inadvertently, ze reacts like a child, closing the door, shutting hir eyes, pretending to sleep; ze feels how he is luring hir back into his world of medicine and psychology, his endless prompting that ze should "go talk to someone" … And the truth, when it comes out, is naked and ugly. Ze's not sure that ze even wants to write it. Put it in print. Why, if it hurts, must ze tell it to the world? Why can't ze just take him in hir arms and hold him? Ze would be lost without him, and even though it always takes days, a week, to get accustomed after so many weeks of absence, ze dreads the thought of really going back to hir (presumably ordinary) solitary state. (*Hir mother never wanted hir to marry and have children, because she thought high of hir, not the opposite, because she saw her own unfulfilled fate in hir; no, not fate, but some projection of self-fulfilment—although her simple, banal, wish was for hir to become a medical doctor.*)

Ze wanted so much to please him … Out of a guilty conscience? No, that will occur to hir only afterwards. J. never evoked pity. Vulnerable yet supercilious, he would hit back hard. Relentlessly. He didn't need to be taken care of, and yet ze pampered him. The first thing they did was to buy a month's membership at the University gym, where he would go working out and swimming while ze were in office. And ze had already made the necessary preparations for their mini-vacation to Namaqualand and Namibia, a skeleton of an itinerary and all four nights' accommodation booked through hotels.com. A bit too meticulous for hir own taste (ze would have preferred to leave at least one night open), but then ze knows from almost thirty years' experience when and when not to pick a fight. The car had also been reserved, two weeks in advance (a lesson learned after having been stuck without a vehicle the previous weekend). But ze lets J. do the driving, to boost his male ego. Besides, he is probably the best driver, less hot-headed and with a more reliable sense of direction. On the day of departure, only two days after his arrival, ze leaves office before three, to have a good margin for the first day's drive, to Lambertsbaai, but it takes almost an hour just to get out of Stellenbosch. And after missing the junction with the coastal road at Piketberg, they have to climb the Cedarberg anyway, via Clanwilliam, and arrive only just before dark.

I AM READING *October*, the latest novel by Zoë Wicomb—perhaps the writer I most closely identify with, even more, or for other reasons, than with Señor C. Her position between academia and fiction more evident, and problematic; the complicated relation to South Africa embodied, as they would say, the in-betweenness of neither-nor, living in Scotland, returning to Cape Town every now and then, with affectional bonds to Namaqualand. Kliprand is the gravity centre of the novel, the forsaken "home" to which the exiled Mercia, a 52-year old writer and academic, newly abandoned by her Scottish partner, is called by her broken left-behind alcoholic brother Jake.

Swaartland and Namaqualand come to life through the reading. I imagine the barren hills in sparkling spring gown, and the indifferent look of a tall Namaqua girl outside a grocery store in one of the roadside villages strikes me as if I had caught the green gaze of Sylvie, Jake's "tart" of a wife, and caretaker of him and their son Nicky.

It is my intention to pass by Kliprand on the way back, a detour of some 200 kilometres on dirt roads, but in the end, we will decide not to. Yet it is as if I had been there, in Zoë's imagination.

Antjie Krog insisted, when we met, that no black person has ever been the protagonist of a novel by a white or coloured South African writer. I immediately brought up Sylvie as proof to refute her. (I could as well have taken the example of the albino narrator of *Zebra Crossing*, by Antje's own colleague and protegée Meg Vandermerwe, which I will read on my return to Sweden, and which will make Antjie's culturalist assumption even more incomprehensible.) But the truth is that they are exceptions, and, moreover, the albino is of course an apposite "white", and way back in Sylvie's god-forgotten ancestry there is a mythical Boer benefactor, providing a drop of "respectable blood" to the Namaqua family line. The reversal of the degenerate seed, but mirroring the same race line.

Sylvie, the Good-Time girl in the butcher's shop, loves to pose before the camera and take pictures of herself with the self-timer. One of the memorable passages of the novel is a curiously erotic one, when she imagines setting up the camera in the shop:

> *The moon just about skimming the window so that an eerie film-set light is cast over everything. Over the streamers of sausage that gleam as moonlight lifts out speckles of shiny white fat. She, Sylvie, having stripped all her clothes, would coil the sausage around her nakedness. Carefully, slowly, starting at her feet.* Hitse! *What a* gedoente *getting it round and round herself, coils of marbled sausage cool against her skin. Neatly, like an Egyptian mummy, a queen wrapped in time. And if the sausage skin should break? Ag, the sausage meat would stay, plastered to her skin, grafted onto her. Sylvie, the Sausage Girl, brand-new as a baby, at one with her handwork.*[1]

What if a white male, say André Brink, had pictured a black girl like that! I muse at the certain outcry, but immediately sadden at the afterthought; am I, de facto, forever inhibited by the boundaries I have set out to transgress?

---

[1] Wicomb 2014: 118–119.

TRAVELOGUE

LAMBERTSBAAI, or more accurately Lambert's Bay, evokes the association to a subtropical Outer Hebrides, no, not subtropical, but something Norse; Norwegian, Icelandic or Scottish. Halfway to Namaqualand, the sea wilder and more frightening than ze has seen anywhere, and ice cold even in summer. Fish and bird country. For some reason, they have always been drawn to these barren places, Northern Norway, the Faroe Islands, Chiloé; they'd surely gone to Malvinas, too, even South Georgia, if they had been offered the opportunity. A strange kind of affinity in alienation, or an embarrassing recognition, Afrikaner pop on the TV, resembling what in Norway thirty years ago was known as *svensktopps-musik*.[2] Even the hairdos are reminiscent of a pre-broken Scandinavia.

Bird Island, the tourist attraction in front of the harbour, had its momentary glory as a defiant Guano republic, before the Empire crushed it under its heel. Decades later, Lambert's Bay was to become one of the British strongholds in the Anglo-Boer war. They walk the bird-made island in blistering white light and later, as the sun sets, pay their visit to the overgrown graveyard. It is like living a travelogue; in hir mind ze can easily translate the barren experience to laconic prose, or the conception of it, if not the actual words, but ze quickly dismisses the idea of trying; it would be too ... *cheap* ... a paraphrase of Chatwin, at best; but, then, who remembers Chatwin, anyway?

He used to be one of hir favourite authors through the '80s and well into the '90s, although ze never particularly identified with him (*too British, too snobbish; the lingering association goes to Sotheby's*). Has he even stood the test of time, ze wonders. Chatwin's kind of travel writing belongs to another era, anyhow, regardless of style.

At Isabella's restaurant, facing Bird Island, they have two bottles of wine with the meal. Ze likes travelling with J. It is as if travelling were their element, an inter-zone in which they both navigate with ease, a state of flow that suits their restless natures; adventurousness brought them together in the first place and keeps them forever attached. Neither of them has any problem resting in the self, but being together is more enjoyable when they move, less irritating, funnier. This journey is turning into a late platonic honeymoon, confirming their mature marriage,

---

[2] Pop music in Swedish, often in a country and western style.

celebrating the astounding fact that they have spent a lot more than half their lives together. Sorrow, loss and infidelity have, to the surprise of both, made their unlikely alliance resilient.

After dinner, they walk into the salty dark down Voortrekker straat, to a bar where the town's few blacks hang out; a fat Boer behind the counter, two brothers to be precise, possibly even twins, the one serving the beer avoids hir look, as if ashamed on hir behalf, or his own. Nobody else seems to notice their intrusion. A man in his thirties, apparently a regular, plays Whitney Houston on the video jukebox, again and again, miming perfectly, every single phrase, and as ze observes him from the corner of hir eye ze suddenly starts crying, discreetly yet uncontrollably. Ze can't explain why, but simply lets hirself go with the emotion, comforting and unsettling, like another premonition; the wake of the South Atlantic flood.

SOME THREE MONTHS later, back in Malmö, I will take part in an Art performance: Black British artists in blue overalls on board the Sugar Ship. The passengers are supposed to deposit three memories: one about a moment when they felt belonging, one about when they felt like aliens and one about when their identity was challenged. I dislike the questions, but fill in the forms (like a "duktig flicka" [good girl] as my Canadian colleague Susan describes her own dutiful compliance). For the identity one, I will write about the discomfort of being white in South Africa and realising that black South Africans don't make the distinction between South African whites and foreigners. (It is of course a constructed and not really "embodied" memory; I really can't remember my "identity" ever being seriously challenged, whereas my usually solid "I" has been destabilised many times, deliberately and not.) For the belonging one I will write: In cosmopolitan places, where in a way the very notion of belonging is negated. A stranger among strangers. Preferably in the global South.

THE VOID

THE HOSTESS at Sir Lambert's guesthouse has a stroke of madness in the big bluish-grey eyes. She says "this place is getting too green for me" and goes great length to advice J. on the best short cut to the North, digging out a worn road atlas that looks like a relic from the 1960s, turning over the maps with a finger that she wets with the tip of her tongue, back and forth, only to finally conclude that it be safest to take the main road back to Clanwilliam and get on the N7 again.

N7 is a straight line cut in the semi-arid desert, a sparse flow of fast-moving trucks in both directions, occasional cars like their own silver Polo, peaking at 170 when they have the road to themselves. Ze imagines the burned autumn landscape covered in spring flowers, and the glimpse of a high-cheeked Namaqua girl outside the desolate grocery store in a roadside village becomes as familiar, almost intimate, as if ze had looked into the laughing eyes of Zoe Wicomb's curious double. Ze enjoys sitting in the passenger's seat, dozing off in silly thoughts or just contemplating the uniform landscape, the vastness of earth and sky, smiling to hirself at signs of hardship and despair, *Bitterfontein*, *Allesverloren*, signposts pointing into the void of the Northern Cape, *Calvinia*, *Kliprand*, *Vaalputs*, *Pofadder* ...

OCTOBER MEANS SPRING in the Southern hemisphere, but this is autumn, and that is also what the novel suggests to me, saturation, the melancholy of fulfilment. A year later I will meet Zoë Wicomb at the Institute, something I could never have fathomed on the road through Namaqualand ... A year passes so quickly. A life. (The melancholy of return.)

The next year I am staying in Cape Town, visiting Stellenbosch. Tables turned. The prejudice about Cape Town – which I used to embrace – is that it's white, English, liberal; a leisure town for the well-off and non-guilty. I remember that it struck me at Bill Kentridge's performance that the audience was (practically) all white, almost carnivalesque, masquerading as caricatures. But that is not what I see in the streets, not even on the beachfront. In Cape Town I fully understand what Heribert and Kegila meant when they claimed that South Africa, as opposed to Europe, has an acceptance for difference.

Zoë tells me about the struggle with a novel that isn't coming out (*how she is even at the verge of giving it up*). It resonates with my own doubts, the all but joyful side of the writing process, distractions, dementia, the fear of forgetting. Zoë would dread to perform for fear of losing the words. Reading is one thing, a comfort zone, or pretending not to read from a paper, but improvisation is hazardous. She is so warm and welcoming, and witty; her features are more Namaqua than I had imagined; the high cheekbones, the roguish glimpse in the eyes, more like Sylvie than the apparently autobiographical self. What she says about language is truly intriguing; how the gap between the *beskaaft Afrikaans* and the *zwaart Afrikaans* is widening. One would imagine the opposite, that the language would strive to return to its creole origin, to restore the cleansed-out non-Dutch synonyms, especially since the black majority of Afrikaans-speakers is taken as hostage in the on-going language struggle against English. But Zoë notes that it is rather the other way around, a return to the colonial Dutch. The street signs in Stellenbosch are becoming void of "y"s. The Afrikaans y—which originates in a misreading of the Dutch "ij"— is being abolished to the extreme of hypercorrection; one Anthony respelling his name Anthonij. Zoë grew up bilingual, but has lost her Afrikaans. She realised it when she heard Breyten Breytenbach speak (in the heated debate) and she could hardly figure out what he said.

[RIGHTS OF PASSAGE]

*ÖVERGÅNGEN från tredje till första person sker omärkligt; jag är knappt
ens medveten om det, och osäker på vilket som är mer distanserat respek-
tive mer intimt. Språkbytet däremot kräver omställning, som att kliva
ur en förklädnad och i en annan, men inte heller där är det längre
självklart vilken jag är mest bekväm i. Jo, svenskan ligger förstås närmare
mina tankar, eller i varje fall mina känslor, det vore förmätet att påstå
något annat. Men jag kommer allt oftare på mig själv med att göra även
anteckningar på engelska, också när det inte är relaterat till något jag
läser. Kanske ska jag reservera ett rum för svenskan, ett lager (lustigt nog
hittar jag först inte det adekvata svenska ordet för "layer"), som dock i
den slutliga texten ändå måste översättas (kanske av någon annan), efter-
som svenskan och engelskan inte ar likvärdiga. Spanska och engelska hade
fungerat, även om det förstås hade reducerat läsekretsen avsevärt, medan
svenska är som afrikaans; det skulle fungera för min mikroskopiska
svenska läsekrets. Jag tänker på Stephanus bok* Nagmusiek, *om den afri-
kaanske tonsättaren Arnold van Wyk, där afrikaans och engelska vävs
samman, liksom fiktion och biografi, dock inte nödvändigtvis med över-
ensstämmande gränser. Men för att nå utanför den afrikaanska offentligheten, som i storlek är någonstans mellan den danska och den svenska,
men snarare jämförbar med den (icke-existerande men möjliga) skandi-
naviska offentligheten, måste de afrikaanska partierna översättas till
engelska. Aryan föreslog att de engelska partierna i den upplagan på mots-
varande sätt borde översättas till afrikaans, så att man fick två spegelver-
sioner och de enspråkiga skulle vara tvungna att läsa båda.*

*Könsbytet, eller genusväxlingen, är dock den största utmaningen och
jag är inte helt övertygad om beslutet att hålla fast vid det tredje könet.
Komplikationen blir dubbel i gestaltningen av sexuella relationer. Vem
är* hens *motpart? Man eller kvinna. Den förestående katastrofen får
helt olika konnotationer beroende på denna spegelvändning ...*

[The passage from third to first person goes imperceptibly, I am
hardly even aware of it, and not sure as to which is the most distanced or the most intimate. The change of language, by contrast,
craves a conversion, like stepping out of one disguise and into
another, but even here it's no longer self-evident which one I find
most comfortable. Of course, Swedish is closer to my thoughts, or at
least my feelings; claiming the opposite would be presumptuous. But

it happens more and more often that I catch myself taking notes in English, even when it's not related to anything I'm reading. Maybe I ought to reserve a room for Swedish, a layer (*curiously, I have to think twice to remember the Swedish word "lager"*) which in the end will have to be translated anyway (supposedly by somebody else), since Swedish and English are not equal. Spanish and English would work, although that of course would have reduced the readership substantially, whereas Swedish is like Afrikaans; it would only work for my microscopic Swedish readership. I think of Stephanus' book *Nagmusiek*, about the Afrikaner composer Arnold van Wyk, in which Afrikaans and English are interlaced, like fiction and biography, albeit not necessarily with corresponding boundaries. But in order to reach out further than the Afrikaans-speaking public sphere, which in size is somewhere between the Danish and the Swedish, but comparable to the (non-existent yet plausible) Scandinavian public sphere, the Afrikaans part of the book had to be translated to English. Aryan suggested that the English part in that edition should be translated to Afrikaans, so that there were two mirroring versions, and the monolingual would have to consult both.

The sex change, or gender conversion, is however the chief challenge, and I am not as yet fully convinced that I should stick to the third gender. The complication doubles in the narration of sexual relations. Who is *hir* counterpart? Man or woman. The imminent catastrophe attains completely different connotations depending on that mirror twist.]

Here I am moreover treading on territory that is largely unknown to me, and *booby-trapped* at that [*a more intriguing expression than the Swedish* försåtminerad]. Easy prey—white, senior, male, straight— with as yet shallow or (at best) *random* knowledge of the immense gender studies literature; not because I dismiss the gender dimension (*on the contrary, as you will see, my interrogation is increasingly focusing on sex and race*), but possibly due to my general scepticism (which in this case may translate as *prejudice*) about anything that borders on identity politics. I am aware that my intention can and probably will be misinterpreted, but the purpose is neither to provoke nor to offend. An anarchist at heart, I instinctively side with the queers. Yet, I am in the process also coming to realise that the inner homophobe is more devious than the rather inoffensive racist.

INGLORIOUS BASTERS

AT THE TIME ze is unaware of a parallel journey, some two hundred kilometres inland, in the 1870s; the expulsion of the semi-nomadic *Basters*, from the lost grazing lands of the Northern Cape to enforced settlement in German South West Africa. The bastards of Rehoboth[3] were to be the object of German anthropologist Eugen Fischer's meticulous investigation: *Die Rehobother Bastards und das Bastardisierungsproblem beim Menschen. Anthropologische und ethnologische Studien am Rehobother Bastardvolk in Deutsch-Sudwestafrika.*[4] Conducted just after the first genocide of the twentieth century, the extermination of the defiant Herero and Nama, Fischer's study of "the effects of miscegenation" became the catalyst for a century of horror. Steven Robins, whom ze recognises from the Anthropology department and its on-going seminar series *Indexing the Human*, is to trace this genealogy of eugenics in his *Letters of Stone* (2016), the story of his father's escape from Nazi Germany to South Africa, and the fate of the family of his father and those of so many others, who were trapped in Hell, to eventually be deported and murdered.

The Basters had in the mid-nineteenth century been pastoralists around the Amandelboom Rhenish mission (now Williston). In the 1860s, they entered into escalating conflict with the expanding *trekboers*. Basters and trekboers were both largely livestock farmers in competition for land and water with wealthier white wool farmers in the region. These better-off farmers persuaded the Cape colonial government to enforce land laws that gradually privatised the commons, culminating with the Land Beacons Act in 1865, which made the semi-nomadic way of life impossible and forced the Basters to move northwards and settle in Rehoboth. Their forced departure created business opportunities for Jewish merchants such as Steven Robins' granduncle Eugen Robinski, who had arrived in Cape Town in 1888, after escaping prison in Königsberg, and proceeded on the gruelling six-hundred-kilometre

---

[3] The *Basters*, as they nowadays proudly call themselves, were originally descendants of Boer father and, usually, Khoi or San mother. The division lines were blurry between basters, trekboers, *Griqua* and other Afrikaans-speaking groups in the Cape in the nineteenth century. The current Baster population in Namibia is estimated at around 35,000 (*Unrepresented Nations & Peoples Organization*, https://unpo.org).

[4] Originally published in Jena 1913 and republished in a revised ("politically corrected") version in Graz 1961.

journey northwards to Williston, where he bought up a number of dis-
possessed Basters' town and farm properties.[5]

The Rehoboth Basters, who four decades earlier had joined the trekboers on brutal "bushman hunts", virtually exterminating the San population of the Amandelboom area, now willingly aided the Germans in
their murderous campaign against the Herero and Nama. The victim
turned perpetrator, or double victim. *The Double Agent.* Jews in South
Africa, many of whom had barely escaped the Holocaust, often supported apartheid, openly or silently. And Afrikanerdom turned, after the
war, into the most fervent ally of the state of Israel. The kinship of the
neighbourhood bullies, to quote one of Dylan's least memorable songs.

THE PURITY DISCOURSE is never as manifest as in questions of
gender and sexuality. Anything that challenges the (bipolar) heterosexual norm is abominated, and especially the ambisexual, the
polyamorous, the third gender, the hermaphrodite (*with the curious exception of the* hijra *of the Indian subcontinent, most notably in
Muslim Bangladesh*). Cheryl Stobie notes the increasing prevalence
of bisexuality in South African novels after 1994,[6] and asks what
that might signify in a society previously dominated by an either/
or mind-set. Does it point towards a "utopian wonderland beyond
gender",[7] or, in Stobie's own metaphoric conception,

> an imaginary zone somewhere in the double rainbow of gender/
> sexuality and race/ethnicity, a zone with a wretched history which
> also offers the possibility of a broader, more inclusive and generous
> future?[8]

Transition (to democracy), as defined by Homi Bhabha, is the
"'hybrid' moment of political change", when people become

---

[5] Robins 2016: 74–75.
[6] Behr 1995; Dangor 2001; Willoughby 2002; Heyn 2003; Adair 2004, and others.
[7] Michel 1996: 60, in Stobie 2007: 270.
[8] Stobie 2007: 270.

"free to negotiate and translate their cultural identities in a discontinuous intertextual temporality of cultural difference".[9] (*My computer wants to autocorrect* intertextual *to* intersexual.) Bisexuality functions textually to contribute to a discourse of multiplicity and change, which triggers powerful emotional reactions.[10] (Importantly, this discourse refuses both the familiar binary discourse of heteronormativity and its less familiar counterpart homonormativity; neither-nor, beyond binaries, *over the rainbow* would perhaps be a more apposite metaphor for the utopian gesture of transition.)

The sympathetic reading of the infamous Mark Behr's novel *The Smell of Apples* (1995), with its "contaminated and contaminating bisexual double agent",[11] is particularly intriguing. Before becoming an informant for the ANC, Behr had been a spy for the apartheid government at Stellenbosch University, recruited by the threat of being exposed for his "closeted gay experiences". The double agent, an incarnation of political shame and personal amorality, "is metaphorically covered in filth, is inseparable from that filth".[12] Filth, more than dirt, intrinsically associated with *shit.*

Identity formation, according to Judith Butler, is "the mode by which others become shit".[13] [*That is an astonishing statement! Identity politics, the politics of (communal) excretion. But beware of the turning tables, the contradiction in terms, the word contamination so contaminated with negative meaning that it is almost unusable.*]

The ambiguity of the bisexual, as opposed to homosexuality's inversion (mirroring) of the heterosexual norm. (*Adam after the Fall, bisexually torn between sameness and difference.*[14]) Why did it take hir so long to affirm hir bisexuality, *and why do I—subconsciously, yet very deliberately—switch to third person (and third gender) when I enter into this domain?* Why is it easier for (white Western) women

[9] Bhabha 1988: 13, 22, in Stobie 2007: 7.
[10] Stobie 2007: 170.
[11] Ibid.: 153.
[12] Hemmings 1993: 129–130, in ibid.: 152.
[13] Ibid.
[14] Stobie 2007: 271, with reference to Patton & Sánchez-Eppler 2000.

writers to be self-exposing, putting their most intimate selves at play, literally?[15] ... Aryan pointed my attention to Chris Kraus, whom I frankly had never heard of before, and Kraus brought me to Maggie Nelson.[16] Can I be as frank as them? Am I not obliged to? Anything else is hypocrisy. The ultimate challenge. If I really want to grapple in-depth with contamination and creolisation, I mustn't be prudish.

Ironically, what ze is approaching here, the supposed peripeteia *of this "interlude", is something comparatively innocent. The last night in Sea Point, ze will summarise hir revisit to the Cape with the scent of pussy on hir fingers.*

[15] Curiously, Stobie's study of the South African transition literature found that female authors were less likely than their male counterparts to explore bisexual or homosexual themes. Especially black women writers were conspicuously absent.

[16] Kraus 2016 [1997]; Nelson 2015.

LIMBO

No country for tourists. The Fish River Canyon, the second largest in the world, is closed because of the killing heat. Off season in the Honeymoon Suite. The hostess asked if they were celebrating something. "*No? Just life ... Enjooooy!*" After checking out at the border, they had driven straight to the Orange River Camp ten kilometres further along the dirt road, on the riverbank, facing South Africa. Only when they were napping on the honeymoon bed after sharing the compliment bottle of sparkling wine, did J. realise that they never checked into Namibia. So, they quickly got dressed and drove back to the border, queuing up to get the entrance stamps in the passports. More than three hours elapsed in no man's land, but no one had noticed, luckily.

This somewhat symptomatic incidence is hir remaining memory of that last journey, a comfort in the desolation` ... *No, there is no comfort in recalling anything, only pain, and self-pity. What did ze think ze was doing? Playing God, as the deceived Lisa suggested after hir double betrayal, the last time ze was unfaithful in the flesh, not only the mind, entertaining two lovers simultaneously. Memories of all the evil ze inflicted on J. pop up, the extremes that they have been through ever before and after; and still he stayed by hir, to his mother's and his friends' discrete or open disapproval. And now ze inflicted this on hirself.* Three weeks after the Namibian excursion, on J.'s last night in Stellenbosch, fifteen minutes before they were going to the student cinema to see the unbearably pretentious *Interstellar*. After a moment of mutual stupor, he wrestled hir down, bended the mobile out of hir hands and locked himself into the toilet. While he was reading hir chats with the myriad mistresses, ze laid paralysed with the head under the pillow exorcising the evil spirits of vanity and insanity. *This is not happening. This is not happening.* But it was. And after a quarter of an hour that could have been any quantum of time, past, present and future tense, ze hears his measured words, sober and clear: "You realise that this is the end. I never want to see you again". Then, in a toneless voice, as detached from the body, hurt distilled to disdain, the coup de grace: "You are pitiful. Go hang yourself!"

The melodrama of their life together. Devastated, shattered to crumbs; was this hir ultimate pathetic way of expressing hir passionate love? Yes, not sexually passionate yet uncompromising, intensely intimate, the kind of love ze never experienced in hir happy fragile family, the numb affection of siblings under the scrutiny of demanding parents. Under scrutiny and yet unseen. Ze's a passionate autist, and he knows, he sees through hir, and ze keeps challenging him. Why? When ze realises that he is actually leaving hir, it is like the final verdict. Game over. Happy suicide, *as Ronald Laing was reputed to have said to one of his patients* (ze had met Laing and interviewed him on one of his last tours in Copenhagen and the former star in disgrace desperately hung on to this young sympathetic journalist).

The day ze witnessed the meeting of Homi Bhabha and Noam Chomsky on a street corner in Göteborg. That same day, bringing Homi Bhabha to the Book Fair, an apex in hir early academic career, and bringing disaster over hirself, a point of no return, and yet ... Ze has never written about hir disgrace, only remotely hinted at it without touching the gore. Only now when ze has lost everything is ze able to face it. But to what purpose? Evoking pity? Justifying hir pity? Hir pitiful vanity. The self-destructive instinct that ze recognises in some of hir dubious friends. Like Kevin, a brother in misery, ten years ahead into heavy alcoholism, with a similar disastrous vanity and self-contempt—a snake, as he once confessed in a moment of clarity ... Ze can write the evil now in this numb limbo, imagining that everything is lost, just as ze's imagining being in exile. But it is a dangerous exorcism. J. may have dumped hir for real and for ever. He's dependent, economically, emotionally, but he is also unpredictable. Ze believed that he deliberately put a blind eye to hir misdemeanours. He could have disclosed hir secret so easily if he had wanted, but he had to literally catch hir with hir pants down, and ze begged for it. Melodrama. Because ze wanted to put an end to it, too. Ze is weary of wasting hir creative energy courting women around the world, especially building the falsely intimate relationships that inevitably come with these seduction games, snaring hir in a web of contradictory lies. Ze'll just have to delete them completely, just like ze regularly used to stop smoking, instantaneously, when disgust overtook desire. Although these courting games are, or can be, very satisfactory; ze could say, like Sr C. about his alter ego David Lurie, that ze had found a convenient way to solve the problem of sex. (*Did he actually use the word "problem"? Yes, it is an eternal problem, not just an issue or a question.*) A satisfactory solution for a sexagenarian autist. Yes, ze misses the physical contact, but ze passed that line a long time ago. Young flesh is beyond hir aspirations, ze has enough self-distance to realise that. Ze should rather try hard to find hir way back to marital bliss.

Do you remember, ze calls to his shadow, when we went to the family councillor, the young Iranian psychologist whom I met individually, too, a couple of times. The last session ended with his conclusion that there was no hope for reconciliation. And afterwards we went for a coffee at one of the coffee bars around Davidshallstorg, and we laughed at it all.

REFERENCES

Adair, B. (2004). *In Tangier We Killed the Blue Parrot*. Johannesburg: Jacana.

Behr, M. (1995). *The Smell of Apples*. New York: Picador.

Dangor, A. (2001). *Bitter Fruit*. Cape Town: Kwela.

Hemmings, C. (1993). "Resituating the Bisexual Body", in Bristow, J. & A. R. Wilson (eds.). *Activating Theory: Lesbian, Gay and Bisexual Politics*. London: Lawrence and Wishart.

Heyn, M. (2003). *The Reluctant Passenger*. Johannesburg: Jonathan Ball.

Kraus, C. (2016 [1997]). *I Love Dick*. London: Serpent's Tail.

Michel, F. (1996). "Do Bats Eat Cats? Reading What Bisexuality Does", in Hall, D. E. & M. Pramaggiore (eds.). *Representing Bisexualities: Subjects and Cultures of Fluid Desire*. New York and London: New York University Press.

Nelson, M. (2015). *The Argonauts*. London: Melville House.

Patton, C. & B. Sánchez-Eppler (2000). *Queer Diasporas*. Durham, NC: Duke University Press.

Robins, S. (2016). *Letters of Stone: From Nazi Germany to South Africa*. Cape Town: Penguin.

Stobie, C. (2007). *Somewhere in the Double Rainbow: Representations of Bisexuality in Post-Apartheid Novels*. Scottsville: University of KwaZulu-Natal Press.

Wicomb, Z. (2014). *October*. Cape Town: Umuzi.

Willoughby, G. (2002). *Archangels*. Howick: Brevitas Publishers.

CHAPTER 6

Cape Calypso II

In Praise of Relation
(Waiting for Señor C.)

(2018)

© The Author(s) 2020
O. Hemer, *Contaminations and Ethnographic Fictions*,
Palgrave Studies in Literary Anthropology,
https://doi.org/10.1007/978-3-030-34925-7_6

ESSENCE AND RELATION. To what extent do the two central concepts of Édouard Glissant translate to Purity and Impurity? Glissant never refers to Douglas, but that is irrelevant. French and English rarely refer to each other, generally speaking, and poets and anthropologists definitely talk different languages, for the most part unintelligible to each other—although both Douglas and Glissant would be exceptions to that rule. [*Glissant had in fact studied ethnography at Musée de l'Homme for his Ph.D. in philosophy at Sorbonne—which means that he was at the Museum when Sartjie Baartman's genitals were still on display …*]

If Derek Walcott is the Caribbean Homer—for his Antillean Iliad, *Omeros*—who is Glissant? The Antillean Aristotle? … Alliterations are alluring, but other than that, no … The Caribbean Kant sounds like a dirty joke, yet evokes some intriguing connotations. The *Poetics of Relation* in fact refers to Kant's conception of Relation (*and oversees, perhaps, with his biological explanation of race—although it is intriguing that the first philosophical definition of race is centred around* race mixture).[1] … But all these Eurocentric comparisons are fundamentally false, derogatory and condescending. As if mimicry were the only possible relation between the former colonised and the coloniser. I sometimes mockingly turn it around by describing Paris as the European Buenos Aires. But turning tables only confirms the binary, and after all, centre–periphery is possibly the most ingenuous of all binaries. *Ingenuous as opposed to ingenious; I can't stop confusing them.*

BACK TO THE SENSE(S)

ZE HAS ONLY BEEN AWAY over the week-end, as usual, but if feels like an entire week, or more. In fact, the break is an abyss, although ze pretends as if nothing has happened. And although ze senses that it

---

[1] Bernasconi 2010, in Erasmus 2017: 80. Kant's definition from 1775, quoted by Lettow 2014, in ibid.:
Among the subspecies, i.e. the hereditary differences of the animals which belong to a single phylum, those which persistently preserve themselves in all transplantings (transpositions to other regions) over prolonged generations among themselves and which also always beget half-breed young in the mixing with other variations of the same phylum are called races.

must be obvious to everyone that ze is not hir ordinary self, nobody seems to notice; possibly because the group has dramatically changed as March turned April. More than half, maybe two thirds, are newcomers who have not as yet become completely accommodated with the routines. The male predominance prevails, but at last there is a black African constituency, so conspicuously absent during the first two months. Francis is the first new acquaintance. They already met, in Roskilde at a conference that ze co-organised, and even though they didn't talk much then it is like meeting an old friend now.

Francis gives an open lecture on campus about "incompleteness", and besides immediately striking a chord with hir own preoccupation with impurity it is a wonderful tribute to simplicity, which clearly puzzles the Director and the dignitaries of the Institute. Francis evokes one of the humblest and least prestigious Nigerian writers, Amos Tutuola, *The Palm-Wine Drunkard*. (The elaborate paper published a few months after his talk will be the first to draw hir attention to the notion of *conviviality*, as "a currency for frontier Africans". If incompleteness is the normal order of things, natural or otherwise, conviviality invites us to celebrate and preserve incompleteness and mitigate the delusions of grandeur that come with ambitions and claims of completeness.[2]) They share an entire bottle of whisky one improvised evening in Francis' apartment, when an unannounced load shedding impedes hir from returning to hir own, and that is surely the most invigorating intoxication ze has experienced in years.

Apart from Francis, there is Denis, the socio-musicologist[3] who has dedicated years of research to *sounding the Cape*; an amazing exploration of "music, identity and politics in South Africa" that traces that *other*, suppressed history of creolisation (*the key notes of the* Cape Calypso, *as ze wittily presumes, also for later digestion, next year when ze returns to the Cape, and another two years further ahead, when ze will sit in Pietermaritzburg of all places and try to conclude what ze has started here and now*). The bits and pieces are beginning to come together as ze is slowly coming back to hir senses, or *sense* in singular, the intellectual rigor of the critic, whose clarity often

---

[2] Nyamnjoh 2017: 262.

[3] He defines himself as a socio-anthropologist who has conducted research on the social significations of music.

surprises hir; sometimes ze can hardly believe that ze is the author of hir own texts. That goes for the literary writing as well, but the academic endeavours inspire an even fuller estrangement; as if ze the researcher were really another person; someone ze barely knows; someone ze actually may not fancy.

Denis is very decisive for the way the project will eventually evolve, by introducing hir to Glissant. Ze of course knew of the Martinican poet-philosopher before, but only as a secondary source; the principal inspirer of the *Creole Manifesto* which ze had often referred to in the early '90s, eagerly engaged in the emerging globalisation debate, which to hir has always primarily been a discussion about culture, not politics or economics. Yes, *Creolisation* was indeed one of the subthemes of the "circle" ze co-coordinated with Geir Thomas in the Nordic Summer University. [*Occidentalism* was another, although ze doesn't remember what that inversion of Orientalism actually was supposed to imply.]

Next time ze comes to Paris, two years later, ze will search through bookstores for Glissant's work. Ze is going to find more than ze can afford—the Gallimard editions are precious gems—and try to read him in original [*the discovery that ze was able to read French had been such a revelation some twelve years ago, when ze wrote an essay about Rimbaud's time in Ethiopia, and ze will find to hir relief that this parallel world remains open, although requiring considerably greater effort than English and Spanish. But in the end ze will lean on Betsy Wing's excellent English translation of* Poetics of Relation].

RELATION IS NON-HIERARCHICAL and non-reductive; that is, it does not try to impose a universal value system but respects the particular qualities of each community.[4] Yet

[p]articularity is only valuable as long as it is outward-looking and related to other cultures and values. *Essence*, on the contrary, is revealed as complicit with the coercive universalism of the West. So, too, is the correlative notion of *origin*.[5]

Slavery not only cuts the roots (historical origin) but forces the uprooted to transform into another, *new* culture. The space of Relation in the new world has supplanted the linear time span of *filiation* (the chain of ancestry). The transatlantic journey, so beautifully described in all its horror in the opening chapter of *Poetics of Relation*, is a radical rupture.

This boat is a womb, a womb abyss ... This boat is your womb, a matrix, and yet it expels you.[6]

Whereas for the colonists, the (free) migrants from the old to the new world, filiation was transferred to the new space. I come to think of Darcy Ribeiro's categorisation of the Latin American nations in *transplanted* (Argentina, Uruguay), *witness-bearing* (Mexico, Guatemala, Ecuador, Peru, Bolivia) and *new* (Brazil, Cuba, Colombia and the rest) ... Latin America used to be my touchstone, the supposed pilot project for the globalising world, *a world in creolisation*—the latter a radical yet rational assumption and plausible projection in the late 1980s and early 1990s, when Glissant and Swedish anthropologist Ulf Hannerz independently of each other envisioned precisely that.[7] The Caribbean was clearly the cradle of creolisation, but since I had never been to any of the islands, except Cuba, I didn't have a personal relation, as I indeed had to Spanish America.

[4] Glissant 1997 [1990]: 75.

[5] Ibid.: 15.

[6] Ibid.: 6.

[7] Hannerz 1987. The fact that Hannerz and Glissant are not entering into dialogue is not a matter of disrespect—*ninguneo*—but, most certainly, of differing academic traditions, differing languages—Francophone vs. Anglophone—and, perhaps, differing personalities.

What took place in the Caribbean, which could be summed up in the word *creolization*, approximates the idea of Relation for us as nearly as possible. It is not merely an encounter, a shock, a *métissage*, but a new and original dimension allowing each person to be there and elsewhere, rooted and open, lost in the mountains and free beneath the sea, in harmony and in errantry.[8]

In the following paragraph, Glissant makes the distinction between creolisation and *métissage*—which, I assume, also goes for its blunt English correspondent *hybridity*:

> If we posit *métissage* as, generally speaking, the meeting and synthesis of two differences, creolization seems to be a limitless *métissage*, its elements diffracted and its consequences unforeseeable.[9]

But let us not go ahead of the encounters, but dwell on the beauty of the evolving poetics: *the blue savannas of memory or imagination*.[10]

> Just as the first uprooting was not marked by any defiance, in the same way the prescience and actual experience of Relation have nothing to do with vanity. Peoples who have been to the abyss do not brag of being chosen [...] They live Relation and clear the way for it, to the extent that the oblivion of the abyss comes to them and that, consequently, their memory intensifies.[11]
> Our boats are open, and we sail them for everyone.[12]

EASTER

A SUDDEN DAMP COLD hints that autumn is on its way. Two cloudy grey days are followed by an astonishing Indian summer—*the Director suggests that April is the kindest month*—but nights remain

---

[8] Glissant 1997 [1990]: 34 (italics in original).
[9] Ibid.
[10] Ibid.: 7.
[11] Ibid.: 8.
[12] Ibid.: 9.

cool and the temperature in the fifty-meter outdoor swimming pool at the gym drops by a half degree every day. The few remaining times ze goes there ze is painfully reminded of J. The slow pleasurable strokes, breast and back, head underwater, like a sea mammal, the heavy body swift and agile in its natural element. Ze had enjoyed seeing him enjoy, this was hir gift to him. Now ze is almost alone in the pool; last time ze had to get up after two hundred meters, shivering with cold.

How had J. put up with hir all these years? Was it love, affection, or friendship basically? Yes, they had always been friends more than lovers. Like siblings—but not twins, although they were less than ten days apart, both born in November but under different stars. J.'s more than weeklong silence—over a dreadful Easter without resurrection—is tormenting hir, gnawing hir from within. *Had ze expected to be forgiven? Again, and again...* Ze admires his determination, but ze doesn't make sense of it; it's so unlike him, unlike the J. ze has known for more than half hir life. His final decision to dump hir must have matured over a long time. What was the point of no pardon, and when? J. wanted a family, children, but that had (*surprisingly*) never been a matter of serious conflict. Ze used to mock him for being *bourgeois*—a curious invective, that ze hirself had found extremely offensive at the time it was commonly used, in the radical '60s and '70s; now ze spoke it with a smile that annihilated every possible insult. But hadn't ze also wanted to *procreate* into a new generation? Ze was one of five siblings, which was anomalous in modern social-democratic Sweden. When the family had moved from Linköping to Malmö, they were provided with two standard apartments amalgamated into one seven-room residence (on the seventh floor) in the Southern frontline of the expanding city. Their home had always been literally open (the door was never locked) to friends and acquaintances of all the siblings, with a twelve-year age span from the oldest brother to the youngest sister. Ze was number four, a comfortable position of freedom and invisibility, raised by hir brother and two elder sisters, more than hir parents, vulnerable to all the luring dangers of the time (*ze dropped hir first acid when ze was fifteen*), yet protected by the *integrity*— ze can't find a better word—of family ... So, why didn't ze want a family of hir own? Was it a projection of hir mother's frustrated ambitions? *And why did* she *project that on her youngest son and not on her daughters?* Was it simply, as J. repeatedly claimed, in non-ironic response to the mocking accusations of being bourgeois, that ze was too obsessed with hir own self-fulfilment? *That* was a much more hurtful allegation, because it was true. *Or had been the truth at the time, if not now, but what did that matter?* J. was an only child, just like almost all hir friends. Maybe at heart ze was an only child too. But J., unlike hir, dreamed of a family because he never had one.

Two loners forming a couple is a contradiction in terms. And aging childless couples are pathetic and pitiful, regardless of whether they wanted children but couldn't have them or made the deliberate choice to abstain. The barrenness of the relation becomes evident, for everybody else if not the parties themselves; an embarrassing void, the shadow of Death, the discontinuity of living memory... *It all ends here, and for what reason?*

Cheryl will remind hir—when they meet in Pietermaritzburg three years later—that bisexual women are always regarded as being actually heterosexual, whereas bisexual men are supposedly truly gay—that is, the attractor would in both cases be male. But for hir the attractor is definitely female. Ze and J. had, at one sole occasion, joked about "the heterosexual coming out of the closet". But J. wasn't amused. It would have been much easier for him to accept and forgive if ze had been promiscuous with men (*the prototypical gay couple; one monogamous, the other sleeping around*). But then ze would most probably have been dead, like hir six-year-elder cousin, one of the victims of the plague, whose sad death possibly spared hir from that fate, while ze traced equally potentially fatal adventures in other directions. (*Hir cousin's rapid death in aids and hir eldest sister's gradual passing in multiple sclerosis were the two markers for a decade that in retrospect was all about survival.*) No, ze had never been promiscuous for real. Fantasising, a consumer of porn in all varieties, from the magazines that were sold in slot machines in hir puberty to VHS cassettes and even (*at two occasions, both in Stockholm*) strip shows in cellar clubs, before the internet turned that whole smutty industry obsolete. Not excessively, not more than most men (*or women, for that matter*) but it still embarrassed hir like a well-kept shameful secret. J. surely knew (*as hir mother knew about hir father's obsession; as a child of nine or ten ze had come across his hideaway in the closet, a clothes bag filled with magazines—Piff, Paff, Raff, Cocktail— black-and-white, charmingly innocent yet shockingly exciting, disclosing erect nipples and lush pubic bushes*) but J. was curiously prudish and would have been even more embarrassed to say anything. He could thrust himself into hir mouth and hir ass, but that momentaneous frenzy was like a separate dominion that he only occasionally took possession of, and which he apparently could just as well be without. Almost like compliance, to keep hir attached, but never really of importance to himself. Their relation was about something else, something higher, nobler, an intellectual affinity, primarily *homosocial*. Whereas hir inclination, in the professional life, had always been *hetero*social [*a curious word that ze has never used before—very thought-provoking: isn't the prefix hetero- in almost all contexts preferable to homo-;* heterodox, heterogeneous, heteroglossia ...]; ze preferred to work with women, straight or gay didn't matter. In some instances, there was undoubtedly a heteroerotic element, probably to a higher extent than ze was aware of, but not a *sexual* attraction, not on hir part; at least not one that ze would either acknowledge or express. Hir secret desire targeted *other* women, not yet in flesh and blood ... It had started as a virtual game—as it was now, again, although J. rejected that excuse—but inevitably, as in all play, the line of danger had to be transgressed, sooner than later... Ze would rationalise it by diminishing it to a moment of delusion and confusion after hir mother's death, simply an ordinary mid-life crisis, or whatever... But in fact, it had been a watershed moment. Ze could have opted for the straight line at last (*and would most probably have been greeted rather than condemned for it, except by J.'s many friends who would abandon hir as mercilessly as they had warmly adopted hir in the first place*). Ze had even imagined becoming an elderly parent (*certainly a delusion; hir prospective young wife would most likely have discarded hir among the other elder lovers that had preceded hir, or turned hir into a cuckold*). But ze had made the decision to stay with J., and has ever since felt indebted to him for taking hir back.

Now, ze would give up everything else to regain J.'s confidence. Now, that ze finally—physically—*comprehends* that he has irreversibly rejected hir, ze's in limbo. Devastated. *Free*. As miserable as Señor C.

UPROOTING, *ERRANTRY, EXILE* ... The principle of the poetics is *rhizo-matic thought*, which Glissant develops in dialogue with his close friends Gilles Deleuze and Félix Guattari. In Relation, each and every identity is extended through a relationship with the Other.[13]

In Western antiquity, a man in exile does not feel burdened with deprivation—of a nation that does not yet exist. Identification is with a culture (conceived of as civilisation). *It even seems that some experience of voyaging or exile was considered necessary for a being's complete fulfilment.*[14]

During the period of invading nomads, the passion for self-definition first appears in the guise of personal adventure. The root is not important. Movement is. The idea of errantry, still inhibited in the face of this mad reality, does not yet make an appearance. Centre and periphery are equivalent. Conquerors are the moving, transient root of their people.

The West, therefore, is where this movement becomes fixed and nations declare themselves in preparation for their repercussions in the world. The reason for our return to this episode in Western history is that it spread throughout the world. Most of the nations that gained freedom from colonisation have tended to form around an idea of power—the totalitarian drive of a single, unique root—rather than around a fundamental relationship with the Other. [*Which nations, if any, are the exceptions to that rule?*] Culture's self-conception was dualistic, pitting citizen against barbarian. *Nothing has ever more solidly opposed the thought of errantry than this period in human history when Western nations were established and then made their impact on the world.*[15]

The errantry of a troubadour or that of Rimbaud is not yet a thorough, thick (*opaque*) experience of the world, but it is already an arrant, passionate desire to go against a root. The call of Relation is heard, but it is not yet a fully present experience.[16] [*The meaning of opaque is obviously not the opposite of transparent. Is there a contradiction in terms here, or are we simply blinded by imagery? Opaque, not as blurry but as thick, as in Clifford Geertz' thick description?*]

---

[13] Ibid.: 11.
[14] Ibid.: 13 (italics added).
[15] Ibid.: 14 (italics added).
[16] Ibid.: 15.

However, the great founding books of communities were all books about exile and often about errantry, containing the germ of the exact opposite of what they so loudly proclaim. And, it is this "immense paradox" that inspires Glissant to formulate such founding work today, which asserts "the rhizome of a multiple relationship with the Other" and bases "every community's reasons for existence on a modern form of the sacred, which would be, all in all, a *Poetics of Relation*".[17] [*A modern form of the sacred certainly had other connotations in the late 1980s than thirty years later. And further on:*] The thought of errantry is a poetics, which always infers that at some moment it is told. The tale of errantry is the tale of Relation.[18]

> [I]n the poetics of Relation, one who is errant (who is no longer traveller, discoverer or conqueror) strives to know the totality of the world yet already knows he will never accomplish this—and knows that is precisely where the threatened beauty of the world resides.[19]

> The thinking of errantry conceives of totality but willingly renounces any claims to sum it up or to possess it.[20]

WAR BULLETINS

IT MAKES HIR UNEASY to sit comfortably in her spacious room at the Institute while South Africa is literally burning. Seven dead, so far. The TV reports from Durban are like war bulletins; ze watches the footage in awe, the familiar street signs, the city mall, the burning tyres, threatening thugs with *pangas* and *iwisas* and kicked-around strangers running for shelter. A memory pops up from hir last visit to Victoria Market; how ze happened to drive into a *cul de sac* and immediately attracted the attention of a gang of young thugs, like

---

[17] Ibid.: 16.
[18] Ibid.: 18.
[19] Ibid.: 20.
[20] Ibid.: 21.

the ones ze sees rampaging on the TV now, the sudden strike of fear, close to what ze imagines to be the resignation of fate, the last sigh before succumbing to helpless acceptance of quick (at best) and in any case meaningless death. For a white in South Africa there is always a racial dimension to whatever violence. But the post-apartheid variety of black-on-black violence is not, as yet, a threat to whites, nor to the rising black middle-class. *Could it, as in the early transition years, even be instigated by a "third force"?* The flourishing conspiracy theories do not seem too far-fetched, as leading representatives of the Zuma administration keep making dubious statements—the president's own son even calling to violence, in alliance with the Leopard skin pill box king—and since alarmingly little has been done to prevent new massacres after the previous outbursts of rage, in 2008 and 2012. Yet the government looks sincerely baffled, and concerned about the soiled image of the *Rainbow Nation.* Francis, from Cameroon, who has himself been exposed to the contempt for African immigrants and who was one of the first to write about it, compares South African and Nigerian arrogance; while the latter induces respect, he says, the former is *empty.*

Ze has been here for more than two months now. Why doesn't ze get more out of this extraordinary opportunity? The frustration reminds hir of the first revisit to Bangalore, how ze struggled seemingly to no avail with what only a year later, after a second journey, was to become the *Bengaluru Boogie.* Why didn't ze decide on a well-defined, limited project, like writing the paper for the IAMCR conference in Montreal, to which hir abstract has already been accepted? *Why* is indeed the pertinent question, but in this case the answer is simple: *Because ze is not, and will never be, an academic researcher.* But is ze a (literary) *writer* anymore? Will ze ever write another novel? Will ze publish another book in Swedish?

The frustration is also about perceiving to be in the middle of a revolution and not being able to report, let alone make sense of it. The xenophobic wildfire is on television distance, but the *Rhodes Must Fall* campaign is right next-door, the student protests spreading from campus to campus—including Stellenbosch—and gaining momentum as a national protest movement. The otherworldly isolation at the Institute is emphasised to the absurd, the *obscene,* the caricature it is, pushed as it were to its limits.

I READ SLOWLY, chapter by chapter. It's dense, *thick*, and I need to go back and read some passages many times. Relation as a concept is by definition difficult to grasp (comprehend—*com-prendre*). The association to Einstein's Relativity is intriguing: the "powerful and mysterious reason" (as opposed to Descartes' "malicious spirit"), that "provides us with a riddle to decipher".[21]

I am not sure when the idea emerged to let *Poetics of Relation* be the counterpart to *Purity and Danger*. Maybe I touched upon it already during my stay in Stellenbosch, but I couldn't foresee how it might work. Now I'm doing it, whether it works or not, and the challenge is undoubtedly bigger. Is it possible to explain his thought, let alone understand it, without resorting to his conceptual universe—the *écho-monde*, the *chaos-monde*, etc., the terms that Betsy Wing has left untranslated, for reasons explained in her lucid introduction. The text on the back cover makes an admirable attempt at summary, yet clearly addressing a US audience and hence mistakenly stressing the element of identity politics, linking it to discussions of US multiculturalism.

Glissant's biographer, Aliocha Wald Lasowski describes it as an essay of reflection on the modernity in coming. After the cultural dominance of the West, modernity is in Glissant's definition the dynamic of cultures in relation:

> Contre la fixité du *bateau négrier*, dont la raison d'être est une fonction de mort, Glissant décalque cette image par un tableau d'un *bateau ivre* en dérive. Ce zigzag est emblématique des expériences de mise en relation.[22]
> [*This little quote is perfect proof of the difficulty of translation. The elegantly juxtaposed images of the slave ship of death and a "drunken boat" adrift seem blunt, even obscene, in English—and incomprehensible for someone who is not familiar with Rimbaud's poem.*]

In his introduction to the study of Cape Town's musics, Denis-Constant Martin probably makes the most comprehensive condensation of, not only *Poetics of Relation* (*Poétique III*), but also the sequel *Traité du Tout-Monde* (*Poétique IV*, 1997) and *La Cohée du Lamantin* (*Poétique V*, 2005), which have as yet not been translated to English.

Relation is the foundation of the Whole-World (*Tout-Monde*), that totality in process affected and remodelled by creolisation, in which contractions of

---

[21] Ibid.: 134.
[22] Wald Lasowski 2015: 163 (italics added).

space and accelerations of time produce unexpected effects (Glissant 2005: 138). A poetics of Relation answers the obligation to think in terms of worldness (*mondialité*) and not of globalisation (*mondialisation*): a universe that for the first time in history can be envisioned as inextricably multiple and one. The multiplicity of the world thought as *mondialité* accommodates individuals and specificities; it eliminates all contradictions between multiplicity and singularity; but demands a "massive insurrection of the imaginary that will at last lead humans to want themselves and to create themselves (without any moral command) as they really are: a never-ending change, in a perenniality that never congeals. (Glissant 2005: 25)[23]

Yet, the summaries only crudely capture Glissant's thinking, which is intrinsically interwoven with his style of writing. The very structure of the poetics defies the conventional academic treatise: concepts are applied before being presented; they are probed on the outset and only eventually, gradually, defined, in a cyclical, spiral—non-projectile—construction. *Poetics of Relation* is in fact a compilation of public lectures (which also explains the element of "transcribed orality") spanning over exactly a decade, the 1980s, pronouncing the transformation of the decade to come.

ANGLO ARROGANCE AND THE ASSASSIN

MICHAEL RECALLS how the English speakers bullied the Boers in school. When B. J. Vorster gave his first talk to the nation on radio, on 6 September 1966, after the assassination of Verwoerd in Cape Town (*by a "mixed-race, uniformed parliamentary messenger", as Wikipedia describes the culprit*), some of Michael's schoolmates (*including himself?*) even burst out in laughter at the new Nationalist leader's stumbling English.

I made the above note in Stellenbosch, as an illustration of "Anglo arrogance", and included it in the draft of the first part of the diptych, but later took it out and forgot about it. Until my attention recently was drawn to the act itself and the information disclosed within parenthesis. Dmitri Tsafendas, born in Mozambique as the illegitimate son of a Greek emigré and his Mozambican maid, had spent his whole life as a

---

[23] Martin 2013: 63.

racial and familial outcast when he returned to South Africa in 1965. In the preceding twenty-five years, he was deported from or refused entry into the USA, Great Britain, Canada, Israel, Rhodesia, Portugal and Spain. South Africa denied him entry eight times; Greece and Portugal refused him passports. Eight countries detained him in mental institutions or prisons. He became a *cosmopolitan untouchable*, more and less fluent in Greek, English, Portuguese, Spanish, Arabic, German, Italian, Hebrew, Turkish, Shangaan and Afrikaans. On his final return to South Africa, a year before the assassination, he was an outspoken enemy of the apartheid system and an advocate of what he, in conversations with his acquaintances, called a *rainbow nation*. In July 1966, he managed to obtain a temporary position as parliamentary messenger at the House of Assembly in Cape Town. The original plan was to kidnap the prime minister, but since he couldn't find the necessary support among his former comrades in the South African Communist Party (*which he had joined in 1939, after illegally entering the country*) he decided to act alone. The motives for his deed were clearly political, but in the trial, the defence pleaded insanity, to escape the gallows, and the official record filed it as the act of an "apolitical schizophrenic". He was sentenced to lifelong imprisonment (*with severe torture*), first on Robben Island, then at Pretoria Central Prison (*in a special cell next to the execution chamber*), finally at Sterkfontein psychiatric hospital in Krugersdorp, where he died in 1999 at the age of 81.

Only this year (2018), almost two decades after his death, did Tsafendas get a form of redress, in the 2000-page *Report to the Minister of Justice, advocate Tshilio Michael Masutha, in the Matter of Dr Verwoerd's Assassination*, which unambiguously confirms that the killing of Verwoerd was a revolutionary political act, and that this fact was systematically covered up by the authorities.

I learn about this when I happen to come across an article about the forthcoming book release of *The Man Who Killed Apartheid: The Life of Dimitri Tsafendas*.[24] And the most fascinating note is as often parenthetical: shortly before the assassination, Tsafendas had applied for reclassification from "White" to "Coloured". His application had been turned down.

---

[24] Dousemetzis & Loughran 2019. It claims to be the first biography, but Dutch writer Henk van Woerden, who had interviewed Tsafendas in Sterkfontein shortly before he died, wrote the memoir *Een mond vol glas* (1998), which was translated to English two years later as *A Mouthful of glass* (2000). The American edition used the title *The Assassin: A Story of Race and Rage in the Land of Apartheid* (2001).

WE HAVE REPEATEDLY mentioned that the first thing exported by the conqueror was his language. Moreover, the great Western languages were supposedly vehicular languages, which often took the place of an actual metropolis. *Relation, in contrast, is spoken multilingually.* Relation rightfully opposes the totalitarianism of any monolingual intent.[25]

Rather than discovering or telling about the world, a poetics is a matter of producing an equivalent, which would be the Book, in which everything would be said, without anything's being reported. *The World as book, the Book as world…*

> The poetics of language-in-itself strives toward a knowledge that by definition would only be exercised within the limits of a given language. It would renounce the nostalgia for other languages—for the infinite possible languages—now germinating in every literature.[26]

In 2003, the American Indians of Québec proposed a monument to languages with a quote from Glissant translated to all Amerindian languages: *On ne sauvera pas un langue en laissant périr les autres* [One does not save a language by letting the others perish][27] … I come to think of my interview with Ngũgĩ wa Thiong'o, when we were both participants in the 2007 *Time of The Writer* festival. He enthusiastically envisioned an imminent renaissance for African languages like the one for European languages in the Middle Ages. To me that seemed completely naïve and discordant with his otherwise stern political realism. But Glissant is an as ardent defender of multilingualism. His comment on the tower of Babel is that it is possible to build the tower—*in every language.*[28]

> [T]he poetics of Relation remains forever conjectural and presupposes no ideological stability. It is against the comfortable assurances linked to the supposed excellence of a language. A poetics that is latent, open, multilingual in intention, directly in contact with everything possible. *Theoretician thought, focused on the basic and fundamental, and allying these with what is true, shies away from these uncertain paths.*[29]

---

[25] Ibid.: 19 (italics added).
[26] Ibid.: 25.
[27] Wald Lasowski 2015: 408.
[28] Glissant 1997 [1990]: 109.
[29] Ibid: 32 (italics added).

The cultures of the world have always maintained relations among themselves that were close or active to varying degrees, but it is only in modern times that some of the right conditions came together to speed up the nature of these connections. Contacts among cultures—one of the givens of modernity—will no longer come across the huge spans of time that have historically allowed meetings and interchanges to be active but almost imperceptibly so. *Whatever happens elsewhere has immediate repercussions here.*[30]

Finally, the consciousness of Relation became widespread, including both the collective and the individual. We "know" that the Other is within us and affects how we evolve as well as the bulk of our conceptions and the development of our sensibility.

Rimbaud's "I is an other" is literal in terms of history. In spite of ourselves, a sort of "consciousness of consciousness" opens up and turns each of us into a disconcerted actor in the poetics of Relation.[31]

Just as Relation is not a pure abstraction to replace the old concept of the universal, it also neither implies nor authorises any ecumenical detachment. The landscape of your word is the world's landscape. But its frontier is open.

In reality, Relation is not an absolute toward which every work would strive but a totality that through its poetic and practical and unceasing force attempts to be perfected, to be spoken, simply, that is, to be complete.[32]

Katjiepiering

Three years later ze will read through the notes from hir red book (a gift from Deepak in Bangalore) where ze tried to capture the core of all the seminars and activities; notes that ze has meticulously transcribed but only partly, as yet, had time to transpose into consistent narrative or reflection. What will strike hir is the amount and

[30] Ibid.: 26 (italics added).
[31] Ibid.: 27.
[32] Ibid.: 35.

density of material, especially from the last month of hir stay; how
ze must have been absorbent like a sponge in hir bottomless desolation. The question will be what to do with these fractured sketches
of ideas and semi-digested thoughts. Like the barely legible minutes
from a conference with Rob Nixon on "slow violence" (e.g. *exclusion* or *poverty*), ending with the caution not to expand that concept
too much: *we need to detect what violence is* not ... Or the more careful, concentrated annotations from fellow Hans Lindahl's seminar
"*Law and World. Faultlines of Globalisation*". Ze is bad at remembering faces, and ze would not be able to recall his feature even after
a week, but the fantasy image of Hans' grandfather in Colombia,
struggling behind the plough in his Sunday costume, will remain
engraved in hir memory: Enticed to immigrate in the early 1900s,
as part of the then Colombian government policy to "improve the
race", he had suffered immense hardships, like the Misiones Swedes.
His grandson Hans, a third generation Colombian Swede, teaches
Law in Tilburg and speaks no Swedish.

Ze will skim through the notes:

Lawyers are magnificent philosophers—the practice of Law is much
more radical than the theory of Law [...]

The Globe is a thing—whereas the World is not fundamentally a
thing. Phenomenologically speaking, the W is a totality of meaning
relationships [...]

Borders—limits—[*a crucial distinction; one to dwell on*]

The strange need not be foreign, nor the foreign strange ...
Stranger in a foreign land—Foreigner in a strange land—Stranger
among strangers—Stranger among foreigners [*subtle distinctions or
just hair-splitting?*]

[...] Carl Schmitt: Global Law as *nomos* [*c.f. Walter Mignolo!!*]. But
Schmitt would not accept the distinction between border and limit

Reconstitute the public beyond territoriality. A global common
good—a common global space, and vice versa

Representation of a global We' by National Contact Points [*what is
that?*] and CSOs

Global Human Rights as a nomos ("which Schmitt would hate to
hear")

Why is space so crucially important to Law? What is it about the
spatiality of Law that Globalisation brings to the fore?

G is the intertwinement of Heimwelde and Freudwelde [*did ze get that right?* Hir German is pure mimicry... *Freud welde?* Heidegger vs. Freud ...] the intertwinement of the global and the local—bringing close what is far away geographically, and vice versa. [On hir direct question, Hans dismisses the term *glocalisation*, because it implies a hierarchical relation at a lateral level] [...]

Clearly, ze can't bring the whole world into hir project. But the idea of just letting it go, dissolve into oblivion, is saddening ... Yet, if it weren't for these notes, it would already be gone, without a trace in hir selective memory. Except the image of the plough and the indecipherable word *Katjiepiering*, which will still puzzle hir after three years.

In parallel I leaf through Carrol Clarkson's *J. M. Coetzee: Countervoices*, which I bought on one of my recent stopovers in Johannesburg, in an antiquarian bookshop in Melville. The connection Coetzee-Glissant is not as far-fetched as I first thought. Linguistics is a common denominator that I wasn't aware of, and that apparently makes my identification with C. even stranger. It is not a matter of *identification*, though, that makes me consider him to be the foremost living writer. But then, what is it? I'm at loss trying to put words to it. It is a form of reverence, no doubt, similar to what I feel for Borges. But in the case of Borges there is little if any personal affinity. I would feel much more akin to the pathetic Sábato (and like Sábato, although differently, I would have hated to be the subject of Borges' scorn). But, then, I'm not a young aspiring writer anymore, just another admirer, immensely happy that my trajectory for a week (five days to be exact) happened to touch the trajectory of one of the remaining masters. There is a fine line between humility and humiliation that I do not hesitate to thread.

Curiously, the only correspondent relation would be to Swedish writer Lars Norén, with whom I have even less in common, and whom I irrationally without question regard as the greatest Swedish writer ever, all categories. I must have been fifteen when I read his novel *Biskötarna* [The Bee Masters] and managed to buy one of the few remaining copies of *Stupor—Nobody knows you when you're down and out* at the yearly book sale in February, which in my adolescence was one of the major cultural events in Sweden. In its pink cover and awkward format, worn by reading and moving between bookshelves, *Stupor* is most certainly the gemstone in my constantly culled library.

Do I identify with Glissant? It is a strange verb and I do not exactly know what it means—*identity* being a concept that I repel, not "instinctively" but by learning. Do I feel affinity towards him? Yes, but not the same way that I immediately—yet strangely—do with Coetzee (or Norén). Does it have to do with culture? Possibly, to some extent, certainly in the banal sense of common markers; long since forgotten brandmarks, TV personae, etc. Language? English as compared to French … Yes, but C., like G., is from the margins of Empire, an Anglified Boer. The suppressed Afrikaans is like a secret Swedish. More important than language is the mastery of style and metaphors. But it is a solitary planet of immense beauty.

For me, it was an eye-opening experience to participate in the *Time of the Writer* festival in Durban. I was the only participant who had not been published in English (or French), and at that time, I could not imagine writing literary prose in any other language than Swedish. So, the text I read, from my then latest novel, was translated (by a former student). But the eye-opening moment was when I realised that the other participants—from all over Africa; Nigeria, Uganda, Zimbabwe— were also all communicating in their second or even third language.

It is of course a matter of generational experience as well. Glissant, born 1928, is almost my parents' generation (and Borges a young grandparent), whereas Coetzee could have been my eldest brother, like Norén.

The significant detail that I remember from my one meeting with Norén, in his apartment at Hantverkargatan 44 (I remember the exact address as I remember the telephone numbers of my childhood friends), is so odd that I sometimes doubt whether it is memory or fantasy. I was doing an interview for an assignment at the School of Journalism. Norén was then still primarily a poet. His first play had been set up the year before on Dramaten, and quite unanimously pulled to pieces by the critique, and he assured in our interview that he would never write drama again. While we were talking, the phone rang and as he went to another room I casually eyed through the bookshelf and found, inserted among the books of Celan and Hölderlin, a copy of Prince, *the hardcore porn magazine (not to be confused with* Private).

The semblance between Srs. G. and C. becomes evident when the poetics eventually arrives at its core, the process of writing. The following passage corresponds compellingly to Coetzee's reasoning, in *Doubling the Point*, about the two forms of truth, one to fact, the other to something beyond that, something that comes in—or from—the very process of writing.[33]

The literary text plays the contradictory role of a producer of opacity.

Because the writer, entering the dense mass of his writings, renounces an absolute, his poetic intention, full of self-evidence and sublimity. Writing's relation to that absolute is relative; that is, it actually renders

---

[33]Coetzee 1992: 17–18. The adjoining oft-quoted passage, which I have often referred to myself, appears also in Clarkson 2013 [2009]: 44.

It is naïve to think that writing is a simple two-stage process: first you decide what you want to say, then you say it. On the contrary, as all of us know, you write because you do not know what you want to say. Writing reveals to you what you wanted to say in the first place. [...] That is the sense in which one can say that writing writes us.

it opaque by realizing it in language. The text passes from a dreamed-of transparency to the opacity produced in words.

Because the written text opposes anything that might lead a reader to formulate the author's intention differently. At the same time, he can only guess at the shape of this intention. The reader goes, or rather tries to go back, from the produced opacity to the transparency that he read into it.

Literary textual practice thus represents an opposition between two opacities: the irreducible opacity of the text, even when it is a matter of the most harmless sonnet, and the always evolving opacity of the author or a reader.[34]

Señor C.

SEÑOR C.'s PORTRAIT is already up on the board at the coffee machine. And Dorothy, his partner—not a fellow, but a "guest researcher"— has only just arrived (ze spotted her at the end of the corridor and said hello at a distance without realising that it was her). Amazingly, ze didn't even realise until now that they are a couple. Ze had written to Dorothy in her own right—as the author of the foreword to Zoë Wicomb's *David's Story*—explaining how ze looked forward to meeting her at the Institute. The fact that she was now living in Adelaide hadn't rung a bell. Not even her first name, although ze had recently read the correspondence between C. and A., in which they constantly refer to their respective life companions, Dorothy and Siri…

Ze feels ill prepared for this incidental encounter—one of these strikes of luck that make people prone to superstition. But ze has what ze believes to be a trump card, a common acquaintance, the lovely Susanne, who has been a student of both of them. Susanne

---

[34] Glissant 1997 [1990]: 115. The recurring term "opacity" is possibly the most complex of Glissant's concepts. Denis-Constant Martin suggests one of the definitions given by the French dictionary *Trésor de la Langue Française informatisé*:

2. [En parlant d'un corps, d'une substance] Propriété, naturelle ou acquise, d'absorber certaines vibrations électromagnétiques et de ne pas se laisser traverser par certains rayons.

In Martin's words: this definition seems to support Glissant's endeavour to underline the inextricable combination of the idiosyncrasy of human beings, places and cultures with their necessary inclusion in networks of Relation.

unashamedly claimed to have been C.'s favourite student at UCT, at the time of *Disgrace* (in fact, she told hir that there was *another* teacher in those years who perfectly fit the character David Lurie). When the moment comes, the day of his seminar, and ze introduces Susanne to him as he comes down the stair, ze is not sure whether he actually recognises her, but for a moment some spark lights his eyes and softens the stern expression. No, not stern; his face is expressionless. The word *autist* sticks to hir thoughts, like a stigma (in the mind of the beholder). But it is not as if he weren't there, absent, wandering aloof; no, on the contrary, as if he is all too conscious, and uncomfortable, about his own presence.

Not the *womaniser* by look, and yet it is easy to understand that women are attracted to him. (*As if there were a generic* woman.) A certain kind of women, perhaps, that ze would also be drawn to. Like Susanne, their common denominator, whom he had encouraged to become a writer (and whom he will talk to, affectionately, at the reception after the seminar; exclusively, to the deception of the dignitaries who had hoped to mingle in his glory). Like Dorothy, who covers up for his anti-sociality with her spirited openness and warmth. *They* talk, and immediately communicate, but ze never gets to talk to him. Ze didn't expect to, ze wouldn't dream of trying to impose hirself, as some of the other fellows who circle around him at lunch, competing for a seat at the Nobel laureate's table; ze muses with compassionate sympathy at the daily spectacle; his expressionless face as he carries the sorry cellophane-covered lunch plate from the counter: bland vegetables; celery, beetroots—the otherwise creative chef apparently void of imagination when it comes to vegetarian dishes. (*Heribert and Kogila were his neighbours in Cape Town. They recalled him coming with a brown bag from the vegetable store and a giant leek towering like a plume over his head. Kogila laughed warmly at the memory and that image of ridicule is now transferred and forever engraved in hir mind*—giant leek, giant leech ... leach, leash ... *the English words don't really have a meaning to hir as ze plays with them...*) Yes, he is a vegetarian, although not a vegan, whereas Dorothy is a carnivore among the others.

The lunches must be almost as painful as the seminar. (*When asked by Mats, one of the Swedish fellows, what he had thought about the discussion, he responds frankly that it felt awful with all these questions being thrown at him from all directions.*)

What he presents in the crammed seminar room is a condensation of the dialogue between himself (JMC) and psychoanalyst Arabella Kurtz (AK), which at the time has only been published in Dutch. (*It's one of his curious whims, that ze wasn't aware of; to publish the Dutch translation before the English original ... Why Dutch? A subtle vengeance for his Afrikaner childhood?*)

The conversation between the therapist and the author resembles the (Platonic) dialogue between the philosopher and the poet. Truth is the matter.

"If the therapist's interest is to 'make people better'", asks JMC, "does that not entail telling lies, or letting people stick to lies?" Or, formulated as a question to himself (the writer): "How do I tell the story of my life? What is my relation to my life story? What should— or must—I leave out?"

"Free expression is restrained even in the privacy of your own mind", explains AK [*he reads her quotes in a voice with a slightly higher pitch*]. "Psychoanalysis is aimed at setting free the narrative or autobiographical narration".

What is it that impels you to have the patient to tell the truth? Are all auto narratives not fiction? When making up our own autobiographies, are we not free like in our dreams? Why not affirm each other's fantasies, so that there is no reality to crash into?

A narrative like you describe it will be too brittle and tend to fail.

What is the purpose of psychoanalytic therapy? The good-enough? Is truth the only avenue to freedom? Poets have no obligation or allegiance to the truth. Beauty is its own truth. If interminable analysis is not practicable—why not settle with a version of the truth that works? My experience is that truth is often what works. [...]

Hir notes from the seminar, feverishly scribbled down and yet incomplete and partly illegible, will come to life when ze reads *The Good Story* two years later. Not least the passage from the sixth chapter, which stands out as a confession, ambivalent yet ruthless:

I am sure that my dogged concentration, here and in earlier exchanges between us, on the ethical dimension of truth versus fiction comes out of my experience of being a white South African who late in life became a white Australian and, in between, lived for years as a white in the United States, where whiteness as a social reality is more masked than in South Africa or Australia but is still there. That is to say, I have lived as a member of a conquering group which for a long while thought of itself in explicitly racial terms and believed that what it was achieving in settling ("civilising") a foreign land was something to be proud of, but which then, during my lifetime, for reasons of a world-historical nature, had to sharply revise its way of thinking about itself and its achievements, and therefore to revise the story it told itself about itself, that is, its history.

Interestingly, he chooses Australia, his new "home", not South Africa, as the exemplary case in this regard.

I am speaking at a level of generality which makes for the crudest of arguments. Nevertheless, let me start my crude point: that the settler societies in question, the settler societies of today, ought to be riven with self-doubt but are not. They—or their more articulate members—say the following: (a) Our forebears did bad things but they are not to be blamed because they were in the grip of false beliefs and a false understanding of their role in history; (b) we have more enlightened beliefs and a more enlightened understanding of our historical role; and (c) if, as history unfolds, we ourselves are revealed to have mistaken ourselves as deeply as our ancestors mistook themselves, there is nothing we can do about that, that is the nature of history, which is just one story overtaking and supplanting another; therefore, the best we can do is to get on with our lives without more fretting.

I don't want to push the therapeutic analogy recklessly, so let me simply ask the question: *When a society (but for a few dissident members) decides that it does not feel troubled, how can healing even begin?*[35]

Yet Australia also clearly serves as an allegory for the old country and "the tribe or people into which I was born, the Afrikaners".[36] In the eighth chapter he analyses his childhood's "intense tussle" with Afrikanerdom and its tribalist group think, yet disclosing a heartfelt, almost patriotic, respect for the individualist "ordinary Afrikaner", which curiously reminds hir of Borges' ambiguous reverence for the barbarian *gaucho* of the Argentinean Pampa.

[35] Coetzee & Kurtz 2015: 77–80 (italics added).
[36] Ibid.: 109.

Although there was pressure from above, from the more ideological element in the leadership, for organised displays of patriotism or groupthink—for mass rallies or military displays, for instance, such as one associates with Nazi Germany—I never detected much enthusiasm for these among ordinary Afrikaners One should not forget that Afrikaners had their finest hour during the Anglo-Boer War, when they managed to put together an irregular yet highly effective fighting force characterised far more by individualism than by group discipline: men (I hesitate to call them soldiers) felt it was their right to quit the battle lines, saddle their horses, and ride home to their families for the weekend. As a way of life, militarism invites us to discard the individual faculty of judgment, to submit to overriding group passions. Calvinism, the official religion of the Afrikaner state, was and is a religion of reason, suspicious of irrational forces. That is the main reason why the Calvinist churches in South Africa are steadily bleeding to death, as they lose members to the charismatics.

His childhood quarrel with Afrikanerdom was hence not with a system that sought to engulf everyone in its irrationalism, but with *Afrikaner triumphalism*:

[T]he values of the Afrikaner petite bourgeoisie, including its virulent prejudices, dominated public discourse, and if you raised the mildest voice of dissent you would be smitten aside.[37]

Whereas reading the book fills in the blanks of hir hastily scribbled notes, the images and sensory memories of that implausible highlight moment will in the same lapse of time have faded, almost as if it had never happened. Yet ze recalls his discomfort in the seminar room, as ze hirself is always uncomfortable in that same position, in the classroom, at conferences. And one memory persists, for ever engraved: the spark of amusement when ze asked him to what extent the dialogue with Arabella Kurtz should be read as a fiction, with "JMC" as a "semi-distorted version of himself", and the wry smile when he responded by repeating "a semi-distorted version of myself".

---

[37] Ibid.: 109–110.

At hir own seminar a few days later ze is curiously calm, in spite (or because) of C.'s presence at the far end of the table (*listening attentively and taking notes, according to Susanne*). He even makes a comment in the discussion, about Mary Douglas and South Africa, but in the mumbling voice that ze is not able to decipher however hard ze pricks up hir ears—and it will nag hir forever that ze didn't ask him about it at the wine reception afterwards.

BUT, MUSIC, NOT LITERATURE, is the primary vehicle of creolisation. Permissive, *promiscuous* ... At the Cape, which up until 1795 remained an unequalled racial melting pot,[38] the "lechery between Europeans and slaves" went so far as to "dance together stark naked".[39] Literature can only dream of such communion. Denis-Constant Martin's historical inventory of the musics of Cape Town exemplarily applies the poetics of Relation, connecting the Caribbean and the Cape, the Black Atlantic and the less-known itineraries of the Indian Ocean, which have been recently explored by Isabel Hofmeyr and other South African scholars. As a centre for the Southern slave trade route, the Cape became literally a counterpart to the Black Atlantic. The trade was primarily in female household workers, not manpower for the sugar plantations. The binary notions of "slaves" (as African) and "free persons" (as European) were less stable along the Southern route; Hofmeyr even suggests that the circulation of ideas across the Indian Ocean produced a conception of colonialism as more about "a contestation of universalisms" than about local encounters with global forces.[40]

To Martin, the processes through which original musics were created in Cape Town and the Cape region serve to demonstrate "the intensity and protractedness of creolisation dynamics that threaded South African society".[41] If creolisation is an unlimited *métissage*, he moreover suggests, one should consider whether redefining South Africa as a creolising country may clear the ground for overcoming internal conflicts inherited from the past.

> Creolisation is an aspect of Relation, which allows us to conceptualise communication between cultural idiosyncrasies (*opacities*) mutually freed of the toughness of their differences. This implies that particularities are a necessary ingredient of Relation, but also that they have to be permanently redefined and reconstructed; particularities cannot remain disconnecting properties, to be isolated and defended, but should be lived and understood as characteristics or specificities to offer, to share, and to mix.[42]

---

[38] Heese 2006, in Martin 2013: 64–65.
[39] Hoge 1972, in Martin 2013: 73.
[40] Hofmeyer 2007, in Erasmus 2017: 5.
[41] Martin 2013: 67.
[42] Ibid.

The Master could not have expressed it better himself... While reading I recall my faint impression of Denis as a believer, even a convert. The way he referred to Glissant, as a visionary, a prophet, may have resembled, without further comparisons, the reverence paid by followers to, say, Boaventura De Sousa Santos and his "epistemologies of the South". Now I clearly see how doubly mistaken that association was. There is little if anything guru-like about Glissant; what I find disturbing is rather the image of the UN bureaucrat, the editor of the *UNESCO Courier*... One of my Latin American friends who he had met him in that capacity in Paris sometime in the mid-1980s described him as *boring*. Such devastating judgement would certainly have deterred me from discovering his work, when I learned about him through the *Creole manifesto*. But in fact, that was not the first time I came across his name. Only recently, I incidentally found it on the jacket of a Swedish anthology of "South American poetry" from 1962 (including some of the first, poor, translations of Borges); I must have bought (or stolen) it when I was sixteen or seventeen, and it has remained in my library ever since. The text on the jacket refers to a previous book in the same series, an anthology of *negerlyrik*, with Glissant as one of the included "Negro poets" ... Which reminds me of a passage I particularly noticed in Denis' book; the little digression to the USA after the Civil War, when creolised music was racialised, categorised in black and white, excluding "Negro music" from the common tongue of American interracial resonance, while systematically erasing the creole element of white music (country and western especially).[43]

To Glissant, jazz is not only the modern creolised music form *par préférence*. Jazz *is* creolisation. But a more surprising preference—which he shares with Deleuze—is that for Béla Bartok, "*un musicien du Tout-Monde*" who synthesises all the musical sources in his style. Discarding the distinction between "learned" and popular music, emancipated from the major–minor system, in favour of asymmetric and polyrhythmic combinations, inspired by Hungarian folk music and gypsy music, but also Arab popular music, Bartok transgresses the European antagonism between centre and periphery.[44] In 1938, after the *Anschluss*, he leaves for America. There, Bartok encounters jazz and composes *Contrastes* for clarinet, violin and piano, which are interpreted by Benny Goodman.

---

[43] Radano 2003, in Martin 2013: 88.
[44] Wald Lasowski 2015: 377–380.

Vainglory

WHY DOES ZE THINK OF SR. C. as *miserable*? Is it the dryness of the ageing body, seventy-five, approaching his eighties, the old male, truncated, sexless, domesticated like an old woman, Elisabeth Costello (*a character ze finds much harder to conform with than David Lurie*) ...? When, in fact, in his writing, in the [*true*] fictional self of his fiction, he is witty and crystal sharp, with a self-distance and self-insight that would make any living writer envious. He is a philosopher *and* poet ... (like Glissant, although they are probably as different as could be. That unexpected comparison will come as a flash of genius, good or bad, when ze finally arrives at the supposed peripeteia of hir story.) But the banal answer is of course that ze reads hir own misery—and disgrace—into his austerity. (*It will fascinate hir to read* Boyhood *and* Youth *after this encounter—especially* Youth—*and identify so strongly although they are completely different.*)

Somehow, this *is* the core of the venture yet to be named *Cape Calypso*: Hir nothingness, no-oneness, hir thriving in the margin. *Or is ze?* The vainglory—whatever that is. *Ze who had such grand delusions of hir own glory.* And hir complete alienation from the Swedish Parnassus. Hir last novel (the sixth) had been rejected by one publisher after the other. Finally, after almost two years of humiliation, ze decided to publish it hirself, and did not receive one single review. Not even the remaining subscribers to *Sydsvenska Dagbladet* will recall hir name. Whereas the recognition ze has indeed achieved in academia is largely for something ze doesn't really care about. The co-director of *Glocal NOMAD*—someone ze hardly knows. *Everything comes to an end. Ze is struggling now with hir sanity, literally. Without J. ze'll be irreversibly lost. Only writing can save hir. This unfathomable project will be the most demanding one. Hir Sisyphus endeavour...*

FILIATION IS, in Glissant's vocabulary, the hidden cause of both Myth and Epic in the Western world, "its work setting out upon the fixed linearity of time, always toward a projection, a project".[45]

> Westerns mythologies, in contrast [to Buddhist ones], conceive of the individual only insofar as he is a participant in the community. It took the appearance of Christ for the individual as such to sublimate in his dignity the evolution of the community (...)
>   [Christ] consecrates filiation: being a descendant of David and at the same time the son of God who is God. (...)
>   Christian individuation did not result in a return flow of history, as cyclical renewal: on the contrary, by universalizing linear time—*before and after Christ*—it brought a chronology of the human race into common use, initiating a History of Humanity.[46]

Darwinism, although initially opposing the Christian generalisation, is only an objectivised vision of the old filiation applied to the natural universality of all known species. The crucial distinction is instead between (philosophies of) the One and the All. Glissant points to the paradox that in Buddhist thought, for which the aim is to dissolve the individual within the All, there is only individuation, whereas in Western systems of thought, there is only *generalisation*.[47]

> As Mediterranean myths tell us, thinking about One is not thinking about All. These myths express communities, each one innocently transparent for self and threateningly opaque for the other (...) They suggest that the self's opacity for the other is insurmountable, and consequently, no matter how opaque the other is for oneself (no myth ever provides for the legitimacy of the other), it will always be a question of reducing this other to the transparency experienced by oneself. *Either the other is assimilated, or else it is annihilated. That is the whole principle of generalization and its entire process.*[48]

Myth and Epic both contain a hidden violence that absolutely challenges the existence of the other as an element of relation. *Legitimacy* is the consequence (the hidden cause) of both Epic and Tragedy. In the *Iliad,*

---

[45] Glissant 1997 [1990]: 47.

[46] Ibid.: 48.

[47] Ibid.: 49.

[48] Ibid. (italics added).

it is legitimacy that is disrupted by the abduction of Helen (with its threat of *métissage*—mixing the blood of East and West) and legitimacy provides the tragic driving force for the *Odyssey* (Ulysses' and Penelope's faithfulness to each other).

> If legitimacy is ruptured, the chain of filiation is no longer meaningful, and the community wanders the world, no longer able to lay claim to any primordial necessity. Tragic action absorbs this unbalance.
>
> Tragic action is progressive and carried out within opacity, because the violence linked to filiation (the absolute exclusion of the other) cannot be faced head on nor all at once.[49]

Opacity, this other recurrent and ambiguous keyword, is here defined as "that which protects the Diverse".[50] Does diversity necessarily have to do with ethnicity? Probably with colour. Possibly with (the legacy of) slavery. That may be one reason why creolisation has not readily been applied to Europe itself, in spite of the cultural and semantic diversity and constant interchange (intercourse). Take the Caucasus, the epitome of ethnolinguistic variation! Is it not ironic that whites in North America are classified as Caucasians?

> The genealogy of the category goes back to the ancient slave trade of predominantly white women in the Caucasus. Interestingly, as Zimitri Erasmus explains, it was the racialised conception of these (slave) women as the embodiment of beauty that sparked the invention of the "Caucasian race" as white, superior and beautiful.[51]

Take Eastern Europe before the Holocaust! After the massacres, the new or re-emerging nation states are ethnically cleansed—and refuse to receive strangers into their tribal communities. Or take former Yugoslavia, where the ethnical cleansing was commenced during the Holocaust but completed only after the interregnum of Marshall Tito's non-allied socialist regime. Before the Bosnian war, Sarajevo was, as my Croatian colleague Maja casually pointed out, the epitome of *conviviality* without knowing it. [*Oh, the rage still educed at the remembrance of the SerboCroatian carnage.*]

[49] Ibid.: 52.

[50] Ibid.: 62.

[51] Erasmus 2017: 19. The association White–Caucasian can be traced to Johann Friedrich Blumenbach, the father of racial science and race classification: *De generi humani varietate native* (1775).

The connotation to slavery is most probably why creolisation evokes an indefinite uneasiness among white Westerners, as opposed to cosmopolitanism (which may raise objections but not discomfort) or the amiable new catchword conviviality. Slavery, the fundament of the colonial world system, remains a blind spot to the modern European mind. Blind, or, rather, *black*; a reminder of "the underside of Modernity".[52] The suppressed organising category of modernity is *making race*, says Zimitri Erasmus in *Race Otherwise: Forging a New Humanism for South Africa*. I found her new book by coincidence in the university library in Pietermaritzburg, when I was looking for her previous work on the Coloured in the Cape (*which, incidentally, was not to be found in the Stellenbosch university library*), and as soon as I started reading it, I knew that it would become a main reference, besides Glissant.

The "bundle of spoken and unspoken lines" that make up her own family's stories is an illustration of the South Atlantic–Indian Ocean axis, with St. Helena Island and Cape Town as the historical nodes that "tack the two oceans into a quadrangle of *meshworks*".[53] Her mother's ancestry stretches to Eastern Europe (the "Old Country"), Java, and the melting pot of St Helena island, on the paternal Erasmus side, to Dutch settlers and indigenous KhoiKhoi in inland Karoo.

Apartheid flattened South Africa's complex entanglement with Indian and South Atlantic Ocean histories into a racial category—*Coloured*— which Zimitri Erasmus, like Zoë Wicomb, declines to espouse, in defiance of the meta-narrative of racialised destiny.[54] When she joined Wits University in 2011, she refused to tick the box for "coloured" in the compulsory form provided by the HR department. And she has managed to remain "unclassified" in the register, although everybody *sees* her

---

[52] Mignolo 2012, in Erasmus 2017: 25.

[53] Yon 2007, in Erasmus 2017: 6. The direct quote is from Yon, but Erasmus has picked up the term *meshwork* from anthropologist Tim Ingold (2007, 2015) who in his turn borrows from Henri Lefebvre.

When everything tangles with everything else, the result is what I call a *meshwork*. To describe the meshwork is to start from the premise that every living being is a line or, better, a bundle of lines [a knot] (Ingold 2015, in Erasmus 2017: 2).

[54] Erasmus writes (2017: 24).

To paraphrase Zoë Wicomb (1998), my blackness draws its meaning from multiple, overlapping and contradictory belongings and not-belongings. I repeatedly renegotiate these as I move from one place to another inside and outside of South Africa. *This* Blackness defies attempts to give Blackness a general, monologic and definitive meaning.

racial category. In most everyday situations, her dissent is to no avail; if she doesn't tick the box, somebody else will do it for her.

[For a Swede of my generation, it is difficult to fathom the persistence of racialisation. The fact that I more than once have been mistaken for a Latin American immigrant (supposedly a refugee from Chile, Argentina or Uruguay) is a curiosity to joke about—and something that has rather enhanced than prejudiced my professional career. But it takes little imagination to transfer myself to a European near-past, when dark hair and brown eyes were suspicious non-Aryan traits. (It takes a little more effort to imagine a counterfactual near-future South Africa, where being white, or coloured, will be like being Jew or "half-Jew" in the Third Reich, but I have come to realise that this nightmare fantasy is real, not only among whites.) I come to think of Geir Thomas' pamphlet about "the culture terrorism" and his ardent defence of the right *not* to belong to a culture.[55] He was partly speaking for himself, as a non-nationalist Norwegian, but primarily on behalf of the immigrants, who were supposed to assume and embrace their assigned cultural identity. For me, it was never a problem *not* to assume a Swedish identity. "Swedishness" was never imposed on us. I can subscribe to whatever culture I want. But, and this is the crucial difference, I cannot choose not to be ticked in the category "white". The simple reason why these categories persist is that they are read off your skin. In South Africa, before, during and after apartheid, the way of knowing race is by *the look!*]

KAYELITSHA

ZE CAUGHT EDDIE WEBSTER at the coffee machine and they chatted about Jonny Steinberg's decision to return to Johannesburg. "Some of us find a compulsion in living here", Eddie smiled, and when ze quoted Michael Chapman's statement that "living here is like living on adrenaline",[56] he found it to be a very accurate metaphor. "South Africa is a high-risk project. But, then, the whole world is a

---

[55] Eriksen 1993.
[56] Hemer 2012a: 156.

high-risk project now, and South Africa may be a hunch of a future that awaits Europe, and it may be that we are better prepared at dealing with the violent conflicts here".

Yes, but how do you actually get accustomed to the violence? By shutting your eyes and numbing your senses? At that same coffee machine ze repeatedly hears—even from the mouth of a respected ethnographer—the horror stories of people getting robbed and thrown off the train to Cape Town. Ze listens with disbelief, convinced that they are exactly horror stories, feeding the white *angst*, but in the end ze hirself never takes the commuter train, ze hardly ever uses other public transport than taxis, and ze is ashamed to admit it ... Yet ze does walk the streets of Cape Town at night, and ze will take hir Swedish colleagues to mussy Marvel Bar on Long Street, a place they admittedly had not dared to visit alone.

Kayelitsha is some twenty kilometres afar, halfway to Cape Town. In three months, ze has only been to the (modest) metropolis three times, passing in the fast lane through no go land. [*Next year when ze returns, ze will stay on the other side of the black hole, at an apartment hotel in Sea Point; the closest ze will get to Kayelitsha is Athlone— where ze will almost get lost in pursuit of sweet indulgencies...*]

ZIMITRI ERASMUS is an eclectic in the best sense of the word, gathering impulses from many different life worlds and disciplines, and Glissant is but one of her references, and not even the most prominent. Toni Morrison is another, Tim Ingold yet another, from whom she has borrowed the concept *humaning* (as opposed to humanising):

> If becoming human is something we do with other humans and with other sentient and non-sentient beings, then "to human" is a verb; a life-long process of life-in-the-making with others.[57]

But although she only once explicitly refers to Relation, her "meshwork" of theoretical approaches seems impregnated by Glissant's general idea. His conceptions of "filiation" and "legitimacy" correspond perfectly with her reasoning on inheritance and heredity, and the fruitful cross-pollination—*excuse the metaphors!*—is likewise apparent in her subsequent positing that

> creolisation is a beginning in the process of addressing and challenging the normative practice of race classification and the normative ideal presented by a politics of cultivating purity.[58]

The idea of inheritance, to regulate transfer of property, office and title according to genealogies of kin, is transformed into heredity when its legal meaning is transferred to biology. The shift from inheritance to heredity is significant for the concept of reproduction. The former notion of "engendering life" is turned into the idea of

> perpetuation of humans as a species over time by way of heterosexual practices, with genealogy and with an individual's belonging to collective entities such as sex and race.[59]

In other words, what Foucault refers to as biopolitics.[60]

---

[57] Ingold 2015, in Erasmus 2017: xxii.
[58] Erasmus 2017: 97.
[59] Müller-Wille & Rheinberger 2007, in Erasmus 2017: 79.
[60] Foucault 2008.

Caste is, like race, a European invention, going back to the Spanish concept of *las castas*, which purported to establish individual ancestry. This caste system is in turn one of the earliest genealogical designs used for thinking biological heredity, as first developed by Linnaeus and subsequently corroborated by biological theories about the origin of differences within the human species.[61] A similar system with fewer categories was used in British colonies in Africa and elsewhere, evident in archival references to people as "half-castes" or "half-breeds" [*Would that also be the etymology of the Indian "caste system"? The British applied an originally Spanish term to describe the complex system of hereditary stratification that they encountered in India …*].

The Spanish caste system emerged from the concept of blood purity—*limpieza de sangre*—which signified "unsullied Christian ancestry" and was used against Muslims and Jews who converted to Christianity. In the Spanish colonies [*more than in the Portuguese, apparently*], skin colour became a primary marker in the hierarchy of castes. Long before the scientisation of the idea of race in the nineteenth century, missionaries and scholars in colonial America distinguished between lines of "pure ancestry" and lines of "mixed ancestry". The Jesuit José Gumilla (1686–1750) even provided schemata for degrees of mixture across generations of people of "mixed ancestry", according to which it was possible to "dilute" blackness and indigeneity over generations to produce a "completely white" person (already) in the third generation.[62] *Mixture* (as opposed to *métissage?*) was in other words constructed in relation to whiteness as an ultimate goal in the process of propagation. [*Hence the campaigns to* "improve the race" *through immigration of whites in Colombia and other Latin American countries. Hans Lindahl's grandfather in his Sunday costume behind the plough…*]

BITTERSWEET INDULGENCES

WHAT IF SETTING HIR FREE *is J.'s ultimate retaliation?* A hunch of that strange idea passes hir mind, without catching as thought. Now ze can't imagine that next year, when ze will come back to Johannesburg

---

[61] Ibid.: 81.
[62] Mazzolini 2007, in Erasmus 2017: 82–83.

and Cape Town, and another two years ahead in Pietermaritzburg and Durban, hir "affairs", or whatever the secret, still illicit encounters are to be called, may have lost the lure of the forbidden. With J.'s indifference, ze might even be free to write about them. But why would ze? *To affirm hir masculinity?* Ze would laugh out loud at that suggestion now, but a year—three years—ahead it may possibly make hir shudder. *To shock hir colleagues and friends?* No, ze is already beyond that. Besides, the friends who possibly would be shocked—but more likely indifferent—are really J.'s friends. Hir own friendships have rusted and withered, for negligence on hir part, or lack of attention. That is an inoffensive, yet less likable side of hir personality; to abandon people like ze abandons places, without either remorse or ill intent. A curious and inconsistent peculiarity, because ze used to be regarded (*and regard hirself*) as a person of affection and friendship. In hir childhood and youth ze had several friendships that by any standard would be deemed as close and deep. Ze didn't break with them, but neither did ze hold on to them as ze moved on, leaving behind a vacuum of, not bitterness, let alone anger, but consternation and, in some few cases undoubtedly, sorrow.

All the way up into puberty and beyond, ze used to be the kind of person that naturally attracted the attention of others; boys as well as girls, although the latter spell from very early on was ambivalent and fragile. Ze will ponder over it in ever-increasing bewilderment: the series of circumstances that determined hir sexual trajectory (*not* orientation, *because that would presume an inherent characteristic or assumed identity, which ze ardently refutes*); turning away from women was never a deliberate choice, but—more likely—simply a consequence of hurtful experience... Yes, maybe ze was in fact desperately calling for affirmation of hir long suppressed masculinity, revenging the sorry crack-whores-to-be that had sullied hir puberty, by pleasuring lascivious ladies (*mostly single mothers, as it happens*) in their forties or even thirties. Of course, there is something utterly pathetic (*if not miserable*) to the sexagenarian autist's insatiable desire for twenty years younger women, preferably of colour. With hir virtual mistresses ze never disclosed hir real age, and ze will keep fooling hirself by trying to play it down by at least five years. "Judging by your dick", *Katlego will estimate hir to be 57, which, after a second's hesitance, ze will accept.* Yes, nearing Death is most probably, and increasingly so, not just another but the decisive explanation to hir obsession.

Then, why would ze not write about the *icky* stuff? In a year
Chris Kraus will inspire hir, and in three years ze will be further
encouraged by Cheryl, whom everybody tells to "stop writing about
that icky stuff". Ze will never have heard that word and try in vain
to look it up, misspelling it as "*eeky*". Cheryl will be the first to read
a draft of the yet unconceived *Interlude*, and find it "too prudish".
   So, here's to you Cheryl. The myriad masseuses of the three years
to come and pass. An obsession, no doubt, pathological, perhaps;
like becoming the protagonist of one of hir novels. *Shirlene, hir
first and only out-call, in Sea Point on Good Friday, who suddenly,
while dressing, will shed a tear for poor Jesus on the Cross ... Nathalie
("Naughty Nats"), one of the Olivedale housewives in their past-
prime forties that while the suburban boredom away with astrology
and tantraism; she will drive hir all the way to Melville, while stag-
ing a comedy for the 18-year old son in the back, pretending that they
are old acquaintances that have surprisingly reconvened... Tanya,
from Edenvale (another non-posh northern suburb), a former triath-
lon champion who will give hir the sports massage of hir life, and then
soothe the pain with an astonishing GFE.* ["Girlfriend experience" is
a droll term for the unpretentious intimacy between flabby unap-
pealing bodies; casual, *as it were*—the latter an expression that I use
in spite of not fully understanding it; a reminder of my mimicry,
that I am not writing in my native tongue, that I am even trying
to think, and dream, in a language that is not that of my fathers
... I realise that detaching myself is to somehow move away from
the *ethnographic* fiction, back to plain *fiction*. Or is it? In a way I
may simply be taking arduous detours to arrive at conclusions that
are not even my own, such as "*literature can make known even that
which it doesn't fully know*", Beatriz Sarlo's concluding remark about
the premonitory enigma of Borges' short story *El otro duelo*—the
cruel tale of two gaucho soldiers who are sentenced to compete in
a last race, after having had their throats cut—which I have quoted
innumerable times.[63] Sometimes, lately, I have felt that the academic
writing, and even more the UN consultancy lingo, is damaging my
literary language, in a different yet as devastating way as journalism
ever did. Those thoughts come up inevitably, always with *a pang*

---

[63] Sarlo 2003: 229.

of bad conscience—another expression that is not my own—when I occasionally read good literature.] ... *Then, to continue the cavalcade, there's Zolisa who will take hir to the rent-per-hour guesthouse in the outskirts of Pietermaritzburg that ze had already visited a week earlier. Forgetting the time, they will hurriedly dress at the landlady's knocking and escape like merry pranksters; Z. is then going to walk hir from the bus station through dismal downtown PMB and make sure ze gets into a proper cab to hir B&B, because she doesn't want to "read the news tomorrow about a murdered white male" ... There's Sydenham Eve in whose perfumed garden ze will enjoy three hours of lingam worship... And Eden, from "what is now called Zimbabwe", so puzzled by hir casual chit-chat that ze will stop the massage to assure herself: "You are aware that this includes a happy ending?" ... There is going to be numerable others, some of whom ze will barely recall, others that ze deliberately or subconsciously will suppress from recollection.*

But first and foremost, there will be Katlego of Park Lane Village, a stone's throw from Hillbrow, for whom ze will develop an affection that resembles infatuation, although it may be just the vainglory of having attracted a 35-year old Jozi belle. "Born and bred in Johannesburg" as she proudly explains. "Where? In this area?" ze enthusiastically responds, about to share the story of hir primordial visit to Joburg in 1991. "No, in Soweto". And ze will bite hir tongue and blush with embarrassment. Of course! In the 1980s "this area" was exclusively white.

When they first meet, a year from now, Katlego, *Kats*, is living with her five-year old daughter in a two-storey apartment in Park Lane Village's gated community for the emerging black middle class. The stair to the studio is bordered with neatly framed first-day covers from Mandela's presidential inauguration. She has short hair with dyed white trimmings, a tattoo on the left buttock hiding a scar, the slim body exercised every morning to yet fuller perfection. After dropping her daughter at pre-school, she drives all the way to Bryanston to work as a skin therapist in a shop, before going home to her own practice in the evenings.

Blissfully sipping rooibus tea with hot milk after the session, ze will suspect that ze is in fact the only customer. When they say goodbye, Kats gives hir a warm hug and urges hir to come back the next evening, and ze smiles all the way back to Melville, like someone who just discovered the meaning of ASMR. Nevertheless, knowing that such sensational knowledge is best preserved as a secretive memory, ze invents the excuse of a dinner invitation to a colleague at the university, and although ze leaves an opening for "passing by late in the evening", ze will stoically refrain and let that enticing moment pass.

A few weeks later, Katlego's apartment is flooded and the studio destroyed; she loses her job in Bryanston and is evicted from Park Lane Village, and as if that were not enough, her brother is shot dead in a random robbery, after which she moves to Durban to start a new life. When they meet again two years later, she'll be working in a beauty shop in the newly opened Ballito Lifestyle Mall.

Oh, if ze could imagine hirself in three years, at Hops in Ballito ...

Ze sits at the same table as last night, when they had made the absolutely last pizza order (*avocado, feta and bacon, a not bad combination*). Now ze is alone, in the peculiar mix of guilt and assurance that ze has grown accustomed to. The sea at dusk is terrifying. A lonely—*black*— surfer is waiting to rise on his board. Now he finally stands up, and balances on the edge of the abyss, a moment of grace before the inevitable fall ... Ze has come down to the coast over the weekend to prepare for next week's seminar; hir second in Pietermaritzburg, and although the first was seven years ago, ze worries that ze may repeat hirself, and that someone in the audience will notice. Ze is weary of hir own formulations, ze will never get over the fundamental discomfort of speaking in public, and yet ze returns "like a moth to the chandelier" (*Ivan's image from the crashed Café Europa in* The Restless Supermarket, *which for some reason has stuck with hir*). Just as ze keeps flirting with disaster ... Ze recalls Kats' mocking imitation of hir comment on the Lifestyle Mall, *"a bit too fancy to my taste"*, and the annoying assumption that ze *"probably never had touched a black person's hair"*. Lingering fragments of their conversation, as if ze were indeed the ethnographer, interviewing hir most intimate informant about the secrets of the tribe. Kats is unhappy in Durban and yearns to return to *cosmopolitan* Joburg (*yes, she actually uses that expression*), while unashamedly admitting that she *hates Indian and Zulu men alike* ... Now the surfer comes walking on the shore, moulting his skin. He is not black at all (*how could ze even imagine that?*); he was just wearing a wetsuit.

Would that fragment of a future vision be of comfort in hir present misery? [Looking back from that three-year distant not-yet, trying to revive that horrible Easter, the emblematical *Bad Friday*, with the Institute closed and all the fellows gone on holiday, I really can't tell.]

.... Ze shudders at the passing hunch of a not-yet thought and logs on to hir *Kik* account.

THE PURE ANCESTRY comprised not only *Blancos* (*gachupines* and *criollos*), but also *Negros* and *Indios*. The categories of mixed ancestry were *Mestizos, Mulatos* and *Zambos*. In other words, not only whiteness, but also blackness and indigeneity were defined as *states of purity*. But whiteness as purely superior and blackness/indigeneity as purely inferior.

The term "creole" begins with *criollo*, as the classification of Spaniards born in the colonies. But in the late eighteenth century, peninsular Spaniards (*gachupines*) start to derogatorily refer to criollos as "half-breeds" or *mestizos*. In the seventeenth century, *mulatos* and *mestizos* had enjoyed the right of access to ecclesiastical office on the condition that they were born of a legitimate marriage (*which was a rare occurrence*). If not, they were deemed "the offspring of lust" and such offspring were considered to be "living signs of shame, ambivalent creatures torn between different cultures and loyalties, and therefore a threat to empire and race".[64]

The association of "mixed ancestry" with a dishonourable status, illegitimacy, shame and concupiscence, hence circulated in the Western imaginary already in the 1600s. The South African race category Coloured is, as Zoë Wicomb has demonstrated, founded on this centuries-old discourse of shame.[65]

The meaning of Creole also gradually shifted, to become a category for Europeans who had "gone native" and "fallen from European grace". Those described as creole were primarily judged by the degree to which they were "full-blooded" and "cultivated Europeans". At the Cape, slaves were valued by their presumed proximity to European-ness, biologically and culturally. Later, their descendants were judged by the "impurity of their blood" and their "lack of ancestral indigeneity". These properties were measured against both European-ness in the metropole and "native-ness" in the colony.[66]

Yet, while Creole signified degeneracy, it was, as Stuart Hall notes, never historically, and is not today, fully fixed racially.[67] The offspring of the Cape melting pot, still, after three hundred years, does not show signs of physical homogeneity.[68] For the Cape, and South Africa, the

[64] Spanish jurist Juan de Solórzano Pereira, 1647, cited in ibid.: 85.
[65] Wicomb 1998, in Erasmus 2017: 85.
[66] Erasmus 2017: 86 [Erasmus 2011].
[67] Hall 2003, in Erasmus 2017: 86.
[68] Heese 2006, in Martin 2013: 65.

year 1795, when the Dutch lost the colony to the British, marks a historical turn of immense symbolic importance. The Dutch colony had been solidly hierarchised—a brutal and ruthless slave society—but it was also a hotbed of miscegenation and cultural exchanges, and the borders between racial and social categories were still, in the late eighteenth century, relatively blurred. Until 1795, colour or race had not been a legal obstacle to social advancement in Cape Town and its immediate surroundings.[69] [*The English, not the Dutch, laid the foundation for apartheid! Why does that ascertainment fill me with a sense of satisfaction? Because it confirms my own prejudice?*] Yet, only at the turn of the twentieth century, when Cape Town is a "real kaleidoscope of people, colours and sounds", does the ideology of separation become officially promoted in government circles, *and that is under the premiership of Cecil Rhodes.*[70]

From the Union government 1910 and onwards, racial inequality was increasingly entrenched in law. The Population Registration Act of 1950 stipulated three categories: White, Native (divided into "tribes") and Coloured—with Indians as a sub-category of Coloured—and provided the following definitions.

(iii) "coloured person" means a person who is not a white person or a native; ....
(x) "native" means a person who in fact is or is generally accepted as a member of any aboriginal race or tribe of Africa; ...
(xv) "white person" means a person who in appearance obviously is, or who is generally accepted as a white person, but *does not include a person who, although in appearance obviously a white person, is generally accepted as a coloured person.*[71]

But the categories changed over time. From 1951, "native" is replaced by "bantu", since referring to African people as native might legitimise their claim to land and citizenship rights. In 1978, "bantu" is replaced by "black". The Black Consciousness movement contested such narrow use of the word "black", arguing that it was *not* a race category but rather a global political

---

[69] Ibid.

[70] Martin 2013: 89 (italics added).

[71] *The Population Registration Act* No. 30 of 1950, section 1, quoted in Erasmus 2017: 88 (italics added). Erasmus explains these loose common-sense constructions of race, with low reliance on bio-scientific calculations, as a consequence of the recent Holocaust.

identification premised on resistance to white supremacy. Black would in other words comprise all oppressed non-whites—including "Coloureds" and Indians. (*Yet, as Erasmus points out, Steve Biko's position was somewhat ambiguous. Asserting that a society divided by race is a "deliberate creation of man" and not part of a "natural order", he at the same time romanticised African culture as "pure" and "close to nature". And he found the mobilising on the basis of race to be a strategy appropriate "at this stage of our history".*[72])

Post-1994 census categories remain closely correlated with those used by the apartheid regime. The enduring five categories are: White, African, Coloured, Indian and Other.

THE ANCESTORS OF HUMANKIND

THE KHOENA AND SAN peoples are the foundation for the South African creolisation process—the cultural common denominator. They never formed a unified and homogenous community but a plurality of people speaking related languages. They interacted with each other and inter-mingled with the incoming Bantu-speaking people to such an extent that a larger cluster of distinct but interconnected cultures emerged—"not a mosaic of more or less autonomous communities, but rather genuine 'chains of societies', which evolved over time, depending on economic, political or climatic conditions".[73] This constitutive openness and capacity for absorption is later also extended to the European settlers moving in from the South and the slaves brought along the East Indian trading route from Madagascar and Mozambique, and the deported political prisoners from Batavia ....

In spite of being the lowest of the lowest in the social hierarchy, the myth of the *Khoisan* (a contested colonial term) construes them as the ancestors of humankind as a whole. "The coloured people" evoke this myth as descendants of the first occupants of the land, thereby on the one hand claiming a history as a cultural group (in response to the apartheid logic) while on the other re-attaching

---

[72] Erasmus 2017: 42–43.
[73] Martin 2013: 350, referring to Amselle 1990 and Olivier & Valentin 2005.

themselves to all other peoples and reinserting themselves in a global humanity. In other words, the perhaps most exemplary illustration of the concepts of Relation and *Tout-monde* (*Whole-World*, in Martin's translation). Yet, Khoisan activists are now raising claims to be dissociated from the Coloured and recognised as a First Nation. Although the Khoena and San may be despised as inferior—primitive—they are revered as *authentic*—the noble savage—whereas the Coloured seem forever doomed as corrupted and stained.

*To be racialised is to be subjected to the signifier whiteness. To believe we can
see that we "have" black or white bodies obscures the way in which whiteness
produces both this way of seeing and the subject who looks.*[74]

ASKING HOW AND WHY we come to see race as inscribed on the body suggests that there is more to race than its social construction, its historical, material and power effects. In pursuit of this "more", Erasmus relies
on her US American colleague Kalpana Seshadri-Crooks' Lacan-inspired
thought that racial difference comes to the modern subject's rescue by
offering the *fiction of wholeness-of-being*.

The "more" to race lies in "the look" as measure of the order of racial
difference which adjudicates claims to being human, supports and defends
the fantasy of a whole, self-contained subject, and in the process transforms the being who looks as well as the one looked at.[75]

[*This key sentence takes a couple of readings to grasp.*] Erasmus follows up
and suggests that when whiteness fails in its promise of wholeness, blackness can be called upon to step up to the challenge. She refers to "recent
appeals on the part of some young middle class black people in South Africa
to have white people excluded from their worlds".[76] One example is from
the wake of the #RhodesMustFall campaign, when student activist Chumani
Maxwele allegedly shouted that "the statue fell; now it's time for all whites
to go", and stated that "we must not listen to whites, we do not need their
apologies, they have to be removed from UCT, and have to be killed".[77]

Another #Rhodes Must Fall leader, Athabile Nonxuba, put it in less
extreme, yet as radical terms, as "an oath of allegiance that everything
to do with the oppression and conquest of black people by white power

---

[74] Seshadri-Crooks 2000, in Erasmus 2017: 55.

[75] Ibid.: 58.

[76] Erasmus 2017: 58–59.

[77] The alleged statements by Maxwele are quoted from Gerda Kruger, Director of UCT's
Communications and Marketing department, in her article "Facts related to suspension
and disciplinary charge against Mr. Chumani Maxwele", *Daily News*, 5 June (Erasmus
2017: 59). Maxwele incited the campaign on 9 March 2015 by throwing human faeces at
the statue of Cecil Rhodes, at the foot of the steps to the university's convocation hall. The
statue was removed one month later, on 9 April.

must fall and be destroyed".[78] Subsequently, the call among the militant black youth is to abandon the project of "transformation" altogether, in favour of "decolonisation". And, as one of the more articulate #Rhodes Must Fall advocates, Sizwe Mpofu-Walsh, explains:

> The core difference between this approach and post-racial pragmatism is that all social questions are linked to race. Race is no longer a separate problem, to be dealt with independent of "the economy". Instead, it infuses every debate, every social interaction. Students have demonstrated this by combining the struggle over high fees with the question of racial justice: financial exclusion is racialised, and merely the new form of an old problem. Thus, to fix South Africa is to fix racial oppression, and vice versa.[79]

Mpofu-Walsh's suggested remedy is one of his responses to what he deems to be "10 myths in South African politics"; in this case, the alleged myth that "racial justice is unjust".

Interestingly, Zimitri Erasmus never directly refers to the "decolonisation" debate, but the address is obvious when she states that "offering blackness as a totality in opposition to whiteness remains faithful to the perceptual grid of the colonial imaginary".[80] Toni Morrison refers to this use of blackness as "elusive sovereignty".[81]

A seemingly radically different but as elusive form of sovereignty is advocated by sociologist Xolela Mangcu. He proposes "a political multi-racialism" in an anti-racist democracy which regards racialised experiences as "nothing remarkable". In practice, this means enabling different racial groups to work towards a common purpose, that is, a "joint culture" which is directed by "the culture shared by the majority group".[82] Erasmus pulls this argument to pieces, finally posing the rhetorical question in which ways power would work differently in assimilation in "the opposite direction" from the way it has worked to date.

Blackness, when performed as a fiction of sovereignty in opposition to whiteness, is produced by existential uncertainty and anxiety about

---

[78] Mpofu-Walsh 2017: 77.
[79] Ibid.: 77–78.
[80] Erasmus 2017: 59.
[81] Morrison 1997, in ibid.
[82] Mangcu 2015, in Erasmus 2017: 38.

belonging. For Seshadri-Cooks, racial anxiety emerges from the installation of whiteness in the place of the object of desire, that is, in the place of the "more than" of the subject. This place "should have remained empty".[83] The whiteness that fills it is not only contingent on shifting power relations, but unattainable for the black subject. For people considered *mixed race* ("coloured"), both whiteness and blackness are installed in the place of the object of desire. *And neither is attainable.* (Racial anxiety is in their case produced by neither being accepted as fully white, nor being considered *authentically* black.)

People considered "authentically black" also experience racial anxiety when faced with ethical quandaries about race. At UCT's Fuller Hall residence, where members of the #RhodesMustFall movement took charge of serving food and barred white, coloured and Indian students from entering the dining hall, some black students reportedly had mixed feelings about this and felt bad for the friends left outside.

Here, "the look", on the part of the "people at the doors", produces blackness as a totality which ties it to a narrow notion of African descent as visible. It excludes those who do not "look African" because blackness is conflated with African-ness.[84]

REVOLUTION IN THE AIR

THE INSTITUTE IS secluded from campus and ze hasn't seen much of the emerging *Open Stellenbosch* movement, other than the rather peaceful turmoil in front of the Social Sciences building, where passers-by are approached with flyers. None of the peaceful agitators approach hir, though, and ze is reluctant to approach them, deliberately refraining from acting as a reporter (*or ethnographer*), or simply out of the natural shyness ze managed to suppress during twenty years as a journalist; ze likes to believe that many if not most actors become performers to overcome their stage fright, and, yes, ze'd certainly rather

---

[83] Seshadri-Cooks 2000, in Erasmus 2017: 60.
[84] Erasmus 2017: 61.

be the infamous fly-on-the-wall observer than the pathetic wannabee activist. Somehow—and this hunch will become ever more evident in retrospect, while also serving as a convenient excuse—ze instinctively refutes the "decolonisation" discourse, without as yet being able to articulate hir concerns. And yet ze rejoices, of course, at the rupture in the *dorp's* self-deceptive complacency. The university, who recently had restored order after the sudden and mysterious death of its first black vice-chancellor, is now shaken, if not rocked, to its foundation. Ze can recall the sense of revolution in the air, although ze had been in hir puberty during the student movement of the late '60s and largely experienced it through hir elder siblings, and in peaceful Malmö at that, where there wasn't even a university at the time. A teenage anarchist, opposing the Marxist hegemons, waving the red and black flag of the defeated Spanish anarcho-syndicalists, "betrayed by the Fascists and Stalinists in unison", as ze solemnly wrote in the dedication of hir first book of poetry and prose, which ze presented as hir last year project in high school. Yes, a rebel at heart, ze still remains a rebel with another cause.

The admirably prolific Aryan will in the coming year make a documentary trilogy about the Open Stellenbosch *movement. It will be his project during his next stay as a fellow at the Institute; but he will, not very surprisingly, be forbidden to show it at his seminar. Ze will watch the films a year later on hir computer, and ze will have an argument with him when they meet, in Aryan's home in Greyton, a former hippie town in the highlands on some three hours driving distance from Stellenbosch. Ze will be pondering all the way over why these films immediately upset hir in a way that the Marikana threnody did not. Is it Aryan's own conspicuous silence, which ze at first reads as silent agreement? Aryan answers frankly that at the moment it is better to keep quiet and listen. Nobody in the younger generation would be interested in what he may have to say, anyway. If he speaks his opinion it will be discarded as the words of a 50-year old white male. Better wait till things mature ...*

But then, that is the way Aryan usually works; staying in the background, letting the images speak, and leaving the interpretation to the viewer. No, hir uneasiness has rather to do with what Zimitri Erasmus later so eloquently will elaborate as the tyranny of "the look", which "produces the tyranny of identity politics whether on the part of dominant or subjugated people".[85] [*Here, she draws on Black studies scholar John E. Drabinski's comparative reading of Paul Gilroy and Emmanuel Lévinas. Contra Lévinas' famous face-to-face metaphor, the look of racialised identity politics does not see a naked face. Nor does it see a single face. It sees a face dressed in clothes of race, and it sees many, possibly "hordes" of the same face at once.*[86]]

But is it because hir white face is regarded by default as an effigy of the colonial oppressor? Or is it on the contrary, which in reality is just the reflection of the same, for being disregarded, deemed irrelevant—ignored, at best, as long as ze stays in the margin? Tables turned. Ze may hesitantly consent with the general accord that now is a time for whites to shut up and listen; ze can whole-heartedly understand the suppressed anger that inevitably must come out (surprised, as anyone, that it hasn't already come out much more violently), and ze may even agree that it is a valuable learning experience for whites to be subjected to the "look" and feel race inscribed on their own bodies... Yet, why become intermediary for identity politics that go against the grain of non-racialism and vernacular cosmopolitanism, against all the aspirations associated with the now scorned Rainbow *nation, the embodiment of the spirit of the Freedom Charter, which Glissant enthusiastically evoked as testimony to* "la créolisation en marche"[87]?

The raw footage, mostly from the ugly university interior, is void of aestheticism; lengthy, tiring discussions unfold in occupied classrooms, slowly but steadily nipping the initial enthusiasm in the bud. To hir, that oh so familiar, almost banal, revolutionary repression that eats its own children, is the lasting, depressing imprint, whether intentional or not. Yes, if interpretation lies in the eye of the beholder, Aryan may believe himself to be the fly on the wall, but he is not shutting up. Not at all.

[85] Erasmus 2017: 63.
[86] Drabinski 2012, in ibid.
[87] Wald Lasowski 2015: 176.

I AM GOING BACK AND FORTH in my notes and underlinings. There is no other way to approach Glissant; to grasp his thoughts in glimpses of understanding. Glimpses of clarity and poetic beauty—yet respecting the opacity, which should never be confused with obscurity. Now let us try to summarise the things we don't yet know.

How have cultures—Chinese or Basque, Indian or Inuit, Polynesian or Alpine—made their way to us, and how have we reached them? What remains to us of all the vanished cultures, collapsed or exterminated, and in what form? ... Our experience of this confluence will forever only be one part of its totality ... *Not knowing this totality is not a weakness. Not wanting to know it certainly is.* Consequently, we imagine it through a poetics: this imaginary realm provides the full-sense of all these always decisive differentiations.[88]

A lack of this poetics would constitute a failing, he writes, and then comes one of the typical one-liners: *Similarly, thought of the Other is sterile without the other of Thought.*[89] This witty word game in fact encloses a crucial argument and its elaboration ought perhaps to be quoted *in extenso*, but I let it stand as a riddle, like some of the following catch-word definitions of the poetics' elusive subject:

[Relation is] what the world makes and expresses of itself.[90]
Relation is open totality ... Relation is movement.[91] [*The distinction between totality and totalitarian is crucial; this is one of the few passages where Glissant explicitly discusses race, as a "nonprime element", like violence, that* introduces the totalitarian into relation...]
[Relation] always changes all the elements composing it and, consequently, the resulting relationship, which then changes them all over again.[92]
[Relation] is the boundless effort of the world: to become realised in its totality, that is, to evade rest.[93]
Relation cannot be "proved", because its totality is not approachable.[94]

[88] Ibid.: 154 (italics added).
[89] Ibid.
[90] Ibid.: 160.
[91] Ibid.: 171.
[92] Ibid.: 172.
[93] Ibid.
[94] Ibid.: 174.

Relation does not present itself as anything new. Indiscriminately, it is new-ness.[95] [*Salman Rushdie's affirmation of melange and hotchpotch inevitably comes to mind: "A bit of this and a bit of that is how newness enters the world".[96]*]

Eventually, these one-liners are condensed and concentrated in the form of a poem, "That Those Beings Be Not Being", and the one sentence I quote here may perhaps not be crucial, but it is the most beautiful:

Relation contaminates, sweetens, as a principle, or as flower dust.[97]

VERKRAMPTE VOLKEKUNDE

AT THE LAST SEMINAR in the *Indexing the Human* series at the Arts and Social Sciences building, Senior Professor Kees van der Waal talks about "the long walk from Volkekunde to Anthropology". It is a fascinatingly frank auto-ethnography. As a Dutch immigrant, the young Kees identified with his compatriot Verwoerd, who (like Eiselen) compensated his being an *uitlander* by becoming the sternest Afrikaner nationalist. When the fight flared up within Afrikanerdom in the late '60s, between *verkramptes* (cramped) and *verligtes* (enlightened), he sided with the winning cramped conservatives, who regarded the races as subspecies in the human physical anthropology, and anthropology as a biological science which identified five racial subspecies [*how, ze wonders, do they correspond to the prevailing five categories?*]. Although not (as yet) militating as a member, he was sympathetic to the extremist *Broederbond* and *Ossewabrandwag*,[98] and a sworn enemy to "structural functionalism". His guiding light was Peter Coertze's "positive apartheid"

[95] Ibid.: 177.

[96] Rushdie 1992.

[97] Glissant 1997 [1990]: 185.

[98] Afrikaner *Broederbond* (Brotherhood), founded in 1918, was a secret, Calvinist and exclusively male organisation dedicated to the advancement of Afrikaner interests. *Ossewabrandwag* (Ox-wagon sentinel) was established in 1939, in commemoration of the *Great Trek* a hundred years earlier, as an anti-British and pro-German organisation that

(the preferred euphemisms were *self-development* and *good neigh-bourliness*[99]). Only after moving to Johannesburg for his doctoral studies, at then Rand Afrikaans Universiteit, now University of Johannesburg, did he start to question Volkekunde. The moment of conversion—which he actually compares to Saul's conversion—appears in a discussion on "development and race", when it dawns on him that he is a myopic conservative racist. A painful theoretical and methodological repositioning ensues, culminating in 1983 with the agonizing decision to break with the *Doktorvater* [*a curious term, ze is not sure whether he means his supervisor at RAU or his ideological mentor, Coertze, who had succeeded Eiselen as chair of Volkekunde in Pretoria*]. Now, in anger over his last fifteen years of delusion, he joins the Broederbond in order to change Afrikanerdom from within. "A serious error of judgment", as he laconically comments.

At the Q and A after his talk, someone in the audience—a young Afrikaner student—asks him if there isn't anything in Volkekunde that ought to be retained. Kees pauses for a second before responding with a firm "*NO!*".

---

opposed the Union government's participation in the War. It was dissolved as a separate body after the War, absorbed into the National Party, whereas the *Broederbond* continued to play a crucial role in South African political life until 1994.

[99] Dubow 2014: 278–279.

THE SUGGESTION THAT WHITENESS puts itself in the place of the object of desire implies a relationship between sex and race in the constitution and regulation of racialised bodies and subjectivities.[100] Regulation of sex goes back to the Gregorian reforms of the eleventh century, when the Catholic church established celibacy and prohibited marriage between kin up to the seventh generation. That is how the concept of *inheritance* emerges in the realm of the Law.[101] A biological notion of *heredity* begins in the 1830s, but its antecedents have already shaped the idea of incest as a taboo and the cultural logic of prohibition embedded in the taboo against incest is central to the making of racialised subjectivities.[102] The moral aspect regulates who is family, prohibiting sexual relations with family. In parallel, the juridical prohibition of sexual relations across race implies that one should have sex and propagate only within the racial family, i.e. a reversal of the incest taboo. Seshadri-Crooks explains this seeming contradiction by the suggestion that premises for the racial segregation emerge from a cultural or symbolic register of "purity", separateness and inequality, and not from a moral system.[103] [*Racial incest* is an intriguing concept, indeed. The inevitable—unsought—reconnection to Mary Douglas is also rewarding, although Seshadri-Crooks does not refer to her. Nor does Erasmus.]

Today, legal prohibitions of "miscegenation" are gone, but intimate relationships across race remain culturally and politically undesirable (if not taboo) among both black and white South Africans, as evidenced by the *Reconciliation Barometer*.[104] And it is not only a matter of conventional conservatism; in some radical "anti-racist" feminist circles, black men (and lesbian women) who marry white women are questioned about their political reliability.[105] *Making Love in a War Zone* is the telling title of Professor emeritus Jonathan Jansen's interviews with ten interracial couples in The Free State, who have gone against the grain,

---

[100] Seshadri-Crooks 2000, in Erasmus 2017: 61.

[101] Müller-Wille & Rheinberger 2007, in ibid.

[102] Seshadri-Crooks 2000, in ibid.

[103] Ibid.: 62.

[104] *Institute for Justice and Reconciliation* 2014, in ibid. The yearly *South African Reconciliation Barometer* gives detailed statistics on social mobility since 1994 (https://www.ijr.org.za/).

[105] Chigumadzi 2015, in Erasmus 2017: 62.

often in defiance of their own families. (Jansen, like Erasmus, draws on his personal history in the study of what he calls "the national obsession of South Africa".)[106]

The "coloured" who are living proof of interracial intimacy are of course especially prone to be subject for racialised sexual claims. The coloured woman, close to whiteness and therefore an object of desire for black men (and equally desirable as "exotic" for the white male), is often constructed as *lascivious*, as a fatal threat to the preservation of the (racial) family. [I can't help associating to the seemingly opposite, affirmative sexualisation of *la mulata* in some Latin American countries—especially Brazil, where she has nearly attained the status of a national symbol. I recall an ironic but not so amused appeal from one of the organisers at the Frankfurt Book Fair in 1994, when Brazil was the "guest of honour": "Don't send more *mulatas!*". I wonder what the projected national self-image was the next time Brazil was in focus in Frankfurt, in 2013. As I note that South Africa strangely enough is yet to become the guest of honour in Frankfurt, another memory comes as readily to mind: the inauguration sometime in the early 2000s of the Swedish consulting company Sigma's new premises in Malmö's former harbour area. For the occasion, the CEO and philanthropist Dan Olofsson, with strong affiliations in KwaZulu-Natal, had brought a group of traditional Zulu dancers, including bare-breasted teenage girls, whose supposedly "natural" and "non-sexualised" performance evoked a racialised voyeurism of a far less innocent kind.]

But, just like "the look", the hope to "preserve the race" is self-deceptive, infected with bad faith. Today's recurring ideas of "roots", "origins", "kinship", "lineage" and "descent" rely heavily on the metaphor of the human family as proof of human sameness. Assumed familial sameness begins with one's biological parentage, written in the genes, and seems to inform what one "looks like". (The internationally spread

---

[106]Jansen 2017. A little farming town in The Free State, which Jansen describes as "the Mississippi of South Africa", was the location of a scandal in 1971, when 19 of the community's citizens were charged with breaking apartheid's Immorality Act, which forbade interracial intercourse. The story of the trial of "the Excelsior 19" is told in fictionalised form in Zakes Mda's novel *The Madonna of Excelsior* (2002).

story of Sandra Laing is an illustrative example.[107] Born and raised by parents who were classified as "white", Sandra was reclassified when she was ten years old because she "looked black" and was subsequently expelled from school and *disinherited* by her father.[108]) [*I muse on the verb "disinherit", which Erasmus has underlined; the gravest form of dispossession, a punishment at par with expulsion, and (also) a key to undo one of human history's most fatal delusions. Disinherit … defiliate; to break the chain of filiation? Glissant's suggestion to replace the primordial and sacred legitimacy provided by filiation, is* l'étendue, *which Betsy Wing translates as "expanse".*[109]]

In addition to the idea of race as biological inheritance, history and politics determine one's race as a *social* inheritance. Irrespective of their social positioning, black people in former colonies are assumed to inherit poverty and disadvantage. *Black is the face of poverty.*[110] The long-established connection between race and culture has moreover produced the notion of race as *cultural* inheritance, and people considered of mixed race are often seen to lack or to be confused about "their culture". In conflation with these three modes of inheritance, a South African person's race is administratively inherited via apartheid's race classification of the person's parents. One is Black, Coloured, Indian or White by bureaucratic fiat.[111] And thus apartheid is inherited by the next generation. And the next … *Perpetuum immobile.*

REVOLUTION SUSPENDED

THE MAIN AUDITORIUM in the former B. J. Vorster building is filling up to the last chair. One can feel the expectation in the air, as if everyone present senses the dignity of the moment. Stellenbosch

---

[107] Sandra Laing's story is told in Stone, J. (2007). *When She Was White: The True Story of a Family Divided by Race* (New York: Miramax). Stone's book is in its turn the base for the British-South African feature film *Skin* (2008), directed by Anthony Fabian.

[108] Erasmus 2017: 65.

[109] Glissant 1997 [1990]: 53.

[110] Erasmus 2017: 65 (italics added).

[111] Ibid.: 66.

may be peripheral in the overall scheme, although the epicentre of the uprising is only forty kilometres away, but time and place concur in this very moment as living history in the making. Achille Mbembe is Cameroonian, like Francis, hence *kwerekwere*, and his accompanying spouse (Sarah Nuttall) is moreover a white South African (sometimes taken for a Swede), but even the pink berets[112] who make up a substantial part of the audience, respect Mbembe as a brother and comrade. (*Sarah, who is also Achille's colleague and co-researcher—formally his superior as Director of WISER, Wits Institute for Social and Economic Research—stays markedly in the background, as low-key presenter and moderator.*)

Ze finds a chair on the far side of a back row and happens to sit down next to Marlene van Niekerk, whom ze had met briefly in Malmö the year before and whose work, both as literary writer and critic, ze greatly admires. (They had exchanged some emails but never as yet found an opportunity to meet in Stellenbosch.)

Mbembe's speech turns out to be a rhetorical masterpiece; supporting the students' claims for radical change and embracing the general idea of decolonisation, yet drawing clear boundaries as to what it should and should not entail, and calling for moderation. Ze listens attentively and scribbles in the red notebook, now and then exchanging a look with Marlene, who nods in amusement and agreement; *mesmerised* is the word that comes to mind to describe their mutual awe. The notes, as ze transcribes them much later (in fact only *three* years later!) will, although fractured and incomplete, retain that lucidity that in retrospect will appear as premonitory:

The current times in South Africa require clarity, *he says, and states from the outset that* the Cecil Rhodes issue was dealt with successfully, as Rhodes has nothing to do on a university campus twenty years after freedom. Bringing down statues is not a way to erase history, but to demythologise it and put it to rest. That is what memory, properly understood, is supposed to accomplish.

What, *he continues*, has the bringing down of Rhodes to do with 21st century decolonisation of the university? Are we dealing with the past

---

[112] The pink beret is the symbol of the followers of the expelled former leader of the ANC Youth League, Julius Malema, whose radical breakaway party *Economic Freedom Fighters*, EFF, won 6.35 per cent of the votes in the 2014 elections. (In the 2019 elections, they will be the biggest winners and reach 10.79 per cent.)

because we can't face the future? On the contrary, this is bringing back the future, which has been absent the last decades. [And] South Africa's future is irreversibly linked to that of the continent ... [We must] put an end to South African isolationism, to the extra-legal execution of black Africans in the streets and townships. [We must strive for] deprivatisation and rehabilitation of public space. Seventy per cent of the land is in the hands of thirty per cent of the people. Changing that is the condition for mutual survival in this country. Democratization (is) to make the promises of the Freedom Charter real ...

And here comes the key sentence that ze knew, as ze scribbled it, that the reporter ze declines to be would have used as the catch phrase:

South Africa is the only country in the world where a black majority is ruling over a substantial, influential white minority. That is, the reverse from the USA [*the ruthless reporter would have rephrased that as "the USA in reverse", but this is, nota bene, in Obama's time.]*

Further down in the notebook a more curious remark, that ze also vividly will recall:

Coming from West Africa to Joburg or Cape Town, one is struck by the luminosity. Why do the universities here look like prisons?

But the core of the address is his definition of decolonisation as the "decommissioning of absolute knowledges" with the caution not to confuse this with either "de-westernisation"—"The Western archive does not belong to the West alone"—or "Africanisation"—"Mobuto's ideology; predatory projects masquerading as africanisation".

Our struggles—The Black archive—are not only for us, but for Humanity ... What we need to do is re-centre the continent. The choice is between national chauvinism (Hitlerism) and *Afropolitanism*; that is, a recapturing of the nineteenth century dream of an African nationalism which is inclusive.

In the Q&A session afterwards, a student wants to know "where we are in relation to Black Consciousness and non-racialism". Achille Mbembe unexpectedly responds that we need to *banalise whiteness*. Whites are not everywhere, *he says*, yet smilingly admitting that this may be difficult to grasp in Stellenbosch. We need to make a disconnect between racism and xenophobia.

> We couldn't beat them militarily. We beat them morally. Moral capital is important to have when you don't have military power. Now we are losing that moral capital.

And then, the conclusive remark, the rhetorical coup-de-grace:

> Democracy is revolution suspended. (*pause*) We can't go back to "one settler, one bullet", unless we wish to topple democracy.

> *Transparency no longer seems like the bottom of the mirror in which Western humanity reflected the world in its own image. There is opacity now at the bottom of the mirror.*[113]

EXPANSE, AS OPPOSED to Filiation, is a rather straightforward and easily acceptable metaphor for a community's—or individual's—problematic (threatening) relation to the other. Expanse connotes "openness" and "risk", both constituent elements of Relation. *Opacity*, as opposed to Transparency, is less self-evident, ostensibly even contradictory. When hypothetically demanding the "Right to Opacity", Glissant phrases the supposedly indignant opponent's expected counterargument:

> Now it's back to barbarism! How can you communicate with what you don't understand?[114]

He carefully responds: If we examine the process of "understanding" people and ideas from the perspective of Western thought, we discover that its basis is this requirement for transparency. In order to understand and thus accept them we have to measure their solidity with an ideal scale that provides ground for comparisons and judgments. Accepting differences upsets the hierarchy of this scale. But we need perhaps to bring an end to the very notion of a scale. Displace all reduction.[115]

His suggestion is to refer, not to Humanity but to the exultant divergency of humanities, whereby thought of self and thought of other become obsolete in their duality.

> The right to opacity would not establish autism; it would be the real foundation of Relation, in freedoms.[116]
>
> [*Plural of humanities and plural of freedoms. But Relation is singular!*]

---

[113]Glissant 1997 [1990]: 111 (italics added).
[114]Ibid.: 189.
[115]Ibid.: 190.
[116]Ibid.

Against the "false transparency" of a world dominated by the West, he posits "the penetrable opacity of a world in which one exists, or agrees to exist, with and among others".[117] The latter strikes me as an exemplary definition of *conviviality* (as opposed to "false cosmopolitanism").[118]

---

[117] Ibid.: 114.

[118] Denis-Constant Martin comments that this sentence also echoes what according to Paul Ricœur should underlie the human "*visée éthique*" (ethical goal/purpose/aim): "*Une vie bonne, avec et pour autrui, dans des institutions justes*" [A Good Life With and for Others, Within Just Institutions] (Ricœur 1992 [1990]).

GERTRUDE STEIN

IN RONDEBOSCH, a year later ze will see Meg Vandermerwe, who has newly been appointed editor *of New Contrast*, the prestigious literary magazine that Stephen Watson once edited. Although Stephen, in contrast to Ivan, was not a contact ze maintained, it makes hir profoundly sad to learn that he died suddenly from brain haemorrhage four years earlier. Ze vividly recalls their meeting in 1991 at the then newly inaugurated Waterfront. Stephen may have grown conservative, like so many others (not only white former liberals and not only in South Africa), but he was hir instrumental cicerone to the Capetonian culture scene.

Meg welcomes hir with the white poodle Gertrude Stein running in eights around her feet. It may bite, she warns. She has made tarts with cheese and cherry tomatoes, so fresh from the oven that ze burns hir palate, and soothes the pain in sparkling wine (it's a wonder that ze manages to get back to Sea Point). She speaks so fast that ze has troubles following. *I'm chatting your ears off*, as she wittily puts it.

The possibility of exile is a very real concern—she could probably pick and choose from prestige universities in the USK—but she is ambiguously committed to stay in Cape Town. We talk about the continuation of #RhodesMustFall into the ongoing nationwide #FeesMustFall movement; she says she can't detect any visions even faintly resembling those of the former revolutionary thinkers among the new student leaders—but that is perhaps an unfair judgment, regardless of who is making it. It's the times that have changed; the rhetoric of the black consciousness movement was also largely simplistic, and had dubious essentialist elements, but the apartheid state at its most vicious moment left no doubt as to who the enemy were, or the necessity of the resistance struggle.

QUIZ

FIRST QUESTION: *How can "the look" be countered?*
Answer: By means of *adversarial conceptual manoeuvres.* That is, what Erasmus defines as "ways of knowing and of engaging that prise open the cracks in taken-for-granted ideas about race and disrupt repeated reliance on it as a prism".[119] Again, she draws on Seshadri-Crooks, who called for a new *adversarial aesthetics* that will throw racial signification into disarray.[120] They both refer to Toni Morrison's short story *Recitatif* (1983) as a prime example.[121] But Erasmus takes the adversarial manoeuvres further, from the aesthetic realm to that of politics (jurisprudence), with Justice Albie Sachs and "the Walker case" as the illuminating example.[122] In short, the adversarial strategy is to acknowledge the historical effects of race and at the same time contest the use of race as a form of identity politics (which is a variation on Toni Morrison's motto, *"to acknowledge that race matters but refuse to live by its rules"*).

> Historical change invites both black and white people to take account of their intertwined histories and to remake their becoming in the world in ways that contribute to unmaking the racialised injustices of the past.[123]

The *humanism* that Erasmus wishes to forge serves both to critique the continued use of apartheid's race categories and to cultivate *an ethos of*

---

[119] Erasmus 2017: 69.

[120] Seshadri-Crooks 2000: 158.

[121] Sehadri-Crooks' other example is a fascinating analysis of the neo-noir film *Suture* (1993), directed by Scott McGehee and David Siegel.

[122] In 1997, Mr. Walker, a white resident of Constantia Park in Pretoria, complained that the City Council had unfairly discriminated against him on the grounds of race, by suing him and other residents of the area for arrears in respect of rendered municipal services. The background was that they were billed on the basis of a tariff measured by meters, whereas residents of other areas (former black townships) were billed on the basis of a—lower—flat rate per household. Differential billing was part of the City Council's programme to redress the inequalities rooted in apartheid, by both upgrading the services and eventually integrating township residents as civic peers. The case went as far as the Constitutional Court. In short, Justice Sachs' line of argument was to dismiss all claims of discrimination and instead regard the case as one about the rights and responsibilities of citizenship (Erasmus 2017: 66–74).

[123] Erasmus 2017: 74.

contesting inequality and living-together-in-difference.[124] [*This is as close as she gets to a definition of* conviviality, *without using that word. Nor does she ever refer to* cosmopolitanism. *But then, hardly anyone in South Africa does.*] The threshold is a recurring metaphor, the experience of having lived on both sides of the 1990s—"the decade in which everything changed", which "will never happen again"[125]—as her parents had lived on both sides of 1948. Living and *thinking* from thresholds—multiple thresholds—is an act of disobedience against any form of policing thought and practice. Whereas borders are lines of domination, lines of occupation that divide people, thresholds are lines of *relation* which can enmesh people, facilitate their movement and widen their lives. Thresholds are more difficult to police.[126] The threshold hence also denotes a *pluritopic hermeneutics*,[127] for which there are no *original origins* to revive or to which to return. This defies both Eurocentric developmentalist logics and "'the trial' embedded in nativist logics, so prevalent in contemporary South Africa".[128]

> Thought, becoming, humaning and relation are freed to think, to become, to human and to relate not just differently but in an *other* way—*otherwisely.* This freedom enables possibilities—foreclosed by both Eurocentrism and nativism—for imaging something other than a logic of domination, and something other than a logic of victimisation: a logic of *relation.*[129]

[*Although she doesn't write* Relation *with a capital R, she is clearly referring to Glissant, albeit not explicitly. Creolisation is one of four "arts of coming to know otherwise", at par with the adversarial manoeuvres, but her principal Caribbean mentor is Michael Monahan and his philosophy on "the creolizing subject".*[130]]

---

[124] Ibid.: 23–24 (italics added).

[125] Jansen 2009, in ibid.: 24.

[126] Erasmus 2017: 25, referring to Ingold 2007 (italics added).

[127] Mignolo 2012. Argentinean semiologist Walter Mignolo is a member of the influential Latin American research collective *Grupo modernidad/colonialidad.* His elaboration of "border thinking", originally introduced by the late Chicana feminist scholar Gloria Anzaldúa (1942–2004), has greatly inspired Erasmus. (Mignolo has also been a fellow at STIAS.)

[128] Erasmus 2017: 26.

[129] Ibid. (italics added).

[130] Monahan 2011.

The second question, specific to South Africa, is a riddle: *How can non-racialism/cosmopolitanism/creolisation be advocated without being taken as a pretext for the preservation of white privilege?*

Non-racialism as a political idea first appeared in East Africa as opposed to the British colonial *multiracialism*. Yet, in South Africa, its early variety attained a tinge of British imperialism, with the emergence of the mission-educated black elite which had access to vote as British citizens. [*As we have seen, this liberal assimilationism, epitomised in Sol Plaatje's* Native Life in South Africa *(1916), was a favoured object of Afrikaner abomination.*] In the 1930s the liberal non-racialism was challenged by an *anti-colonial* non-racialism, premised on socialist principles, which consequently defied colonial racial codification and refused to participate in institutions for "Natives".

Erasmus draws on the latter tradition of anti-colonial non-racialism, but does not attempt uncritically to recuperate it. Neither does she approve of the common binary between non-racialism on the one hand, as universalist, focused on human rights and equality before the law, and African nationalism and Black Consciousness on the other, focused on the particular, the racialised group and colonialism.

> In addition to my criticism of the linear conception of history embedded in the idea of heredity, my concern is that recent appropriations of Black Consciousness and non-racialism seem to treat the struggles as if they are inheritances in the literal sense of the word—criteria for conducting politics that are passed on to new generations in the way that possessions or things are inherited.[131]

Instead, she sees Black Consciousness of the 1970s and the anti-colonial non-racialism of the 1930s as *beginnings*. While acknowledging these fundamental achievements of a troubled past, the "new humanism for South Africa" that she is sketchily outlining (*forging* is a too strong and somehow incongruous verb) clearly reorients the attention towards the prospective and indeterminate future. Interestingly, at the culmination of her creolising journey of exploration she arrives at the German philosopher of hope, Ernst Bloch.

> For him, human agency is a manifestation of hope, not its source. Coming to know, humaning and the "not-yet" future are open-ended processes with promise.[132]

[131] Erasmus 2017: 45.
[132] Ibid.: 47.

THE TIME OF GLISSANT is the 1980s and 1990s.[133] *Poetics of Relation* is mostly written during the culminating Cold War. Yet there are surprisingly few time markers that might devaluate his observations. It has certainly stood the test of time, although some ambiguities may have become more apparent. He talks about *cultures*, as if they were somehow distinguishable entities, although in constant flux. A certain tendency towards *multiculturalism* was perhaps inevitable in a context of ongoing anti-colonial struggle (culminating with the South African transition). Yet, this is a soft spot—or, rather, an unresolved dilemma.

Reading back and forth, I cautiously search for projections of the future. Like this awkward vision of a post-agricultural South:

(…) Picture an uncultivated land when the factories producing synthetics have provided enough for the stomachs of the chosen few. It would only be used for leisure, for a kind of Voyage in which seeking and knowledge would have no place at all. It would become scenery. That is what would happen to our countries, since it is entirely possible that aforesaid factories would never be located in them (unless they are really responsible for producing too much waste). We would inhabit Museums of Natural Non-History. Reactivating an aesthetics of the Earth will perhaps help differ this nightmare, air-conditioned or not.[134]

An aesthetics of the Earth? His answer to his own question merits a full quote:

In the half-starved dust of Africas? In the mud of flooded Asias? In epidemics, masked forms of exploitation, flies buzz-bombing the skeleton skins of children? In the frozen silence of the Andes? In the rains uprooting *favelas* and shantytowns? In the scrub and scree of Bantu lands? In flowers encircling necks and ukuleles? In mud huts crowning goldmines? In city sewers? In haggard aboriginal wind? In red-light districts? In drunken indiscriminate consumption? In the noose? The cabin? Night with no candle?

[133] Denis-Constant Martin rightly comments that a very substantial part of his work was produced in the 2000s (Glissant 2005, 2006, 2007, 2008), in which he developed many of his ideas. None of the post-*Poetics of Relation* work has however been translated to English and is therefore largely unknown outside the francophone world. But by suggesting that his time is the 1980s and 1990s I mean that his ideas resonated with the epochal shift of the time.

[134] Glissant 1997 [1990]: 150.

Yes, but an aesthetics of disruption and intrusion. Finding the fever of passion for the ideas of "environment" (which I call surroundings) and "ecology", both apparently such futile notions in these landscapes of desolation. Imagining the idea of love of the earth—so ridiculously inadequate or else frequently the basis for such sectarian intolerance—with all the strength of charcoal fires or sweet syrup.
Aesthetics of rupture and connection.[135]

Further on, a more dismal vision of a not-yet that bears a sombre semblance to our present now:

Merely consider the hypothesis of a Christian Europe, convinced of its legitimacy, rallied together in its reconstituted universality, having once again, therefore, transformed its forces into a "universal" value—triangulated with the technological strength of the United States and the financial sovereignty of Japan—and you will have some notion of the silence and indifference that for the next fifty years (if it is possible thus to estimate) surround the problems, the dependencies and the chaotic sufferings of the countries of the south with nothingness.[136]

MARVEL HAZE

HIR LAST WEEKEND in the Cape before going back to Sweden is intended to be a *Grand Finale*. Michael, who has concluded his residency as artist at the Institute, is arranging a small cultural festival with emerging avant-garde artists at an "alternative" gallery downtown, and the *Afrikaaps* cultural collective is giving a musical show warmly recommended by Denis, who will attend himself. For the occasion ze has booked a room at a shabby "boutique hotel" on Long Street. Hir Swedish colleagues Mats and Cecilia—he a philosopher and fellow, she a cultural studies programme coordinator who shares her husband's office at the Institute (*to the Director's annoyance*)—are also spending the night in Cape Town, at a slightly

---

[135] Ibid.: 151.
[136] Ibid.: 191.

fancier hotel a few blocks away. After checking in, before joining the others at the gallery, ze slips into the noisy Marvel Bar across the street for a beer. Two for the price of one is the Happy Hour offer. Being the only white ze hesitates for a moment before lining up in the scrum around the bar desk; ze believes to sense one or two frowns (or at least batted eyelids), but most of the customers are busy balancing their drinks and holding their space on the rapidly filling-up floor; some are already dancing to the loud *black* music— current rap and classical Motown, in a curious aggressive-sentimental brew—that kills any attempt at conversation. Ze only has time for one beer, but agrees with the bartender to have the second on hold till ze comes back (knowing ze most likely will not, and that he will have forgotten anyway).

Maybe Marvel was just the first bar at hand—there are plenty to pick along this section of Long Street—but the choice, be it random, had that hunch of *fate*, which ze was always superstitiously prone to believe in. That evening, and ensuing night, is a blank. Ze will be able to faintly recall a dance performance that impressed hir at the gallery, and ze will remember the feel-good ambience of recognition among the coloured audience at the *Afrikaaps* show, but all details will have vanished, like coiling celluloid film frames that dissolve from the centre.

On the way back from the theatre, ze had suggested that they take a night cap on Marvel Bar. The music split their ears as they approached, the bar so crammed that it spilled out into the street and they could barely make their way through the crowd, let alone reach the bar desk. But when ze finally managed to call the bartender's attention he smilingly nodded (the way ze used to joke that only Malmöites do, by subtly throwing back the head) and ze proudly returned with hir free second beer and the two extras for hir Swedish peers who watched hir balancing manoeuvre in outright horror. They were cornered at one end of the dance floor, just inside the entrance, and could barely move.

As they stand there, beginning to fully realise the precariousness of their predicament, a high-pitch scream cuts through the music wall and draws alerted attention to a huge man by the bar, apparently not one of the locals, probably expatriate (prejudice signals Nigerian or Congolese). He is waving his bare arms, bottle in one hand, blood pouring from a scar under his eye, as two other men, little more than half his size, with joint effort try to escort him to the door. The circle of excited spectators moves with the wrestlers, balancing back and forth; it's like a price fight, or rather like a bear trying to shake off two fretless dogs, with the other dogs standing around with their teeth bared. When he eventually succumbs with raised open hands, he gets thrown out the entrance head over heels and bumps into a parking BMW, whose driver frantically adds to the insult by slamming the car's door in his face. Ze can see from the corner of hir eye how the wounded bully hesitates for a second before looming away, in the fury of someone who will return in five minutes with a machinegun if he can find one. From their position in the corner they don't have a clue as to what actually happened, but the atmosphere is suddenly tense with aggression and fear. The turmoil has set the whole bar in motion, Mats instinctively takes Cecilia under the arm, pushes their way through the door and starts walking hurriedly up street, seemingly without direction. Ze tries to follow *en suite* but nearly loses sight of them before even getting to the pavement. On the verge of returning to hir hotel across the street, ze decides to run after them, if only to say goodnight and somehow apologise (as if ze were personally responsible for the unpleasant incident). The very moment ze catches up, after crossing Pepper street, hir cell phone rings. It is only the second or maybe third time in three months and ze is so taken by surprise that ze doesn't realise at first what it is that buzzes against hir thigh, and ze gets even more stupefied after cumbersomely pulling the phone out of hir jeans pocket and seeing J. on the display. Exhausted from the rush, lightly dizzy from the beer and half-deaf by the music that still pummels in hir head, ze answers with a loud "HELLO!" and starts telling about the evening, with the slightly posy voice that anyone who knows hir immediately will detect and know that ze is not alone. Yet, the truth is that ze is overwhelmed by affection, incredulously hoping—wanting to believe—that this first sign of life in almost a month is a token of truce, if not peace; an assurance that things will eventually go back to normal—again. But J. doesn't respond to hir babbling. He doesn't say a word and for a moment ze thinks that the line is broken. *"Hello?"* Then ze can hear him inhale before he utters this one sentence, with the same low-pitched voice that had solemnly told hir to go hang hirself: *"Will you please erase your dick pics!"* He hangs up before ze gets a chance to speak, mercifully as it were, because ze wouldn't have had anything to say; any excuse or explanation at this point would be futile, at best, and tangle hir up in ever-more devious lies. Mats and Cecilia watch hir literally losing hir balance and bracing hirself against the nearest wall; it happens to be the window to Clarke's bookstore, which conveniently gives hir a chance to save hir face. Ze looks through the window while catching hir breath, blushing with embarrassment, then turns to the couple and waves them off with a forced good night and a smile, well aware that ze must be like the open books at display in the window (one about the eviction of District Six; the other a coffee table folio about the history of wine-making in the Cape). *How could ze be so incredibly stupidly careless?* But that is not what ze thinks in the moment; it's what ze will imagine that ze *normally* would have thought, when ze reflects on what happened many months later. In the moment hir mind is blank, or a blank when ze will try to remember, maybe a *haze* would be a more accurate metaphor in the present, even something reminiscent of a psychosis—which ze experienced in hir young adulthood, in a situation of extreme strain, self-imposed as now. Because ze obviously isn't thinking clearly. Instead of going to the hotel, ze returns to Marvel Bar, in order to "literally get hurt". Yes, ze will recall that impulse, which was inspired by Doung Jahangeer, the Mauritian artist in Durban, who had started his performative *city walks* through the no-go interstices of Durban with exactly that defiant motto. That act of absolute despair—to walk naked into the night, to face the demons, to give up everything—was also a recurrent (melodramatic) motif in hir novels; hence no wonder that —*if* (we can't state it as a fact)—ze reverted to a romantic—no, *Rimbaudian*—confusion of life and letters.

My BEWILDERMENT, at first, when the computer breaks down and makes everything I have written to date inaccessible. A complete nightmare, had it not been that—wise from previous experience—I had saved it all on a USB. Everything except the last minor revisions I made while reading through the draft second register (*Waiting for Señor C.*). Before the breakdown, during three productive days, I had written as much as I could without further immersion into the literature—the diverse reading material I had brought as a travel library to my refuge... The awkwardness of going back to pen and notebook; going back to *normal* in the sense that this was the way I used to write, always by hand before putting the white sheet in the typewriter—also after I had swapped the typewriter for my first computer (*a Zenith, one of the early laptops, certainly too heavy to have on your lap*). Now that seems like ages ago; I had forgotten how much I actually missed that qualitative leap from notebook (or loose scribbled sheets) to the first typed version. That step required concentration, because the typing was a form of print-and-publish, if only for my own eyes. That threshold disappeared in the ever-changeable digital document that can be formatted in whichever way I want.

It's late October and Paris is getting chilly and dark. I'm in a rented one-room apartment in Les Lilas. South Africa and the Cape are distant, but it makes sense to be here when writing about creolisation. Paris is more of a metropole than I had imagined. The diversity of appearances on the metro (11) to Châtelet, République or Belleville. There's the concealment of the big city, but also a kind of calm and relaxation in all the turmoil of the rush-hour traffic that I haven't even experienced in New York—which would be the closest comparison. Not London, for reasons that I can't readily specify. French colonialism was ever as brutal as the British, but more egalitarian in principle. London cannot escape its association with decaying Empire, whereas the idea of the Republic somehow saturates Paris ... *Saturates, permeates...* oh, how I can feel constrained by language, the frustrating inability to fully express what I want to convey (*maybe not only a matter of linguistic inability, but I'd rather not pursue that line of thought*) ... What am I trying to prove? Who am I trying to impress? If it's *ethnography*, what are my data? Whatever does *auto*-ethnography imply? When I begin scrutinising my ongoing "project" and its motifs, it all appears as elusive. Illusory. The doubt eats into my usually solid self. I am freezing, I am lonely, I am a ruin. The blank page of the notebook is a horror ... No, writing cannot save me. I am burned out. Everything comes to an end. I have come to the end, and I am starting to realise the full consequences of that simple irreversible fact. What I have been trying for three years to finalise will never be accomplished—even if I try hard to believe that I am getting a little closer each time … It gives some comfort to note that Zimitri Erasmus hasn't succeeded either in bringing her (first) monograph to a proper conclusion; she ends on a brief chapter of "beginnings" and a one and a half page "open closure". But then, *she* has a life story, the experiences of creolisation and racialism (literally) written on her skin, and hence the authority to speak; whereas I am a privileged tourist whose "errantry" is purely philosophical, an imaginary exile from a country and culture that, regardless of whether I consider them as "home", will never expel me. Yes, I defy accusations of "acculturation". I claim my right, as a man, to imagine what it is to be a woman, and as a white, to imagine what it is to be black. I defy anything that even faintly resembles essentialism, and I am allergic to the word *authentic*. But I couldn't easily brush off the objections from a black female student at my seminar in Pietermaritzburg, and I was not entirely comfortable with the endorsement afterwards from one of the student's white teachers. Yes, I may have the right to identify with whomever I want. But to what purpose? By what authority do I speak about "South Africa" (or "creolisation", for that matter)? I may claim to have a longer relation to the country than most of its own inhabitants, who have grown up after the transition. But I don't have the sensory memory of township (or suburb) that Jacob Dlamini evokes in his compelling memoir *Native Nostalgia* (2009)—or Trevor Noah, for that matter, in *Born a Crime* (2016)—and however hard I pressed my literary imagination, I would never be able to construct such memory in a truthful way. Not in South Africa! I did it in my Argentina trilogy, apparently with some success. In my imagining of an Argentinean childhood and adolescence, the main challenge was the lack of memory markers, the small significant details that would signal "authenticity" and convince an *Argentinean* audience of my narrative authority. When I was doing research for my dissertation, I found an inexhaustible source of such memory markers in the enormously ambitious—and also highly questionable—three-volume documentation of the militant insurgency of the 1960s and 1970s, *La Voluntad* [The Will].[137] I used some of the minuscule details, the nerdy kind that

---

[137] Anguita & Caparrós 1997, 1998.

I would have remembered from my own childhood and youth, specific locations (*Lanemos konditori* in Linköping, *Ringbaren* or *Klubb Bongo* in Malmö) or pop songs (like the *Buckle Shoe Stomp*) ... And at the reading of a chapter of *Santiago* on the "Nordic Night" at the Buenos Aires book fair in April 2008, where I was the Swedish representative because I happened to be in town, and Sweden, unlike the other Nordic countries, had not bothered to send one of its prominent authors, I could hear an awe of recognition in the audience at precisely those signal words, which to me were not connected to any memories at all; I didn't have a clue as to who *Litto Nebbia y sus gatos* were or even what their song *La balsa* sounded like. I touched a chord of collective memory, laden with emotion and nostalgia, grief and loss, and it was sheer manipulation on my part. Yet that was my one and only experience as a writer of communicating with a live audience in real time, a communion in the flesh. [*And that memory of what-could-have-been—un unfulfilled not-yet—makes the present muteness of non-reception the more difficult to bear.*]

Although I vehemently oppose Antjie Krog's conclusions about unsurmountable barriers between the life worlds of blacks and whites, I can understand the rationale behind them. As Zimitri Erasmus puts it:

> "[T]he look", the category and the gene are customary; humaning and critical humanism are historically side-lined; continued use of apartheid race categories and recent conceptions of blackness as sovereign are the new.[138]

I, a sexagenarian white male, and a foreigner at that, shall insist to claim my right to imagine being black, or "coloured", but it would be more important—*imperative*—that young black writers, male and female, exercise their right to transgress the racial identity ... Now, back to the communion at the Nordic night in Buenos Aires: *Did my manipulation make the evoked emotions less true?* When I pose that question, I can hear Coetzee's voice (in conversation with Arabella Kurtz). Is the question rhetorical? He never made a black person the focaliser of any of his novels. Michael K. is neither white nor black; his race is undetermined [*I will have to read it again when I get home, to confirm that skin colour is deliberately left out in the description of the characters, with one curious exception:*

---

[138]Erasmus 2017: 136.

one of the soldiers—who would supposedly be white—is depicted by his "dark complexion"]. In fact, he may be read as the incarnation of the creolised Cape ancestry going back to the time of the slave colony when the Khoisan mingled with Dutch settlers and merchants of the Dutch East India Company, slaves from Madagascar and exiled intellectuals from Batavia ... [*Yes, Michael K, with his unspecified Khoisan features. Why didn't I think of him before? He is the missing link between Coetzee and my project* (as if such a link were necessary)].

I could perhaps imagine growing up as (English- or Afrikaans-speaking) white in South Africa, but that is somehow as discomforting as imagining growing up in the Third Reich. How would I know where the line of complicity were to be drawn? How could I have acted *otherwise* (and lived)? I think of Michael, Stephanus, Aryan, the generational peers of my age or some ten years younger; old enough to have had the choice whether to engage in "the struggle" or not; all impeccably liberal or radical, yet capsuled in their privileged predicament—to a much higher degree than a middle-class Swede like myself. The step to abandon that position must have been so huge—even if it were not a lethal decision, as it most probably would have been in the Third Reich—that it was in practice almost impossible. Would they even have been welcomed—or automatically suspected to be infiltrators (*like Mark Behr*)? Or Simon, my five years older fellow at the Institute, who frankly admitted that he had been too cowardly to take a militant stand. How could I judge or condemn him? *How can I judge or condemn my own father?* When does cowardice become a crime? When the choice not to act has immediate consequences for someone else; when saving your own skin implies the sacrificing of another? Voting with the majority in *Bollhuset* in Uppsala was an act of conformism, at best, which indirectly implied the death of tens or hundreds (or thousands) of Jews who might have been admitted to Sweden as refugees ... But then, refugee migrants are now drowning by the thousands in the Mediterranean with the complicit acceptance—willing or not—by all the privileged citizens of the EU.

Michael, from his privileged position, is a facilitator of creolisation, both in his composition—*The Bow project*—and as curator for the young art scene in Cape Town, enabling encounters and collaborations across the divides. Isn't that good enough? Maybe the "good-enough" and the "not-yet" are in fact postulating each other.

POSTCARD CAFÉ

WHATEVER HAPPENED AT THE MARVEL BAR remains a conundrum. That night is a complete blank. Ze got drunk, for sure; the hangover lasted the whole next day. Judging from the smell of hir clothes, ze may even have smoked dagga. But how ze ended up in hir bed is a complete mystery. Somebody must have escorted, if not *carried* hir across the street and all the way up the spiral staircase to hir room. That helpful angel must moreover have put hir in the bed and taken off hir shoes and trousers, letting hir keep the t-shirt and dirty underpants; the angel or demon could well have seized the opportunity to rape hir, and ze will almost wish that he had, in rightful punishment [*is there an English equivalent to the Swedish word* straffknulla? *In ancient China, they had "punishment by horse's cock", as depicted in the catalogue to one of hir childhood's exhibitions at Louisiana; a sample of Phyllis and Eberhard Kronhausen's collection of Erotic Art, which ze will unexpectedly recall in a nostalgic flash.*]

Ze arrives at Leiwater in the late afternoon, just before dark, and starts packing in the evening. In the morning ze makes a frugal breakfast from the left-overs in the fridge and continues to prepare for the journey; without returning to the Institute or saying goodbye to anyone. The taxi to the airport is ordered at 1.30 PM so there is plenty of time. But before hir departure, ze is being picked up for lunch by Marlene. It is the only time slot that they have managed to settle for a meeting. She takes hir to the scenic Postcard café some six kilometres to the southeast, at the entrance to the Jonkershoek nature reserve. She says she uses to go there for inspiration. It's a beautiful day, the air is crisp and the mountain sides clothed in autumn colours. They don't speak much, and ze doesn't feel obliged to chat, the pauses of silence are comfortable, as opposed to the awkward mutual muteness with C.—although his goodbye was warm and heartfelt: "it was nice meeting you". Marlene is relaxed and witty, sharp and outspoken, knowing her friends and foes (*Antjie Krog clearly being among the latter*). The lunch is brief but not hurried, ze eats hir egg and ham sandwich with little appetite but enjoys the company and forgets about time. When Marlene drops hir off in Rattray straat, the taxi is already there. Ze hurriedly fetches hir bags, and ze knows with assured ambivalence that it is not a farewell, but a return.

APARTHEID SOUTH AFRICA is only referred to in passing, as an example among others, in *Poetics of Relation*. But in the sequel *Traité du Tout-Monde* (1997), Glissant dedicates a chapter to Nelson Mandela—"Le temps de Mandela" [Mandela's time]—whom he evokes as an incarnation of Relation.

> C'est l'expérience du Tout-monde qui est au cœur de la vie de Nelson Mandela. Un homme libre et divers dans son unité de courage et de vérité [It is the experience of Whole-world that is at the heart of Nelson Mandela's life; a free and composite man in his unity of courage and truth.][139]

Mandela's time is also Glissant's time. Questioned, or forgotten, they now both seem out of step with the current politics, in South Africa and the world at large.

What would Glissant have said about the current student protests? He would possibly have regarded them as a (nostalgic) reminiscence of the old struggle, driven by the ideology of national independence. Whereas (*he would patiently repeat*) the global interdependence at work today calls for other ideas and approaches. Not the "root identity" of nationalism but a "Relation identity", linked to the conscious and contradictory experience of contacts among cultures, that *exults the thought of errantry and of totality*.[140] [*I have to look up the uncommon word "exult"; the combined praise for errantry and totality is one of these seeming discords that intermittently call the reader from comfort to alert.*] The point being that Root and Relation are not binary opposites. The counterpart to root is *rhizome*. The rhizome maintains the idea of rootedness, but opposes the idea of one totalitarian root. Again: *Rhizomatic thought is the principle behind the Poetics of Relation*.[141]

DÉJÀ-VU

THREE YEARS FROM NOW ze will briefly meet a troubled Sarah Nuttall at WISER.

[139] Wald Lasowski 2015: 175.
[140] Glissant 1997 [1990]: 141.
[141] Ibid.: 11.

When ze tells her about the progress of hir project, Sarah shakes her head. *This is not the time for cosmopolitanism and creolisation. Now is the time for affirmation of blackness (and whiteness). Time may come again. But now that is a dead-end street.* And then she adds, in passing, as to downplay the significance of what she says: *In the end, we may opt for liberalism.*

So, ze asks, *what can you do now as a white intellectual in South Africa? Just shut up?* Sarah shakes her head again. *No, but maybe work at another level.* Like, for example, speaking about non-racialism in schools, which she does, and finds very rewarding.

From hir present horizon this is indeed like a gaze into Dystopia. The spring of 2015 (*autumn in the Southern hemisphere*) is barely the wake of the refugee migration that will rattle the entire European union. Although fascism has reared its head again, figures like Duterte, Trump and Bolsonaro are as yet unimaginable (*although they shouldn't be*: Modi is already elected to power in India). Nonetheless it is a *déjà-vu.*

Mandela's time was also the time of the war in Yugoslavia and the genocide in Rwanda (*which happened while the world media's attention was on South Africa's first democratic elections*)... Then, in the parenthesis between 1989 and 2001, ze had somewhat naïvely projected *Latin America* as a model for the globalised world in making. Even white-washed Argentina had in hir wishful thinking appeared as a pluralist ideal, albeit clearly overshadowed by its Northern historical rival, Brazil—the *Utopia of Uprooting* that ze evoked in hir contribution to an anthology in solidary support of the besieged (and violated) Sarajevo[142] ...

Oh, the rage still evoked by recalling the SerboCroatian carnage, and the Dayton agreement's affirmation of the ethnic cleansing, which, in a way that ze is yet to realise, was a reflection of what had happened generally in Europe after World War II.

Three years from now, ze and J. will have an agitated argument over the symbolic connotations of the World Cup final between France and Croatia. J. finds hir "hang-up" on Croatia (Ustaša, *as ze provocatively calls them*) to be an eccentric whim at par with hir hang-up on Facebook (*as if those were commensurable evils*).

[142]För Sarajevo 1993: 189–207.

To J., Croatia is just the underdog, which he would instinctively support no matter what, whereas *"les bleus"*, regardless of colour and background, represent French arrogance and cowardice (*J. definitely has some hang-up on France*). But to hir, it will be more than a game. Ze is going to watch in silence and suspense. Spellbound. Yes, it's a form of conjuring, although not the kind ze playfully exercises almost every day (*like getting to the mailbox and back before any car passes on the road*). This time it's deadly serious. Like exorcism:

If France wins, there is still hope!

THE POLITICS OF PURITY need neither exemplification nor explanation. They are all over now and it's not difficult to understand their appeal. Identity politics works. But *it also ultimately serves to reinforce the very system that is the source of the symptoms that such politics confines itself to addressing.*[143] What, then, are the politics of *impurity?*

Glissant envisioned a *Politics of Relation* as an archipelago-like configuration of change, and a *politics of creolisation* as the identity that changes in the change.[144] The true radicality of his thought lies perhaps simply in putting an end to an ontological version of identity.[145]

Erasmus suggests *aimance* as a form of affirmative politics grounded in a practice other than identity politics. Aimance, as elaborated in correspondence between the Moroccan philosophers Ghita El Khayat and Abdelkébir Khatibi,[146] is her fourth "art of coming to know otherwise" (the other three being *adversarial manoeuvres, creolisation* and *sociogenesis*). She translates it to "love as political practice", or political will with Eros.[147]

> Love invites beginning, and beginning again, in relation. "Not yet" is a space in which to reconfigure the world (...) "Not yet" is the future in the present ...[148]

*

It may not be a mere coincidence that the formulation of *creolisation* as theoretical approach (and aesthetic strategy) coincided with globalisation and the resurgence of liberalism. (*Not with the neo-liberal market fundamentalism*, nota bene, *which incidentally formed the economic backbone of the 1980s, with its postmodern "happy nihilism". Nor with the neoconservative "clash of civilization" ideology of post 9/11.*) The dynamics of

---

[143] Seshadri-Crooks 2000: 158.
[144] Wald Lasowski 2015: 406.
[145] Noudelmann 2004, in ibid.
[146] Khayat & Khetibi 2010
[147] Erasmus 2017: 143 (italics in original).
[148] Ibid.: 146.

globalisation are akin to those of the early process of creolisation, to the "shock of space and time" of early plantation cultures.[149]

Even enlightened liberals are reluctant to admit that colonialism is the underside of modernity; that the modern world arguably was born in the plantation economies of the New World. Some of their militant opponents to the left, in their turn, fail to acknowledge that the decolonisation they propose de facto also implies de-modernisation.

But the colonial contact cannot be undone. *Relation is the primordial encounter of Modernity.* *Our boats are open.* *Relation is irreversible.*

REFERENCES

Amselle, J.-L. (1990). *Logiques métisses: anthropologie de l'identité en Afrique et ailleurs.* Paris: Payot.

Anguita, E. & M. Caparrós (1997, 1998). *La voluntad. Una historia de la militancia revolucionaria en la Argentina, I-III.* Buenos Aires: Norma.

Chigumadzi, P. (2015). *Sweet Medicine.* Auckland Park: BlackBird Books.

Clarkson, C. (2013 [2009]). *J. M. Coetzee: Countervoices.* Basingstoke: Palgrave Macmillan.

Coetzee, J. M. & D. Attwell (1992). *Doubling the Point: Essays and Interviews.* Cambridge, MA: Harvard University Press.

Coetzee, J. M. & A. Kurtz (2015). *The Good Story: Exchanges on Truth, Fiction and Psychotherapy.* New York: Viking, and imprint of Penguin Radom House LLC.

Dlamini, J. (2009). *Native Nostalgia.* Johannesburg: Jacana.

Dousemetzis, H. & G. Loughran (2019). *The Man Who Killed Apartheid: The Life of Dimitri Tsafendas.* Johannesburg: Jacana.

Drabinski, J. E. (2012). "Vernacular Society: On Gilroy and Levinas". *Levinas Studies* 7: 167–196.

Dubow, S. (2014). *Apartheid 1948–1994.* Oxford: Oxford University Press.

Erasmus, Z. (2017). *Race Otherwise: Forging a New Humanism for South Africa.* Johannesburg: Wits University Press.

Eriksen, T. H. (1993). *Kulturterrorismen: et oppgjør med tanken om kulturell renhet.* Oslo: Spartacus.

---

[149] Lionnet & Shi 2011: 24, 30.

Foucault, M. (2008). *The Birth of Biopolitics: Lectures at the Collège de France*. Ed. by M. Senellart, transl. by G. Burchell. Basingstoke and New York: Palgrave Macmillan.

För Sarajevo!: [en litterär antologi i solidaritet med en belägrad och våldtagen stad i Europa] (1993). Tollarp: Studiekamraten.

Glissant, É. (1997a [1990]). *Poetics of Relation*. Transl. by B. Wing. Ann Arbor: University of Michigan Press [*Poétique de la Relation. Poétique III*. Paris: Gallimard].

Glissant, É. (1997b). *Traité du Tout-Monde. Poétique IV*. Paris: Gallimard.

Glissant, É. (2005). *La cohée du Lamentin. Poétique V*. Paris: Gallimard.

Glissant, É. (2006). *Une nouvelle région du monde. Esthétique I*. Paris: Gallimard.

Glissant, É. (2007). *Mémoires des esclavages, La fondation d'un Centre national pour la mémoire des esclavages et de leurs abolitions*. Paris: Gallimard/La documentation française.

Glissant, É. (2008). *Les entretiens de Bâton Rouge*, avec Alexandre Leupin. Paris: Gallimard.

Hall, S. (2003). "Creolization, Diaspora and Hybridity in the Context of Globalization", in Enzewor, O. (ed.). *Créolité and Creolization*. New York: Distributed Art Publishers.

Heese, H. (2006). *Cape Melting Pot: The Role and Status of the Mixed Population of the Cape, 1652–1795*. Johannesburg: Self-Published [Translation by Delia Robertson of: *Groepe Sonder Grense: Die rolle 'n status van die gemengde bevolking aan die Kap, 1652–1795*. Bellville: University of the Western Cape, 1985].

Hemer, O. (2012a). *Fiction and Truth in Transition: Writing the Present Past in South Africa and Argentina*. Münster: LIT Verlag.

Hemer, O. (2012b). "Hillbrow Blues", in Chapman, M. (ed.). *Africa Inside Out: Stories, Tales & Testimonies*. Scottville: UKZN Press.

Hoge, J. (1972). "Miscegenation in South Africa in the Seventeenth and Eighteenth Centuries", in Valkhoff, M. F. (ed.). *New Lights on Afrikaans and "Malayo-Portuguese"*. Louvain: Peeters/Imprimerie Orientaliste.

Ingold, T. (2007). *Lines: A Brief History*. New ed. London and New York: Routledge.

Ingold, T. (2015). *The Life of Lines*. Abingdon and Oxon: Routledge.

Jansen, J. (2009). *Knowledge in the Blood: Confronting Race and the Apartheid Past*. Stanford: Stanford University Press.

Jansen, J. (2017). *Making Love in a War Zone: Interracial Loving and Learning After Apartheid*. Johannesburg: Bookstorm.

Lionnet, F. & S. Shi (eds.) (2011). *The Creolization of Theory*. Durham, NC: Duke University Press.

Mangcu, X. (2015). "What Moving Beyond Race Can Actually Mean: Towards a Joint Culture", in *The Colour of Our Future*. Johannesburg: Wits University Press.

Martin, D.-C. (1999). *Coon Carnival: New Year in Cape Town, Past and Present.* Cape Town: David Philip.

Martin, D.-C. (2013). *Sounding the Cape: Music, Identity and Politics in South Africa.* Somerset West: African Minds.

Martin, D.-C. (2015). "Le general ne répond pas… Chanson, clip et incertitudes: les jeunes Afrikaners dans la "nouvelle" Afrique du Sud". *L'Homme: Revue Française d'Anthropologie* 215/216: 197–231.

Mazzolini, R. G. (2007). "Las Castas: Interracial Crossing and Social Structure 1770–1835", in Müller-Wille & Rheinberger (eds.). *Heredity Produced: At the Crossroads of Biology, Politics and Culture 1500–1870.* Cambridge, MA: MIT Press.

Mignolo, W. (2012). *Local Histories/Global Designs: Coloniality, Subaltern Knowledges, and Border Thinking.* Princeton: Princeton University Press.

Monahan, M. (2011). *The Creolizing Subject: Race, Reason and the Politics of Purity.* Fordham: Fordham University Press.

Morrison, T. (1997). "Home", in Lubiano, W. (ed.). *The House That Race Built.* New York: Vintage.

Mpofu-Walsh, S. (2017). *Democracy & Delusion: 10 Myths in South African Politics.* Cape Town: Tafelberg.

Müller-Wille, S. & H.-J. Rheinberger (eds.) (2007). *Heredity Produced: At the Crossroads of Biology, Politics and Culture 1500–1870.* Cambridge, MA: MIT Press.

Noah, T. (2016). *Born a Crime: Stories from a South African Childhood.* 1st ed. New York: Spiegel & Grau.

Noudelmann, F. (2004). "Pour une pensée archipélique, Édouard Glissant", in Noudelmann, F., Harvey, R. & E.-A. Kaplan (eds.). *Politique et filiation.* Paris: Éd. Kimé.

Nyamnjoh, F. (2017). "Incompleteness: Frontier Africa and the Currency of Conviviality". *Journal of Asian and African Studies* 52 (3). London: Sage.

Olivier, E. & M. Valentin (2005). "Du mythe à l'histoire", in Olivier & Martin (eds.). *Les bushmen dans l'histoire* 10–38. Paris: CNRS Éditions.

Radano, R. M. (2003). *Lying Up a Nation: Race and Black Music.* Chicago: University of Chicago Press.

Ricœur, Paul (1992 [1990]). *Oneself as Another.* Transl. by Kathleen Blamey. Chicago: University of Chicago Press [*Soi-même comme un autre.* Paris: Seuil].

Rushdie, S. (1992). *Imaginary Homelands: Essays and Criticism 1981–1991.* London: Granta in association with Penguin.

Sarlo, B. (2003). *La pasión y la excepción: Eva, Borges y el asesinato de Aramburu.* Buenos Aires: Siglo Veintiuno Editores.

Seshadri-Crooks, K. (2000). *Desiring Whiteness: A Lacanian Analysis of Race.* London and New York: Routledge.

Wald Lasowski, A. (2015). *Édouard Glissant, penseur des archipels.* Paris: Agora Pocket.

Wicomb, Z. (1998). "Shame and Identity: The Case of the Coloured in South Africa", in Attridge, D. & R. Jolly (eds.). *Writing South Africa: Literature, Apartheid and Democracy 1948–1995.* Cambridge: Cambridge University Press.

van Woerden, H. & D. Jacobson (2001). *The Assassin: A Story of Race and Rage in the Land of Apartheid.* New York: Metropolitan Books.

Yon, D. A. (2007). "Race-Making/Race-Mixing: St Helena and the South Atlantic world". *Social Dynamics* 33 (2): 144–163.

CHAPTER 7

Melville Medley

Perpetual Epilogue to the Faded Hillbrow Blues

(2016)

191
O. Hemer, *Contaminations and Ethnographic Fictions*,
Palgrave Studies in Literary Anthropology,
https://doi.org/10.1007/978-3-030-34925-7_7

Walking the inexistent pavements in Olivedale ...

THE RAIN is pouring from a grey white sky all the way from the airport to the guesthouse. Ze didn't realise that Olivedale is 35 kms from the city centre. When asking hir hostess Sherry-Lynne how to get to downtown Johannesburg without a car, she looks at hir with wide incredulous eyes and answers: "Don't go to downtown Johannesburg!"

It's not one of the posh suburbs, and it's not all white, but people live their suburban lives here without ever setting foot in the city. They shop and dine in the local outdoor malls, around Spar or Checkers, or in nearby *Montecasino*, the huge indoor mall with roofs painted like Italian skies, day and night. Ze goes there starving the first evening after arrival, an expensive quick meal, 120 rand for the Uber in each direction. There is something appealing, and oh so familiar, with the awkwardness, the kitsch, the ugly infrastructure. (*As Aryan will point out when they meet in Greyton a week later, Montecasino is like a free zone, where apartheid is unsettled; in the perverse public space within security walls, whites, Indians, coloureds and the middleclass blacks mingle and even communicate.*) Yes, there is something touchy about decayed kitsch. The imagined Italy. (As Meg says about a scholarship she might be granted; *It's in fucking Rome!*) Why doesn't that Europe appeal to hir? Never did. Ze is just as much a barbarian as hir South African colleagues, but without the colonial hangover.

*

'Erase' is one of the decolonisation buzzwords ...

BEING ERASED. Women being erased by men, blacks by whites, gays by straights. Ze will come up with the counter-suggestion *erace*—but hir wit is not appreciated, or passes unnoticed.

*

An artery of freeways obscenely laid bare, as for a bypass operation ...

THE UBER driver, Lawrence, a law student in his late twenties or early thirties (29, in fact), is to become hir personal driver the coming days (*Fuck Uber!*). It will be far more expensive than if ze had rented a car, but ze is quite happy not to drive in Joburg, and besides ze enjoys Lawrence's company. He has a soundly distanced view on the situation in the country. They talk about the legacy of apartheid, and he tells about the awkwardness in studying law cases from the 1980s, as if there had been no rupture. He was only a boy during the transition and had no strong personal memories of the old regime. Ze asks if his parents took part in the struggle and he shakes his head with an inscrutable smile.

In his smart new Audi A4, Lawrence would appear to be the proverbial BEE, but he's just an ordinary guy, struggling to get his certificate from UNISA and eventually practice as an attorney, while managing to make ends meet by driving for Uber. (*He didn't know the difference between the Commonwealth and the EU. It was somehow all the same, associated with an imaginary white world—Britain, the West, whatever.*)

*

Suddenly the Golden City appears in all its splendour, a modernist mirage, as on Goldblatt's photograph of Joe coming to Joburg with his wife and son ...

THE TRIP from Olivedale to Ponte City and back is one thousand rand. It really feels like an excursion, or a safari. There are tour buses on the driveway to the seven-store garage, but ze can't figure out who the operator is or what kind of tour is being catered. Ze is welcomed by James from *Dlala Nje* in the arcade for youth on the entrance floor. *Dlala Nje* is Zulu for "having fun" and before ze has even fathomed the sensation of actually entering this mythical ghost tower—*the world's first vertical urban slum*—ze is on hir way to the 54th floor in one of the (*how many?*) elevators that were supposedly not functioning during the decades of decay. James takes him to one of the apartments facing (*what direction?*), where ze is received by the co-founder and managing director, Michael L.

Michael tells hir that he used to live in that same apartment for three years (*when he moved in, he was one of the few white tenants; now he has moved on to Melville*). From the window they have a magnificent view over the three *misunderstood areas*, as Michael calls them; Yeoville, Berea and Hillbrow. He talks like a casual salesman. Ponte has now turned into *a beacon of hope for the misunderstood areas*. A little later, he calls it *the Sandton of the area*. All 480 apartments are reportedly rented now, mostly by South Africans and Zimbabweans. The management is charging a premium for security by biometric control [*did ze get that right?*] and has adopted a very discriminatory policy. No Nigerians or Congolese are allowed. And no students. Ten to fifteen percent of the tenants are white.

They look out over Hillbrow. Ze can barely detect Pretoria street in the sunlit haze. Dlala Nje organises street walks every Tuesday (*ze might or might not have wanted to join one; some memories are better left untouched*). There is a lot of street justice in Hillbrow, says Michael. During the xenophobic attacks last year, the minority of native South Africans feared retaliation by the makwerekwere, but the Hillbrow and Berea *afropolitans* did not revenge their brothers and sisters of the townships.

*

THE VIEW to the other side is inwards over the circular shaft—*The Core*— where the pile of garbage rose to the fifth floor (*the* fourteenth, *according to James, but that is clearly an exaggeration*). When cleaned out, the corpses of the suicides appeared—those who didn't die by the fall were eaten alive by the rats. (*Just as many—or more—jumped through the windows on the outside.*) Ever since its inauguration, Ponte City earned a reputation as the Suicide Tower. Not only people throwing themselves, but things being thrown out the windows, have been a major concern through Ponte's history.

> Unidentified flying objects have been waging a reign of terror on pedestrians walking in the grounds of the giant block. The objects range from cast iron statues to beercans, flour and water bombs and bottles. Some objects have also been hurled at pedestrians on nearby pavements (…) [W]alking along the pavements near the skyscraper apartments is highly dangerous – if the death this week of Ponte security guard Harold Thisele is anything to go by. Mr Thisele died after he was struck on the head by a bottle allegedly thrown by tenants at the Ponte City.[1]

*

THE HISTORY of Ponte is documented in a magnificent box with images by South African photographer Mikhael Subotzky and British artist Patrick Waterhouse, supplemented by booklets with texts by various authors, edited by Ivan Vladislavić. It's the result of a six-year project, starting in 2008, after the building had been evicted and another attempted renovation had failed. (*In fact, the decline had started the moment it was opened, in 1976, with an uprising Soweto on the horizon.*)

---

[1] *Out the windows*, text compiled by Ivan Vladislavić in Subotzky, Waterhouse & Vladislavić 2014.

Subotzky & Waterhouse [*sounds like an urban make-over consultancy*] entered the ransacked building and began a systematic inventory of every door, every window, every TV-set, interviewing remaining and incoming tenants and taking their photographs in the notoriously dangerous elevators.

Built for 1500 people, imagined to be young white upward-moving couples, it was to house more than 3500 squatters twenty years later. In 1998, there were serious plans to turn the vertical slum into *the tallest prison in the world*. The idea came from US American architect Paul Silver, who was invited by the city authorities to explore how 2000 awaiting-trial prisoners could be housed close to the courts. After examining various options, Silver suggested Ponte: "It's a lousy apartment building, but a perfect prison".

The conversion plan Silver presented to Correctional Services proposed turning Ponte into 11 vertically stacked prison blocks. Decks were to be constructed over the shaft every five floors, thus creating areas for recreation and observation. Not much would be needed to convert the old apartments into cells – 'each with its own barred picture window' as one journalist put it. All you needed to do was to put locks on the doors.[2]

*

ALTHOUGH the owners of the building fervently supported the prison plan as "an inner-city rejuvenation project", it never happened. Several other, less far-fetched reconstruction attempts have failed after that. The current one is in fact the third since hir earliest acquaintance with the Tower, on that first revisit to Hillbrow in 2006—*or was it even 2005?* ... Ze tries to assume the enthusiasm of *Dlala Nje*, waiting for pizza in the "VIP Area" of the Cito Café on the ground floor, with smartly dressed guys and gals watching a Nollywood soap on the TV, challenging hir preconceptions about hookers and pimps. The Nigerians may be expelled from the apartments but are still running the business. On hir second beer, ze establishes that the Afropolitanism issue requires further interrogation, and that such study will have to be done in Johannesburg, not in Cape Town.

---

[2] *The tallest prison in the world*, note by Ivan Vladislavić in Subotzky, Waterhouse & Vladislavić 2014.

How does afropolitanism relate to creolisation?

*

CAREFUL NOT to get drunk, ze calls Lawrence and walks out of the complex, on to the long dreary ramp, intent on not having hir enthusiasm curbed by the literal hills of garbage, just as ze tries not to be overly depressed by the flickering banners of the student protests: "*Fuck The Rainbow Nation!*"

*

Lost and found in the Troyeville ...

THIS TIME ZE sees Ivan in Rosebank, conveniently on the route from Olivedale. They have met three or four times since the reencounter at De Boekehuis. Their third meeting was in 2011, on hir way to Durban for a two-week guest lectureship at UKZN. The World Cup, which had been the semi-utopian reference-point for hir dissertation, was then still fresh in memory. While waiting for Ivan at the Troyeville, one of the main hubs for the football fans during and between games, ze had been helplessly rapt by a heavy-weight boxing match on the TV over the bar. Ze couldn't figure out whether it was a title match, but ze watched in awe throughout the ten brutal rounds. The white fighter was immediately codified as a Boer, whereas ze impossibly could determine the black boxer's ethnicity. He was like the bull in a bullfight, with a bleeding meat wound on his one cheek, doomed to lose because of that handicap, which was frantically tended to in each break and which he desperately tried to compensate by opening each round in frenzy. By the ninth round they both stumbled like moonwalkers, clinging to each other, absorbing the incredible amounts of beating; then in the beginning of the tenth comes the predictable knockout as the long-awaited relief, a catharsis that passes almost unnoticed in the bar. On hir one side, two chain-smoking mixed-race ladies in multi-coloured hairdos and laughing eyes, on the other a merry company of blacks and Indians downing shots in rainbow colours.

Ze had brought Bolaño's *2666* as a present, after stretch-reading it hirself the preceding days. What fascinated hir the most was the sub-layer that only surfaced at the end; the tracing of the European near-past, by a Chilean descendent ... This time ze thought ze could trace the Croatian heritage in Ivan's solemn face. He was shaken after having been brutally robbed little more than a month ago, yet at the same time still exhilarated by the experience of the World Cup, when people had taken to the streets and temporarily reclaimed the public space. *Was it the remnants of this embryonic public sphere that ze could sense at the bar?*

*

NEXT TIME ze passed by Joburg (three years later) ze would not only eat at the Troyeville's portuguese restaurant but stay in one of the very spartan rooms on top. *Did ze see Ivan then?* Ze can't remember ... *Ivan will remind hir that they actually did have breakfast together one morning. But as they were eating their bacon and eggs, the cleaning staff had mopped down the floors of the dining room with Jeyes fluid, so he wouldn't be surprised if the vile smell of the disinfectant erased the occasion from hir memory.* What ze immediately recalled from that journey was the restless supermarket in front of hir window—*although at 3 in the morning it looked as if it were closed; the man ze had noticed in the afternoon still sat by the entrance, the ironed door half open and the dim light glowing with a blueish sparkle from the interior.* Albertina Sissulo Road dark and silent at night, with an occasional car cruising by. The taxi driver in the archaic Mercedes 220 with ripped leather seats and worn-out switches on the dash-board had never heard of the Troyeville; he drove by the barred hotel entrance twice without noticing it... *now ze remembers the details, because ze found hir notes in a casual diary...* He had driven to Troy street and started looking there, for *any* hotel. His name was Abel, he was from Limpopo, and very talkative. They circled the area for at least half an hour before miraculously eventually reaching the destination. Ze had asked him about the coming elections, and Abel had hissed (*as if imitating Desmond Tutu*) and said: *The ANC is going to lose a lot... That young boy, Malema, is coming... Ooooh!.*

*

NOW, IN ROSEBANK, ze has just read Mark Gevisser's *Lost and Found in Johannesburg*, on Ivan's recommendation. Ze is intrigued by the surprising parallels to Istanbul (obviously inspired by Orhan Pamuk) and, even more, by the Lithuanian connection—or rather the broken connection to the Gevissers' European past; none of the Lithuanian relatives survived the Holocaust. (*As ze will later find out, the great majority of South Africa's Jews—including Meg Vandermerwe—have historical roots in Lithuania.*) Ze had recently been to Vilnius hirself and visited the places of evil, the pockets of amnesia, driven by hir—*in J.'s view "sinister"*—interest in the darkest corners of the human soul [*hir red notebook somewhat cryptically reads:* cosmopolitanism vs. creolisation becomes sharp when put in an Eastern European context].

Ivan has recently returned from Argentina, where he and Zoë Wicomb were the South African representatives in Señor C.'s marvellous connecting of the three Southern nodes, Australia, South Africa and Argentina. Things come together in wondrous ways …

*

Another stop on the way, half a year later …

33 ON 1ST in Melville—a newyorkish kind of guesthouse run by a gay couple—old white, young black in flipflops. Sitting in the backyard with a bathtub-like pool, I just discovered a cockroach on the chair across the table, and another one—or the same, in some Sisyphus circle.

*

The sadness of knowing that this is probably the last night in South Africa in a long time. At Picobella on 4th avenue, which I happen to pass by on my indecisive walk before dusk—up 1st avenue, down 7th street, where I had a coffee in the morning with Michael L. who thanked me for keeping in touch, and then back on 4th without knowing where it would lead. I recognise Picobella as the place where Mariekie took me last time, when I had moved from Sherry-Lynne's B&B to a guesthouse at the far end of 7th street.

Melville is some water hole in this crazy town of brutal beauty and fear. The jacaranda leaves draping the pavements—*not non-existent as in Olivedale but difficult to follow.* Dogs barking as you pass as an unidentified alien, big cars threatening to run over you when you follow the street, non-accustomed to the left-hand traffic. *Oh, but this is so familiar to me, and the sadness comes over me as I finish my meal with a grappa at dusk.*

*

Apropos the apartheid museum …

MARIEKIE SAID that she is tired of feeling guilt. I like to say that she will have to deal with that, possibly for the rest of her life, just as Germany had to let more than one generation bear the guilt of the Holocaust (*yes, they are comparable crimes*), and that every talk about not having to pay a debt anymore is associated with reaction and historical revisionism. Germany is the exemplary state in Europe, but only as long as it keeps paying its debt to history. When right wing populism returns to power in Berlin it will truly be the *Untergang des Aberlandes.*

*

Nats vs. Kats ...

SUMMARISING the tenth visit, that is what South Africa comes down to. Salt and pepper. Blue-eyed Nats, faded beauty but charmingly warm and generous. Bittersweet, hard-working Kats ... *still waiting for hir call, but ze lets the moment pass; yet indeed hoping to be back again in a year or two.*

REFERENCES

Gevisser, M. (2014). *Lost and Found in Johannesburg: A Memoir.* 1st ed. New York: Farrar, Straus and Giroux.

Subotzky, M., Waterhouse, P. & I. Vladislavić (eds.) (2014). *Ponte City: Mikhael Subotzky - Patrick Waterhouse.* 1st ed. Göttingen: Steidl.

Correction to: Bengaluru Boogie

with Photos by Ayisha Abraham

(2013)

Correction to:
Chapter 3 in: O. Hemer, *Contaminations and Ethnographic Fictions*, Palgrave Studies in Literary Anthropology, https://doi.org/10.1007/978-3-030-34925-7_3

In the original version of this chapter, figure text citations were placed throughout. These have been removed.

The updated version of this chapter can be found at
https://doi.org/10.1007/978-3-030-34925-7_3

C1

REFERENCES

Adam, H. & K. Moodley (2013). *Imagined Liberation: Xenophobia, Citizenship and Identity in South Africa, Germany and Canada*. Stellenbosch: SUN Press.

Adair, B. (2004). *In Tangier We Killed the Blue Parrot*. Johannesburg: Jacana.

Amselle, J.-L. (1990). *Logiques métisses: anthropologie de l'dentité en Afrique et ailleurs*. Paris: Payot.

Anguita, E. & M. Caparrós (1997, 1998). *La voluntad. Una historia de la militancia revolucionaria en la Argentina, I-III*. Buenos Aires: Norma.

Appadurai, A. (2006). *Fear of Small Numbers: An Essay on the Geography of Anger*. Durham: Duke University Press.

Appadurai, A. (2013). *The Future as Cultural Fact*. London and New York: Verso.

Appiah, K. A. (2006). *Cosmopolitanism: Ethics in a World of Strangers*. New York and London: W. W. Norton.

Bauman, Zygmunt (1998). *Globalization: The Human Consequences*. London: Polity.

Behr, M. (1995). *The Smell of Apples*. New York: Picador.

Bekker, S. (2010). "Explaining Violence Against Foreigners and Strangers in Urban South Africa: Outbursts During May and June 2008". *The African Yearbook of International Law* 16: 125–149.

Bernabé, J., Chamoiseau, P. & R. Confiant (1993 [1989]). *Éloge de la créolité = In praise of Creoleness*. Edition bilingue français/anglais. Paris: Gallimard.

Breytenbach, B. (1982). *A Season in Paradise*. New York: Persea Books.

Breytenbach, B. (1993). *Return to Paradise*. London: Faber and Faber.

© The Editor(s) (if applicable) and The Author(s),
under exclusive license to Springer Nature Switzerland AG 2020
O. Hemer, *Contaminations and Ethnographic Fictions*,
Palgrave Studies in Literary Anthropology,
https://doi.org/10.1007/978-3-030-34925-7

Butalia, U. (2000). *The Other Side of Silence: Voices from the Partition of India*. London: C. Hurst.

Chigumadzi, P. (2015). *Sweet Medicine*. Auckland Park: BlackBird Books.

Clarkson, C. (2013 [2009]). *J. M. Coetzee: Countervoices*. Basingstoke: Palgrave Macmillan.

Clifford, J. (1986). "Introduction: Partial Truths", in Clifford, J. & G. E. Marcus (eds.). *Writing Culture: The Poetics and Politics of Ethnography*. Berkeley: University of California Press.

Coetzee, J. M. (1988). *White Writing: On the Culture of Letters in South Africa*. New Haven and London: Yale University Press.

Coetzee, J. M. & D. Attwell (1992). *Doubling the Point: Essays and Interviews*. Cambridge, MA: Harvard University Press.

Coetzee, J. M. & A. Kurtz (2015). *The Good Story: Exchanges on Truth, Fiction and Psychotherapy*. New York: Viking, and imprint of Penguin Radom House LLC.

Dalrymple, W. (2002). *White Mughals: Love and Betrayal in Eighteenth-Century India*. London: HarperCollins.

Dangor, A. (2001). *Bitter Fruit*. Cape Town: Kwela.

Das, G. (2002). *The Elephant Paradigm: India Wrestles with Change*. New Delhi: Penguin.

Dlamini, J. (2009). *Native Nostalgia*. Johannesburg: Jacana.

Dlamini, J. (2014). *Askari: A Story of Collaboration and Betrayal in the Anti-Apartheid Struggle*. Johannesburg: Jacana.

Douglas, M. (1966). *Purity and Danger: An Analysis of Concepts of Pollution and Taboo*. London: Routledge & Kegan Paul.

Dousemetzis, H. & G. Loughran (2019). *The Man Who Killed Apartheid: The Life of Dimitri Tsafendas*. Johannesburg: Jacana.

Drabinski, J. E. (2012). "Vernacular Society: On Gilroy and Levinas". *Levinas Studies 7*: 167–196.

Du Toit, P. & H. Kotze (2011). *Liberal Democracy and Peace in South Africa*. Johannesburg: Palgrave Macmillan.

Dubow, S. (2014). *Apartheid 1948–1994*. Oxford: Oxford University Press.

Duschinsky, R. (2013). "The Politics of Purity: When, Actually, Is Dirt Out of Place?" *Thesis Eleven* 119 (1): 63–77.

Eichrodt, W. (1933). *Theologie des Alten Testaments*. Leipzig: Hinrich.

Eiselen, W. W. M. (1920). "Die Naturellevraagstuk: 'n Lesing gehou op 7 Mei 1920 voor die Filosofiese Vereniging van die Universiteit van Stellenbosch".

Eiselen, W. W. M. (1948). "Die Bevolkingsvraagstuk van Suid-Afrika, Sosiologies Beskou met Besondere Aandag aan die Arbeidsgemeenskap van Blankes en Naturelle en die Implikasies van Apartheid," 'n referaat gelewer op die Simposium van i Julie, 1948, van die Jaarvergadering van die Akademie vir Wetenskap en Kuns te Orange Free State.

Erasmus, Z. (2017). *Race Otherwise: Forging a New Humanism for South Africa.* Johannesburg: Wits University Press.

Eriksen, T. H. (1993). *Kulturterrorismen: et oppgjør med tanken om kulturell renhet.* Oslo: Spartacus.

Eriksen, T. H. (1994). "The Author as Anthropologist: Some West Indian Lessons About the Relevance of Fiction for Anthropology", in Archetti, E. P. (ed.). *Exploring the Written: Anthropology and the Multiplicity of Writing.* Oslo: Scandinavian University Press (Universitetsforlaget).

Foucault, M. (2008). *The Birth of Biopolitics: Lectures at the Collège de France.* Ed. by M. Senellart, transl. by G. Burchell. Basingstoke and New York: Palgrave Macmillan.

För Sarajevo!: [en litterär antologi i solidaritet med en belägrad och våldtagen stad i Europa] (1993). Tollarp: Studiekamraten.

Freud, S. (1961). *Civilization and Its Discontents.* 1st American ed. New York: W. W. Norton.

Gellner, E. (1962). "Concepts and Society", in *International Sociological Association. Transactions of the Fifth World Congress of Sociology,* vol. 1. Washington, DC.

van Gennep, A. (1909). *Les rites de passage: étude systématique des rites.* Paris.

Gevisser, M. (2014). *Lost and Found in Johannesburg: A Memoir.* 1st ed. New York: Farrar, Straus and Giroux.

Gibson, W. (1993). "Disneyland with the Death Penalty". *Wired* 1 (4): 51–55.

Gilroy, P. (2004). *After Empire: Melancholia or Convivial Culture?* London: Routledge.

Glissant, É. (1997a [1990]). *Poetics of Relation.* Transl. by B. Wing. Ann Arbor: University of Michigan Press [*Poétique de la Relation. Poétique III.* Paris: Gallimard].

Glissant, É. (1997b). *Traité du Tout-Monde. Poétique IV.* Paris: Gallimard.

Glissant, É. (2005). *La cohée du Lamentin. Poétique V.* Paris: Gallimard.

Glissant, É. (2006). *Une nouvelle région du monde. Esthétique I.* Paris: Gallimard.

Glissant, É. (2007). *Mémoires des esclavages, La fondation d'un Centre national pour la mémoire des esclavages et de leurs abolitions.* Paris: Gallimard/La documentation française.

Glissant, É. (2008). *Les entretiens de Bâton Rouge,* avec Alexandre Leupin. Paris: Gallimard.

Gourevitch, P. (1998). *We Wish to Inform You That Tomorrow We Will be Killed With Our Families: Stories from Rwanda.* New York: Farrar, Straus and Giroux.

Hall, S. (2003). "Creolization, Diaspora and Hybridity in the Context of Globalization", in Enzewor, O. (ed.). *Créolité and Creolization.* New York: Distributed Art Publishers.

Hassim, S., T. Kupe, & E. Worby (eds.) (2008). *South Africa: Go Home or Die Here: Xenophobia and the Reinvention of Difference in South Africa.* Johannesburg: Wits University Press.

Heese, H. (2006). *Cape Melting Pot: The Role and Status of the Mixed Population of the Cape, 1652–1795*. Johannesburg: Self-Published [Translation by Delia Robertson of: *Groep Sonder Grense: Die rolle 'n status van die gemengde bevolking aan de Kap, 1652–1795*. Bellville: University of the Western Cape, 1985].

Hemer, O. (2003). "Indiens Moment 22" (India's Catch 22), unpublished reportage.

Hemer, O. (2011). *Writing Transition: Fiction and Truth in South Africa and Argentina*. Diss. Oslo: University of Oslo.

Hemer, O. (2012a). *Fiction and Truth in Transition: Writing the Present Past in South Africa and Argentina*. Münster: LIT Verlag.

Hemer, O. (2012b). "Hillbrow Blues", in Chapman, M. (ed.). *Africa Inside Out: Stories, Tales & Testimonies*. Scottville: UKZN Press.

Hemer, O. (2014). *Argentinatrilogin* (e-book). Stockholm: Vulkan.

Hemer, O. (2015). "Bengaluru Boogie: Outlines for an Ethnographic Fiction", in Hansen, A. H., Hemer, O. & T. Tufte (eds.). *Memory on Trial: Media, Citizenship and Social Justice*. Berlin: Lit Verlag.

Hemer, O. & H.-Å. Persson (2017). *In the Aftermath of Gezi: From Social Movement to Social Change?* Basingstoke: Palgrave Macmillan.

Hemer, O., M. Povrzanović Frykman, & P.-M. Ristilammi (eds.) (2020). *Conviviality at the Crossroads: The Poetics and Politics of Everyday Encounters*. Basingstoke: Palgrave Macmillan.

Hemmings, C. (1993). "Resituating the Bisexual Body", in Bristow, J. & A. R. Wilson (eds.). *Activating Theory: Lesbian, Gay and Bisexual Politics*. London: Lawrence and Wishart.

Heyn, M. (2003). *The Reluctant Passenger*. Johannesburg: Jonathan Ball.

Hofmeyr, I. (2007). "The Black Atlantic Meets the Indian Ocean: Forging New Paradigms of Transnationalism for the Global South—Literary and Cultural Perspectives". *Social Dynamics* 33 (2): 3–32.

Hofmeyr, I. (2018). "Southern by Degrees: Islands and Empires in the South Atlantic, the Indian Ocean and the Subantarctic World", in Bystom, K. & J. R. Slaughter (eds.). *The Global South Atlantic*. Fordham: Fordham University Press.

Hoge, J. (1972). "Miscegenation in South Africa in the Seventeenth and Eighteenth Centuries", in Valkhoff, M. F. (ed.). *New Lights on Afrikaans and "Malayo-Portuguese"*. Louvain: Peeters/Imprimerie Orientaliste.

Illich, I. (1973). *Tools for Conviviality*. New York: Perennial Library.

Ingold, T. (2007). *Lines: A Brief History*. New ed. London and New York: Routledge.

Ingold, T. (2015). *The Life of Lines*. Abingdon and Oxon: Routledge.

Jansen, J. (2009). *Knowledge in the Blood: Confronting Race and the Apartheid Past*. Stanford: Stanford University Press.

Jansen, J. (2017). *Making Love in a War Zone: Interracial Loving and Learning After Apartheid*. Johannesburg: Bookstorm.

Kaganof, A. (2014). *Night is Coming: Threnody for the Victims of Marikana* (Digital Video). Cape Town: African Noise Foundation.

Kakar, S. (1996). *The Colors of Violence*. Chicago: The University of Chicago Press.

Kentridge, W. (2015). *Refuse the Hour*. A collaboration with Philip Miller, Dada Masilo, Catherine Meyburgh, Peter Galison. Cape Town. 26 and 27 February 2015.

Kraus, C. (2016 [1997]). *I Love Dick*. London: Serpent's Tail.

Krog, A. (1999). *Country of My Skull*. London: Vintage.

Krog, A. (2009). *Begging to Be Black*. Cape Town: Random House Struik.

Kross, C. (2002). "W.W.M. Eiselen: Architect of Apartheid Education", in Kallaway, P. (ed.). *The History of Education Under Apartheid, 1948–1994: The Doors of Learning and Culture Shall Be Opened*. New York: P. Lang.

Lionnet, F. & S. Shi (eds.) (2011). *The Creolization of Theory*. Durham, NC: Duke University Press.

McClintock, A. (1995). *Imperial Leather: Race, Gender and Sexuality in the Colonial Contest*. New York and London: Routledge.

McNeill, J. T. & H. M. Gamer (eds.) (1938). *Medieval Handbooks of Penance*. New York: Columbia University Press.

Maimonides, M. (1956 [1881]). *The Guide for the Perplexed*. 2nd ed. New York: Dover Publications.

Malinowski, B. (ed.) (1938). *International Institute of African Languages and Cultures. Memorandum XV, Methods of Study of Culture Contact in Africa*.

Malouf, D. (1990). *The Great World*. London: Chatto & Windus.

Mangcu, X. (2015). "What Moving Beyond Race Can Actually Mean: Towards a Joint Culture", in *The Colour of Our Future*. Johannesburg: Wits University Press.

Marinovich, G. (2016). *Murder at Small Koppie: The Real Story of the Marikana Massacre*. Cape Town: Penguin.

Martin, D.-C. (1999). *Coon Carnival: New Year in Cape Town, Past and Present*. Cape Town: David Philip.

Martin, D.-C. (2013). *Sounding the Cape: Music, Identity and Politics in South Africa*. Somerset West: African Minds.

Martin, D.-C. (2015). "Le general ne répond pas… Chanson, clip et incertitudes: les jeunes Afrikaners dans la "nouvelle" Afrique du Sud". *L'Homme: Revue Française d'Anthropologie* 215/216: 197–231.

Mazzolini, R. G. (2007). "Las Castas: Interracial Crossing and Social Structure 1770–1835", in Müller-Wille & Rheinberger (eds.). *Heredity Produced: At the Crossroads of Biology, Politics and Culture 1500–1870*. Cambridge, MA: MIT Press.

Memories of Madness: Stories of 1947 (2002). K. Singh: *Train to Pakistan*; B. Sahni: *Tamas*; Manto: *Stories*. New Delhi: Penguin.

Michel, F. (1996). "Do Bats Eat Cats? Reading What Bisexuality Does", in Hall, D. E. & M. Pramaggiore (eds.). *Representing Bisexualities: Subjects and Cultures of Fluid Desire*. New York and London: New York University Press.

Mignolo, W. (2012). *Local Histories/Global Designs: Coloniality, Subaltern Knowledges, and Border Thinking*. Princeton: Princeton University Press.

Millin, S. G. (1924). *God's Stepchildren*. London: Constable.

Mngxitama, A. (2009). "We Are Not All Like That: Race, Class and Nation After Apartheid", in Hassim, S., Kupe, T. & E. Worby (eds.). *Go Home or Die Here: Xenophobia and the Reinvention of Difference in South Africa*, 189–208. Johannesburg: Wits University Press.

Monahan, M. (2011). *The Creolizing Subject: Race, Reason and the Politics of Purity*. Fordham: Fordham University Press.

Morrison, T. (1997). "Home", in Lubiano, W. (ed.). *The House That Race Built*. New York: Vintage.

Moulinier, L. (1952). *Le Pur et l'impure dans la Pensée des Grecs, d'Homére à Aristote*. Paris.

Mpe, P. (2001). *Welcome to Our Hillbrow*. Scottsville: University of KwaZulu-Natal Press.

Mpofu-Walsh, S. (2017). *Democracy & Delusion: 10 Myths in South African Politics*. Cape Town: Tafelberg.

Müller-Wille, S. & H.-J. Rheinberger (eds.) (2007). *Heredity Produced: At the Crossroads of Biology, Politics and Culture 1500–1870*. Cambridge, MA: MIT Press.

Naipaul, V. S. (1964). *An Area of Darkness*. London: Deutsch.

Nair, J. (2005). *The Promise of the Metropolis: Bangalore's Twentieth Century*. New Delhi: Oxford University Press.

Nelson, M. (2015). *The Argonauts*. London: Melville House.

van Niekerk, M. (1999 [1994]). *Triomf*. Transl. by Leon de Kock. London: Little, Brown.

Noah, T. (2016). *Born a Crime: Stories from a South African Childhood*. 1st ed. New York: Spiegel & Grau.

Noudelmann, F. (2004). "Pour une pensée archipélique, Édouard Glissant", in Noudelmann, F., Harvey, R. & E.-A. Kaplan (eds.). *Politique et filiation*. Paris: Éd. Kimé.

Nyamnjoh, F. (2017). "Incompleteness: Frontier Africa and the Currency of Conviviality". *Journal of Asian and African Studies* 52 (3). London: Sage.

Olivier, E. & M. Valentin (2005). "Du mythe à l'histoire", in Olivier & Martin (eds.). *Les bushmen dans l'histoire* 10–38. Paris: CNRS Éditions.

Pani, N., Radhakrishna, S. & K. G. Bhat (eds.) (2010). *Bengaluru, Bangalore, Bengaluru: Imaginations and Their Times*. New Delhi: Sage.

Patton, C. & B. Sánchez-Eppler (2000). *Queer Diasporas*. Durham, NC: Duke University Press.

Rabie, Jan (1964). *Die Groot Anders-Maak*. Cape Town: Human & Roseau.

Radano, R. M. (2003). *Lying Up a Nation: Race and Black Music.* Chicago: University of Chicago Press.

Rao, M. (ed.) (2002). *The Asia Pacific Internet Handbook: Episode IV: Emerging Powerhouses.* New Delhi: Tata McGraw-Hill.

Reilly, J. (2012). *Shame: Confessions of an Aid Worker in Africa.* Cape Town: Jillian Reilly (e-book: lulu.com).

Ricœur, Paul (1992 [1990]). *Oneself as Another.* Transl. by Kathleen Blamey. Chicago: University of Chicago Press [*Soi-même comme un autre.* Paris: Seuil].

Robertson, R. (1992). *Globalization: Social Theory and Global Culture.* London: Sage.

Robins, S. (2016). *Letters of Stone: From Nazi Germany to South Africa.* Cape Town: Penguin.

Rosenberg, D. (2002). *Cloning Silicon Valley: The Next Generation High-Tech Hotspots.* London: Reuters.

Rushdie, S. (1992). *Imaginary Homelands: Essays and Criticism 1981–1991.* London: Granta in association with Penguin.

Saer, J. J. (1997). *El concepto de ficción.* Buenos Aires: Seix Barral.

Sanders, M. (2002). *Complicities: The Intellectual and Apartheid.* Durham, NC: Duke University Press.

Sanders, M. (2007). *Ambiguities of Witnessing: Law and Literature in the Time of a Truth Commission.* Stanford: Stanford University Press.

Sarlo, B. (2003). *La pasión y la excepción: Eva, Borges y el asesinato de Aramburu.* Buenos Aires: Siglo Veintiuno Editores.

Sartre, J.-P. (1948). *Anti-Semite and Jew* [*Réflexions sur la question juive*]. New York: Schocken Books.

Seshadri-Crooks, K. (2000). *Desiring Whiteness: A Lacanian Analysis of Race.* London and New York: Routledge.

Singhal, A. & E. M. Rogers (2001). *India's Communication Revolution: From Bullock Carts to Cybermarts.* New Delhi: Sage.

South Africa, Truth and Reconciliation Commission (1999). *TRC Report, vol. 1–5.* London: Macmillan.

Steinberg, J. (2014). *A Man of Good Hope.* Johannesburg and Cape Town: Jonathan Ball.

Stobie, C. (2007). *Somewhere in the Double Rainbow: Representations of Bisexuality in Post-Apartheid Novels.* Scottsville: University of KwaZulu-Natal Press.

Subotzky, M., Waterhouse, P. & I. Vladislavić (eds.) (2014). *Ponte City: Mikhael Subotzky - Patrick Waterhouse.* 1st ed. Göttingen: Steidl.

Söderblom, S. (2009). "Anteckningar om senfärdigheten – om ansatser till konstnärlig forskning inom det litterära området", in Lind, T. (ed.). *Konst och forskningspolitik: konstnärlig forskning inför framtiden.* Stockholm: Vetenskapsrådet.

Tilly, C. (2006). *Why?: [What Happens When People Give Reasons... and Why]*. Princeton, NJ: Princeton University Press.

von Tunzelmann, A. (2007). *Indian Summer: The Secret History of the End of an Empire*. London: Simon & Schuster.

Vaknin, S. (2011). *Malignant Self-Love: Narcissism Revisited*. Prague: Narcissism Publishers.

Vandermerwe, M. (2013). *Zebra Crossing*. Cape Town: Umuzi.

Vladislavić, I. (2002). *The Restless Supermarket*. Claremont: David Philip.

Vladislavić, I. (2007 [2006]). *Portrait with Keys*. London: Portobello.

Volkan, V. (2006). *Killing in the Name of Identity*. New York: Ingram.

Wald Lasowski, A. (2015). *Édouard Glissant, penseur des archipels*. Paris: Agora Pocket.

Watson, G. (1970). *Passing for White: A Study of Racial Assimilation in a South African School*. London: Tavistock Publications.

Wicomb, Z. (1998). "Shame and Identity: The Case of the Coloured in South Africa", in Attridge, D. & R. Jolly (eds.). *Writing South Africa: Literature, Apartheid and Democracy 1948–1995*. Cambridge: Cambridge University Press.

Wicomd, Z. (2006). *Playing in the Light*. New York and London: The New Press.

Wicomb, Z. (2014). *October*. Cape Town: Umuzi.

Wicomb, Z. (2018). *Race, Nation, Translation: South African Essays, 1990–2013*. Johannesburg: Wits University Press.

Willoughby, G. (2002). *Archangels*. Howick: Brevitas Publishers.

van Woerden, H. & D. Jacobson (2001). *The Assassin: A Story of Race and Rage in the Land of Apartheid*. New York: Metropolitan Books.

Yon, D. A. (2007). "Race-Making/Race-Mixing: St Helena and the South Atlantic world". *Social Dynamics* 33 (2): 144–163.

Index

A

Abomination, 51, 53, 171
Aboriginal, 149, 172
Acculturation, 178
Adam, Heribert, 43, 49, 50, 72, 73, 102
Adversarial conceptual manoeuvres, 169
Aesthetics
  Aesthetics of the Earth, 172
Africanisation, 164
Afrikaans, 38, 60, 75, 79, 97–100, 121, 126, 180
Afrikaaps, 173, 174
Afrikanerdom, 58, 101, 131, 132, 158, 159
Afropolis, 14
  Afropolitanism, 164, 195, 196
Ahlmark, Per, 33
Ahmedabad, 18, 20
Aimance, 185
Allesverloren, 8, 96
Anarchism, 28

ANC, 43, 47, 57, 63, 68, 102, 163, 197
Ancestry, 53, 92, 111, 139, 180
  mixed ancestry, 143, 148
  pure ancestry, 143, 148
Anglo-Boer War, 94, 132
  South African War, 79
Anglo-Indian, 24, 25, 35
Anima, 61
Animal, 59, 61, 73, 108
Anschluss, 135
Anthropology, 3–5, 38, 44, 100, 158
Anti-Colonial, 171
Anti-Semite, 81
Apartheid, 8, 9, 12, 14, 38–43, 45–47, 53, 57, 58, 63, 70, 81, 82, 101, 102, 121, 139, 140, 149, 150, 158, 161, 162, 168, 169, 179, 182, 192
  Apartheid Museum, 198
Appadurai, Arjun, 20, 26, 72
Appiah, Kwame Anthony, 5
Aramburazo, 46

Argentina, 3, 9, 24, 31, 43, 63, 111,
  140, 183, 198
Argentina trilogy, 4, 71, 178
Askari, 47
ASMR, 146
Athlone, 141
Atlantic
  Black Atlantic, 134
  South Atlantic, 95, 139
Atonement, 46
Australia, 19, 38, 63, 130, 131, 198
Authenticity
  authentic, 13, 151, 178
Autism, 166
  autist, 105, 129, 144
Autobiography, 45, 130
Auto-ethnography, 7, 158, 177

B
Baartman, Sartjie, 108
Balkan, 48
Ballito, 147
Bangalore, Bengaluru, 18, 19, 21–23,
  26, 27, 29, 35, 63, 72, 118, 123
Bangladesh, 101
Bantustan, 40, 43
Baraka, 68
Barbarian, 13, 39, 57, 116, 131, 192
Bartok, Béla, 70, 135
Bastard, 53, 58, 59, 71, 85, 100
Baster
  basterskap, 58
  bastertaal, 58
  bastervolk, 58
Batavia, 150, 180
Bauman, Zygmunt, 31
Bechuana, 54
Behr, Mark, 101, 102, 180
Berea, 13, 193, 194
Bhabha, Homi, 101, 102, 105

Biko, Steve, 150
Biology, 142
Biopolitics, 142
Bird Island, 94
Bisexuality, 101, 102
Bitterfontein, 96
Black Consciousness, 82, 149, 164,
  168, 171
Blackness, 139, 143, 148, 152–154,
  179, 183
Black-on-black violence, 118
Bloch, Ernst, 171
Boekehuis, De, 14, 196
Boer, 53, 54, 61, 73, 79, 92, 95, 120,
  126, 196
Bolaño, Roberto, 196
Bollhuset (Uppsala), 66, 180
Bolsonaro, Jair, 183
Border, 7, 13, 28, 60, 62, 63, 72, 80,
  85, 99, 104, 124, 149, 170
Borges, Jorge Luis, 5, 126, 127, 131,
  135, 145
Brahmin, 24, 33
Brazil, 111, 161, 183
Breytenbach, Breyten, 58, 59, 81–83,
  97
Brink, André, 93
British
  British colonies, 143, 171
  British imperialism, 171
  colonial rule, 39
Broederbond, Afrikaner, 158, 159
Brown, Norman O., 71
Bruin-mense, 38, 82, 85
Bryanston, 146, 147
Buddhism, buddhist, 137
Buenos Aires, 13, 90, 108, 179
Burton, Sir Richard, 23
Bushman
  bushman hunt, 101
Butalia, Urvashi, 49

C

California ideology, The, 29
Calvinia, 96
Calvinism, 132, 158
Cameroon, 118
Cantonment, The, 22
Cape, The, 8, 41, 60, 85, 100, 103, 109, 134, 139, 148, 173, 176, 177
Cape Town, 2, 43, 55, 56, 70, 79, 83, 91, 96, 100, 119–121, 129, 134, 139, 141, 144, 149, 164, 168, 173, 180, 195
Caribbean, 6, 8, 108, 111, 112, 134, 170
Carmichael, Stokely, 45
Caste, 32, 49, 74
  caste hierarchy, 27, 74
  caste system, 74, 143
Caucasus, *Caucasian*, 138
Cedarberg, 91
Chapman, Michael, 140
Chastity, 34, 49
Chatwin, Bruce, 94
Chiloé, 94
Christ, Christian, 54, 77, 137, 143, 173
Chronology, 62, 137
City, The, 7, 14, 22, 24, 42, 61, 70, 117, 169, 192, 195
Civil Rights Movement, 23
Clanwilliam, 91, 96
Clarke's Bookstore (Cape Town), 176
Clarkson, Carrol, 126, 127
Clifford, James, 5
Coertze, Peter, 158, 159
Coetzee, J.M., 6, 54, 126, 127, 131, 179, 180
Cold War, 172
Collaboration, 22, 47, 68–70, 80, 180
Colombia, 63, 111, 124, 143

Coloured, 13, 25, 41, 57, 63, 82, 84, 92, 121, 139, 140, 148–151, 154, 161, 162, 174, 179, 192
Commonwealth, The, 193
Communalism, 27, 61
Communal violence, 2, 27
Complicity, 47, 81, 82, 84, 180
Conqueror, Conquest, 22, 116, 117, 122, 152
Contamination, 5, 6, 8, 9, 42, 52, 57, 63, 68, 70, 102, 103
Convergence, 4, 27
Conviviality, 60, 109, 138, 139, 167, 170
Cooke Town, 31, 35
Coolie, 73, 74
Coon Festival, 41
Coorg, 72
Copenhagen, 105
Corruption, 26, 27
Cosmopolitanism, 22, 45, 60, 139, 167, 170, 171, 183, 198
  cosmopolitanism from below, 28
  vernacular cosmopolitanism, 30, 156
Creolisation, 3, 8, 53, 57, 103, 109, 111, 112, 119, 134, 135, 138, 139, 142, 150, 170, 171, 177, 178, 180, 183, 185, 186, 196, 198
Creole Manifesto, 6, 110, 135
Criollo, 148
Croatia, 183
Cross-genre, 3, 6, 8
Cuba, 111
Cubbon Park, 22, 31
Culture(s), 38, 41, 43, 57, 58, 63, 64, 73, 85, 110, 111, 116, 119, 123, 128, 140, 148, 150, 153, 157, 162, 168, 172, 178, 182
  culture terrorism, 140

D
Dala, Zainub, 83
Dalit, 23, 27, 33
Dalrymple, William, 23
Darwin, Charles, 43
David, 137
Decolonisation, 153, 155, 163, 164,
  186, 192
De Klerk, F.W., 79
De La Rey, Koos, 79
Deleuze, Gilles, 116, 135
Delhi Case, The, 18, 27
Democracy, 7, 33, 63, 69, 101, 153,
  165
  democratisation, 164
Descartes, René, 119
Desire, 105, 115, 116, 144, 154, 160,
  161
De Sousa Santos, Boaventura, 135
De-westernisation, 164
Dirt, 41, 44, 48, 68, 80, 92, 102,
  104
Disgrace, 129
Dissertation, 3, 4, 7, 56, 62, 76, 178,
  196
Diversity, 32, 41, 43, 138, 177
Dlala Nje, 193–195
Dlamini, Jacob, 47, 68, 178
Dominance, Domination
  cultural, 119
  male, 76
  racial, 82
Douglas, Mary, 2, 40, 41, 44, 51, 52,
  60, 61, 64, 67, 68, 71, 72, 74,
  78, 81, 83, 108, 133, 160
Drabinski, John E., 156
Durban, 23, 42, 45, 79, 83, 117, 126,
  144, 147, 176, 196
Durkheim, Émile, 44
Dutch, 48, 79, 97, 121, 130, 139,
  149, 158, 180
Duterte, Rodrigo, 183

Dylan, Bob, 101
Dystopia, 183

E
Einstein, Albert, 119
Eiselen, Werner, 38, 57, 58, 158, 159
Electronic City, 29
El Khayat, Ghita, 185
Emergency, State of, 39, 69
Epic, 137
Erasmus, Zimitri, 82, 108, 134,
  138, 139, 142, 143, 148–150,
  152–156, 160–162, 169–171,
  178, 179, 185
Eriksen, Thomas Hylland, 4, 140
Eros, 185
  eroticism, 71, 74
Errantry, 112, 116, 117, 178, 182
Essence, 108, 111
eThekwini, 83
Ethiopia, 42, 110
Ethnicity, 101, 138, 196
Ethnographic fiction, 8, 25, 63, 145
Ethnography, 3, 5, 108, 177
EU, 90, 180, 193
Eugenics, 100
Europe, 2, 8, 20, 57, 58, 82, 96, 138,
  141, 173, 183, 192, 199
  Eastern Europe, 12, 138, 139
Exile, 43, 45, 56, 63, 105, 116, 117,
  168, 178
Expanse, 162, 166

F
Facebook, 29, 30, 183
Faroe Islands, The, 94
#FeesMustFall movement, 168
Fiction, 3–5, 7, 62, 71, 91, 99, 130,
  132, 136, 145, 152, 153
Fictionalisation, 4

Filiation, 111, 137, 138, 142, 162, 166
First Nation, 151
Fischer, Eugen, 100
Fish River Canyon, 104
Foucault, Michel, 142
Fox News, 27
France, 183, 184
Francis, Pope, 31
Fraser Town, 31
Freedom Charter, The, 156, 164
Free State, The, 160, 161
Freud, Sigmund, 72, 125
Frontier, 27, 29, 109, 123
Fundamentalism, 28, 185

G
Gaucho, 131, 145
Geertz, Clifford, 116
Gemeinschaft, 61
Gender, 7, 18, 34, 53, 99, 101, 102
Genealogy, 100, 138, 142
Generalisation, 137
Genetic variation, 8, 56
Genocide, 20, 28, 39, 100, 183
German Democratic Republic, 9
Germany, 43, 73, 198, 199
Gesellschaft, 61
Gevisser, Mark, 197
Gibson, William, 22
Gilroy, Paul, 60, 156
Glissant, Édouard, 2, 6, 82, 108, 110–112, 116, 117, 119, 120, 122, 126–128, 135–137, 139, 142, 156–158, 162, 166, 170, 172, 182, 185
Globalisation, 6, 31, 110, 120, 124, 185, 186
Glocalisation, 125
God, 44, 53, 104, 137
Goldwater, Barry, 48

Goodall, Jane, 30
Goodman, Benny, 135
Gopal, Ram, 35
Gourevitch, Philip, 20
Greece, 27, 121
Greek, 5, 44, 77, 120, 121
Greyton, 155, 192
Group Areas Act, 39
Guano republic, 94
Guattari, Félix, 116
Gujarat, 20, 32, 33
Gumilla, José, 143

H
Hall, Stuart, 148
Hani, Chris, 68
Hannerz, Ulf, 111
Harlem Renaissance, 14
Hell Fire Club, 48
Heredity, 142, 143, 160, 171
Herero, 100, 101
Hermaphrodite, 18, 34, 101
Hermeneutics
  pluritopic hermeneutics, 170
Heteronormativity, 102
Hierarchy, Social, 74, 150
Hijra, 101
Hillbrow, 12–15, 146, 193–195
Hindu, 25, 30, 32, 34, 73, 74
  Hindu nationalism, 22
History, 4, 12, 23, 35, 47, 63, 64, 76, 84, 101, 109, 116, 120, 123, 131, 137, 150, 161–163, 171, 176, 194, 199
Hofmeyr, Isabel, 134
Holiness, 52
Holocaust, 20, 27, 39, 101, 138, 149, 197, 198
Homeland, 40, 63
Homonormativity, 102
Houston, Whitney, 95

Humanism, 169, 171
humaning, 142, 179
Humour, 72
Hybrid, 5, 25, 52, 54, 57, 101
    hybridity, 53, 58, 112

I

Identity, 43, 49, 53, 58, 73, 80, 95,
    109, 116, 126, 140, 144, 179,
    182
    identity politics, 2, 99, 102, 119,
    155, 156, 169, 185
Iliad, The, 137
Immigration, 13, 143
Immorality Act, 45, 161
Impurity, 2, 3, 8, 44, 46, 54, 61, 72,
    108, 109, 148, 185
Incompleteness, 109
Indian Ocean, 134, 139
Indigeneity, 143, 148
Indirect rule, 39
Individuation, 137
Informatisation, 29
Ingold, Tim, 139, 142, 170
Inheritance, 142, 160, 162, 171
Interregnum, 42, 62, 83, 138
Israel, 20, 101, 121
Istanbul, 27, 35, 79, 197
Italy, 192

J

Jahangeer, Doung, 176
Jansen, Jonathan, 160, 161, 170
Java, 139
Jazz, 45, 48, 135
Jew, Jewish, 20, 45, 49, 66, 73, 77,
    100, 101, 140, 143, 180, 197
Johannesburg, 7, 14, 55, 126, 140,
    143, 146, 159, 192, 195, 197
July Systems, 19

K

Kaffir, 59, 73
Kaganof, Aryan, 69
Kakar, Sudhir, 73
Kannada, 22, 25, 27
Kant, Immanuel, 108
Karnathaka, 72
Karoo, 38, 139
Kashmir, 27
Kayelitsha, 140
Kentridge, Bill, 70, 96
Khatibi, Abdelkébir, 185
Khoena, Khoikhoi, 150, 151
Khoisan, 150, 151, 180
Khomeini, Ayatollah, 6
Kirschner, Cristina, 63
Kliprand, 91, 92, 96
Königsberg, 100
Kraus, Chris, 5, 6, 103, 145
Krog, Antjie, 75, 79, 80, 92, 179, 181
Kronhausen, Phyllis and Eberhard,
    181
Kurtz, Arabella, 130–132, 179
KwaZulu-Natal, 161
Kwerekwere, pl. *Makwerekwere*, 13, 49,
    50, 163

L

Laing, Ronald D., 105
Laing, Sandra, 162
Lal Bagh, 21
Lambert's Bay, 94
Land Beacons Act, 100
Language, 22, 34, 58, 60–63, 79, 82,
    97, 98, 108, 111, 122, 126–128,
    145, 150, 177
Late Nite News, 63
Latin America, 8, 30, 111, 183
Law, 38, 58, 61, 67, 75, 100, 124,
    149, 160, 171, 192
Le Corbusier, 38

Legitimacy, 137, 138, 142, 162, 173
Leiwater, 51, 55, 181
Les Lilas, 177
Lévinas, Emmanuel, 156
Leviticus, 51, 52
Liberalism, 183, 185
Libertarian socialism, 28
Lindahl, Hans, 124, 143
Linux spirit, The, 29
Literature, 2–4, 14, 54, 61, 99, 122,
    134, 145, 146, 177
literary practice, 2, 4
Lithuania, Lithuanian, 197
Load shedding, 39, 60, 109
London, 55, 177
Long Street (Cape Town), 141, 173,
    174
Look, The, 140, 152, 154–156, 161, 169
Love, 23, 70, 90, 93, 104, 113, 173,
    185
Lund, 56, 75
Lurie, David, 105, 129, 136

M
Madagascar, 150, 180
Magic, 44, 60
Maimonides, 51
Majority, 20, 27, 66, 70, 80, 97, 153,
    164, 180, 197
Malan, D.F., 38
Malema, Julius, 50, 163
Malmö, 13, 18, 33, 45, 56, 75, 95,
    113, 155, 161, 163, 179
Malvinas, 94
Mandela, Nelson, 48, 79, 146, 182,
    183
Mander, Harsh, 23, 31
Mangcu, Xolela, 153
Marikana, 69, 70, 155
Martin, Denis-Constant, 41, 53,
    79, 119, 120, 128, 134, 135,
    148–151, 167, 172

Marvel Bar (Cape Town), 141, 174,
    176, 181
Masculinity, 144
Matrilineal, 77
matrilinearity, 49
Maxwele, Chumani, 152
Mbembe, Achille, 163, 164
McClintock, Anne, 53
Mediterranean, 137, 180
Melting pot, 134, 139, 148
Melville, 14, 126, 145, 146, 193, 198
Memory, 2, 12, 18, 22, 25, 33, 48,
    69, 75, 77, 95, 104, 112, 114,
    117, 124, 125, 127, 129, 132,
    146, 161, 163, 178, 179, 193,
    194, 196, 197
Meshworks, 139, 142
Mestizo, 148
Métissage, 112, 134, 138, 143
Mignolo, Walter, 124, 139, 170
Millin, Sarah Gertrude, 54
Million Programme, 45
Mimicry, 38, 108, 125, 145
Minority, 20, 25, 53, 72, 74, 77, 82,
    164, 194
Miscegenation, 23, 53, 54, 70, 100,
    149, 160
Misiones, 4, 25, 124
Mission, 100
    mission education, 58, 171
Mixing, 52–54, 56, 58, 68, 108, 138
Modernity, 14, 39, 40, 64, 119, 123,
    139, 186
Modi, Narendra, 32, 33, 183
Monahan, Michael, 170
Monolingualism, 99, 122
Montecasino, 192
Montesquieu, Charles-Louis de
    Secondat, 5
Montreal, 8, 118
Moodley, Kogila, 43, 49, 50, 72, 73
Morin, Edgar, 69, 70
Morrison, Toni, 142, 153, 169

Moulinier, Louis, 44
Mozambique, 120, 150
Mpe, Phaswane, 13
Mpofu-Walsh, Sizwe, 153
Mulato, 148
    mulata, 161
Multilingualism, 122
Multinationalism, 82
Multiracialism, 171
Muslim, 25, 27, 32, 34, 73, 101, 143
Mysore, 22, 24
Myth, 14, 137, 150, 153

N
Naipaul, V.S., 21, 74
Nama, 100, 101
Namaqualand, 42, 91, 94, 96
Namibia, 42, 91, 100, 104
Narcissism, 28, 72
    predatory narcissism, 20
Nationalism, 2, 8, 22, 164, 171, 182
National Party, 38, 159
Native, 145, 149, 171, 194
    going native, 148
Nazi Germany, 66, 100, 132
Necklacing, 50, 68
Neo-apartheid, 73
Neo-conservativism, 185
Neo-liberalism, 43
Neo-nationalism, 2
New Contrast, 168
Newness, 158
New World, 8, 31, 111, 186
New York, 46, 162, 177
Ngũgĩ wa Thiong'o, 122
Nigeria, 127
Nixon, Rob, 124
Noah, Trevor, 178
Non-racialism, 156, 164, 171, 183
Nonxuba, Athabile, 152

Norén, Lars, 62, 126, 127
Nostalgia, Nostalgic, 30, 35, 62, 122,
    179, 181, 182
Not-yet, 147, 171, 173, 179, 180
Novel, 3–5, 8, 13, 14, 54, 62, 63, 71,
    74, 83, 85, 91–93, 96, 97, 101,
    102, 118, 126, 127, 136, 145,
    161, 176, 179
Nuttall, Sarah, 163, 182

O
Obama, Barack, 23, 68, 164
Observatory, 13
Öcalan crisis, 27
Odyssey, The, 138
Olivedale, 145, 192, 193, 196, 198
Ollantaytambo, 75
Olofsson, Dan, 161
Opacity, 2, 127, 128, 137, 138, 157,
    166, 167
Open Stellenbosch movement, 154, 155
Oppenheim, Joshua, 69
Orality, 120
Origin, 5, 22, 53, 97, 111, 143, 161,
    170
Ossewabrandwag, 158
Österlen, 75

P
Pakistan, 27
Palme, Olof, 33
Paris, 5, 8, 70, 108, 110, 135, 177
Park Lane Village (Johannesburg),
    146, 147
Partition, The, 34
Pat Garrett and Billy the Kid, 71
Perpetration, 50
    perpetrator, 20, 23, 43, 47, 50, 69,
        72, 73, 81, 101

Phillips, Anne, 79
Philosophy, 6, 83, 108, 137, 170
Pietermaritzburg, 8, 109, 114, 139,
144, 146, 147, 178
Piketberg, 91
Plaatje, Sol, 54, 171
Plantation culture, 186
Plato
platonic dialogue, 130
Poetics, 112, 116, 117, 120, 122,
123, 127, 157
Pofadder, 96
Pogroms, 20, 27
Pollution, 44, 49, 61, 67, 68, 72, 74,
81
pollution rules, 76
sex pollution, 77, 78
Ponte City, 13, 193, 194
Population Registration Act, 149
Populism, 2, 199
Post-apartheid, 69, 118
Postcard Café (Stellenbosch), 181
Post-modernity, 64
Pragmatism, 61, 153
Pretoria, 56, 159
Pretoria Central Prison, 121
Pretoria Street (Johannesburg), 12,
13, 15, 194
Primitive, 2, 44, 60, 64, 76, 151
Projection, 73, 90, 113, 172
project, 3, 4, 7, 22, 42, 56, 62, 63,
65, 70, 75, 80, 110, 111, 118,
125, 136, 137, 140, 153, 155,
164, 177, 180, 183, 194, 195
Promiscuity, 74
promiscuous, 47, 114, 134
Property, 142
propertied, 33
Psychoanalysis, 130
psychoanalytic, 74

Purity, 2, 8, 44, 49, 53, 58, 81, 83,
101, 108, 142, 143, 148, 160
politics of purity, 8, 39, 185

Q
Québec, 122

R
Race, 19, 42, 45, 53, 54, 80, 92, 99,
101, 108, 124, 137–140, 142,
143, 145, 148, 149, 152–154,
156–161, 169, 179
race categories, 148, 149, 169, 179
race classification, 138, 142, 162
Racial
racial anxiety, 154
racialise, 135, 138, 139, 152, 153,
156, 160, 161, 169, 171
racial justice, 153
Rainbow Nation, 118, 121, 156
Ravan Press, 12
Reader, Reading, 7, 12, 19, 24, 25,
39, 42, 43, 48, 55, 66, 80, 83,
91, 97, 99, 102, 104, 126, 128,
132, 135, 139, 152, 156, 172,
177, 179, 182, 196
Reclassification, 121
Reddy, Rajesh, 19
Rehoboth, 100, 101
Relation, 6, 32, 60, 61, 76, 77, 82,
91, 99, 108, 111, 112, 114–117,
119, 122, 123, 125–128, 134,
137, 142, 143, 151, 154, 157,
158, 160, 164, 166, 170, 178,
185, 186
Poetics of Relation, 7, 82, 108, 110,
111, 117, 119, 120, 122, 123,
134, 172, 182

Relativity, 119
Reproduction, 142
Reservation, 27, 32
Resnais, Alain, 33
The Restless Supermarket, 12, 147, 197
Rhizome, 117
 rhizomatic thought, 116, 182
Rhodes, Cecil, 2, 50, 53, 149, 163
#Rhodes Must Fall movement, 118,
 152–154, 168
Ribeiro, Darcy, 111
Rimbaud, Arthur, 110, 116, 119, 123
Ritual, 19, 44, 50, 61, 65, 67, 69
Robertson, Roland, 6
Robertson Smith, William, 44
Robins, Steven, 100, 101
Rogers, Everett, 29
Rome, 192
Rondebosch, 168
Root, 46, 52, 57, 81, 111, 116, 161,
 182, 197
Rosebank, 196, 197
Rouch, Jean, 69, 70
Rushdie, Salman, 5, 6, 83, 158
Rwanda, 20, 183

S
Sachs, Albie, 169
Saer, Juan José, 5, 8
San, 100, 101, 150, 151
Sanders, Mark, 47, 53, 58, 81, 82
Sarajevo, 138, 183
Sarlo, Beatriz, 46, 145
Scandinavia, 9, 48, 94
Schmitt, Carl, 124
Schreiner, Olive, 53
Sea Point, 103, 141, 145, 168
Sedibe, Glory, 47
Separate development, 38, 53
Seshadri-Crooks, Kalpana, 152, 154,
 160, 169, 185
Sexuality, 49, 53, 77, 101

Shame, 45, 54, 102, 148
Silver, Paul, 195
Singapore, 22
Singh, Manmohan, 23
Sjöblom, Ulla, 33
Slavery, 111, 138, 139
Slum, 14, 29, 193, 195
Snobs, The, 48
Solidarity, 35, 76
Somali, 42, 49, 84
Sophiatown, 14
Soweto, 42, 69, 146, 194
Spain, 9, 121
Species, 44, 52, 137, 142, 143
Spencer, Herbert, 44
Springbok Pub, The, 84, 85
Srishti, 23, 32, 33
Steinberg, Jonny, 49, 56, 140
Stellenbosch, 38, 39, 42, 48, 56, 69,
 70, 75, 84, 85, 91, 96, 97, 102,
 104, 118–120, 139, 155, 162,
 163, 165
Sterkfontein, psychiatric hospital,
 121
St. Helena Island, 139
Stobie, Cheryl, 7, 101–103
Stockholm, 30, 45, 66, 79, 114
St. Paul, 77
Stream of consciousness, 7
Street children, 23
Student movement, 155
 student revolt, 2
Subotzky, Mikhael, 194, 195
Sugar Ship, The, 95
Svensktoppsmusik, 94
Swaartland, 91
Sweden, Swedish, 4, 7, 22, 26, 35, 45,
 46, 48, 56, 62, 63, 66, 79, 92,
 94, 98, 99, 111, 113, 118, 124,
 126, 127, 129, 135, 136, 140,
 141, 161, 173, 174, 179–181
Symbolism, 67, 72
 symbolic system, 74

T

Tamil, 22, 25, 27
Tanganyika, Lake, 30
Tanzania, 30
Tearle, Aubrey, 12
Terence, Publius Terentius Afer, 5
Theoretical fiction, 6
Thick description, 116
Third Reich, 140, 180
Tilly, Charles, 42, 56
Time of the Writer, 83, 122, 126
Times of India, 23
Tipu Sultan's fort, 22
Totalitarian, 116, 157, 182
Totality, 117, 119, 123, 124, 153,
    154, 157, 182
Tourist, 31, 94, 104, 178
Tout-Monde, 119, 151
Tragedy, 5, 137
Transdisciplinary intervention, 63
Transformation, 3, 7, 13, 14, 30, 35,
    120, 153
Transgression, 4, 41, 83
Transition, 2, 7, 9, 12, 47, 52, 58, 67,
    101–103, 172, 178, 193
    Transition trilogy, 80
Transparency, 2, 26, 128, 137, 166,
    167
Travelogue, 94
Trekboer, 100
Tribe, 13, 60, 85, 131, 147, 149
    tribal, 38, 58, 138
Triomf, 14
Troell, Jan, 33
Troubadour, 116
Troyeville, 196, 197
Trump, Donald, 183
Truth, 66, 74, 81, 90, 92, 114, 127,
    130, 175, 182
    Truth and Reconciliation
        Commission (TRC), 47, 70, 81
Tsafendas, Dmitri, 120, 121

Turning Torso, 13
Tutuola, Amos, 109
Tylor, Edward Burnett, 43, 44

U

Uber, 192, 193
UNESCO Courier, 135
Union, 39, 53, 54, 183
    Union government, 149, 159
UNISA, 193
Universality, 137, 173
Uppsala, 66, 180
Urbanity, 30
USA, 19, 20, 135, 164
Ustaša, 183
Utopia, 101, 102

V

Vaalputs, 96
Vagabond, 31
Vandermerwe, Meg, 92, 168, 197
Van der Waal, Kees, 158
Van Gennep, Arnold, 52, 66
Van Niekerk, Marlene, 14, 163
Van Wyk, Arnold, 98, 99
Van Wyk Louw, N.P., 82
Varanasi, 18, 19, 21
Verkramptes, 158
Verligtes, 158
Verwoerd, Hendrik, 38, 58, 84, 120,
    121, 158
Victoria Market (Durban), 117
Vilnius, 197
Violence
    communal violence, 2, 27
    mass violence, 20
    sexual violence, 23, 26
Virginity, 77, 78
Vladislavić, Ivan, 12–14, 194, 195
Vlakplaas, 47

Volkekunde, 38, 57, 84, 158, 159
Voortrekker, 58, 95
Vorster, B.J. (John), 38, 84, 120, 162

W
Walcott, Derek, 108
Wald Lasowski, Aliocha, 119, 122,
    135, 156, 182, 185
Waltic, 79
Waterhouse, Patrick, 194, 195
Watson, Stephen, 85, 168
Webster, Eddie, 140
Western
    culture, 116
    imaginary, 148
    mythology, 137
    thought, 137, 166
Western Cape, 8, 47, 69, 79
Whiteness, 130, 143, 148, 152–154,
    160, 161, 164, 183
Wholeness, 20, 52, 152
Wicomb, Zoë, 54, 85, 91, 93, 96,
    128, 139, 148, 198
Williston, 100, 101
Wing, Betsy, 110, 119, 162

WISER, 163, 182
World Cup, 183, 196, 197
Writing, 4, 6, 7, 14, 62, 63, 66, 80,
    94, 97, 110, 118, 120, 127, 136,
    145, 177
Writing Culture, 5

X
Xenophobia, 2, 13, 39, 43, 72, 73,
    165
xenophobic violence, 2, 49, 50

Y
Yeoville, 193
Yugoslavia, 138, 183

Z
Zambia, 77
Zuid-Afrikanerdom, 58
Zulu, 42, 147, 161, 193
Zuma, Jacob, 43, 63, 118

The manufacturer's authorised representative in the EU is Springer
Nature Customer Service Centre GmbH, Europaplatz 3, 69115 Heidelberg,
Germany. If you have any concerns regarding our products, please
contact ProductSafety@springernature.com

Printed and bound by CPI Group (UK) Ltd, Croydon, CR0 4YY
24/04/2026
02096317-0001

For EU product safety concerns, contact us at Calle de José Abascal, 56–1°, 28003 Madrid, Spain or eugpsr@cambridge.org.

www.ingramcontent.com/pod-product-compliance
Ingram Content Group UK Ltd.
Pitfield, Milton Keynes, MK11 3LW, UK
UKHW021923280426
470499UK00018B/375